MISOGYNOIR TRANSFORMED

INTERSECTIONS: TRANSDISCIPLINARY PERSPECTIVES ON GENDERS AND SEXUALITIES

General Editor: Suzanna Walters

Sperm Counts: Overcome by Man's Most Precious Fluid
Lisa Jean Moore

The Sexuality of Migration: Border Crossings and Mexican Immigrant Men
Lionel Cantú, Jr.
Edited by Nancy A. Naples and Salvador Vidal-Ortiz

Moral Panics, Sex Panics: Fear and the Fight over Sexual Rights
Edited by Gilbert Herdt

Out in the Country: Youth, Media, and Queer Visibility in Rural America
Mary L. Gray

Sapphistries: A Global History of Love between Women
Leila J. Rupp

Strip Club: Gender, Power, and Sex Work
Kim Price-Glynn

Sex for Life: From Virginity to Viagra, How Sexuality Changes throughout Our Lives
Edited by Laura M. Carpenter and John DeLamater

The Bully Society: School Shootings and the Crisis of Bullying in America's Schools
Jessie Klein

One Marriage under God: The Campaign to Promote Marriage in America
Melanie Heath

Respect Yourself, Protect Yourself: Latina Girls and Sexual Identity
Lorena Garcia

The Tolerance Trap: How God, Genes, and Good Intentions Are Sabotaging Gay Equality
Suzanna Danuta Walters

Fat Gay Men: Girth, Mirth, and the Politics of Stigma
Jason Whitesel

Geisha of a Different Kind: Race and Sexuality in Gaysian America
C. Winter Han

Queering the Countryside: New Frontiers in Rural Queer Studies
Edited by Mary L. Gray, Colin R. Johnson, and Brian J. Gilley

Beyond Monogamy: Polyamory and the Future of Polyqueer Sexualities
Mimi Schippers

Brown Bodies, White Babies: The Politics of Cross-Racial Surrogacy
Laura Harrison

Botox Nation: Changing the Face of America
Dana Berkowitz

Misogynoir Transformed: Black Women's Digital Resistance
Moya Bailey

Misogynoir Transformed

Black Women's Digital Resistance

Moya Bailey

NEW YORK

NEW YORK UNIVERSITY PRESS

NEW YORK UNIVERSITY PRESS
New York
www.nyupress.org

References to Internet websites (URLs) were accurate at the time of writing. Neither the author nor New York University Press is responsible for URLs that may have expired or changed since the manuscript was prepared.

Library of Congress Cataloging-in-Publication Data
Names: Bailey, Moya, author.
Title: Misogynoir transformed : black women's digital resistance / Moya Bailey.
Description: New York : New York University Press, [2021] | Series: Intersections : transdisciplinary perspectives on genders and sexualities | Includes bibliographical references and index.
Identifiers: LCCN 2020047212 | ISBN 9781479865109 (hardback) | ISBN 9781479878741 (paperback) | ISBN 9781479890491 (ebook) | ISBN 9781479803392 (ebook)
Subjects: LCSH: African American women in social media. | Social media—United States. | African American women in popular culture—United States. | Misogynoir—United States. | African American women—Social conditions.
Classification: LCC PN4565.A47 B35 2021 | DDC 302.23089/96073—dc23
LC record available at https://lccn.loc.gov/2020047212

New York University Press books are printed on acid-free paper, and their binding materials are chosen for strength and durability. We strive to use environmentally responsible suppliers and materials to the greatest extent possible in publishing our books.

Manufactured in the United States of America

Also available as an ebook

For Mama and Daddy

We cannot sit on our behinds waiting for someone else to do it for us. We must save ourselves.
—Mary Ann Weathers, "An Argument for Black Women's Liberation as a Revolutionary Force," 1969

CONTENTS

Although I did not know it at the time, I started writing this book as an undergraduate at Spelman College. I was on the road to becoming a medical doctor when two things happened that made me shift course: I fell in love with women's studies, and I got international attention as one of the leaders of a small pushback on campus against the rapper Nelly. Both events profoundly shaped my thinking about the way Black women are treated in society and moved me to coin the term "misogynoir," which in turn led to this book.

As a first-year student from tiny Fayetteville, Arkansas, I was appalled when Dr. Beverly Guy-Sheftall told the Spelman College entering class of 2005 about Sarah Baartman's experiences as a human exhibit in Europe during the early nineteenth century. Baartman, a young Khoisan woman from what we now recognize as South Africa, was displayed throughout Europe to paying white audiences as an example of the animalistic and inferior nature of the African woman. Implicit in Baartman's display was a comparison between her body and that of the white women who viewed her. European scientists equated Baartman's anatomical differences with sexual deviance, drawing conclusions about her sexuality and subsequently, the sexuality of Black women from her form. Her butt and genitalia were used to justify racist and sexualized violence as well as the continued enslavement of Africans in the "New World."[1] Dr. Guy-Sheftall explained that the exploitative way Baartman's body was treated in life and in death was made possible under the guise of "objective science, " though what Baartman actually endured was objectification through scientific racism and sexism. In my first week at Spelman, before I had even attended a class, Dr. Guy-Sheftall had challenged my thinking by describing the differential treatment Black women experienced on a global stage. After that moment, I knew I wanted to take every class I could with her.

I was awakened to the profundity of the unique nexus of experience that is Black and woman on this planet and throughout colonial history.

Along with enrolling in Dr. Guy-Sheftall's classes, I took classes with fellow feminist professor Dr. M. Bahati Kuumba (Dr. K), who gave me the final nudge into the open arms of the comparative women's studies major at Spelman. As I was matriculating, I also got involved in the feminist political organizations on campus, all of which were supported by the Women's Research and Resource Center, the home of the comparative women's studies department. It was Dr. K who asked, "You are taking all the classes. Why not be a major?" When she put it that way, there was no room for rebuttal. But in truth, I was a willing convert, despite still having every intention of attending medical school—but that was not to be.

As a nineteen-year-old junior and then president of the Feminist Majority Leadership Alliance (FMLA), I showed the group Nelly's music video for the song "Tip Drill," which had started airing on the late-night television show *Uncut* on BET (Black Entertainment Television). The video featured, most memorably, a scene where Nelly slides a credit card down the crack of a Black woman's butt. Our group decided to name him our Misogynist of the Month, not knowing that the Spelman Student Government Association had agreed to partner with Nelly and his foundation JesUs-4-Jackie to hold a bone marrow registration drive on our campus in an effort to save the life of his sister, who had leukemia.[2]

FMLA raised questions about the misogynoir in his video and lyrics, and when we heard that Nelly was invited to campus, it seemed only fair that we ask him about the way he represented Black women since he was asking us for our help. Nelly declined our offer to talk about his music. Instead, he went to the press, twisting the story such that it seemed that Spelman canceled the bone marrow registration drive because of the video, an assertion that many still believe today, though we orchestrated our own drive.[3] The story garnered national and eventually international headlines, both praising and condemning Spelman students for daring to talk back to the music.[4]

It was a hard lesson in the hypervisibility and invisibility of being a Black woman.[5] Nelly felt entitled to our assistance with saving his sister's life but did not feel that he had to address us, the Black women who dealt with the fallout of his video and lyrics in our day-to-day lives. As young Black women, we felt the impact of the video and lyrics in the form of street harassment in the United States and abroad. We dealt with assumptions about our sexual availability to men in the form of unsolicited commentary on our bodies, on our clothing, and on our time. He used his celebrity, built on the bodies of Black women, to urge people to support an underappreciated cause, the health of Black women. Black women are far less likely to find a matching bone marrow donor than their white woman counterparts, in part because of Black people's deep distrust of the systemic racism in medicine, which makes them less likely to volunteer to donate. What was not quite clear to me in 2004 was the irony of using a fame garnered through limiting representations of Black women while refusing to address that decision and also wanting support from those very same Black women.

I wasn't quite able to connect the dots between popular media representations of Black women and my and other Black women's experiences with discriminatory housing practices, intimate partner violence (IPV), street harassment, employment discrimination, and ill treatment from healthcare providers, but my interest in the role media plays in shaping the perceptions of Black women became all-consuming, such that the goal of becoming a medical doctor morphed into getting a doctorate to investigate the role that media representations play in the treatment of Black women patients by white doctors. I learned about the ways historical popular culture seeped into the consciousness of supposedly objective future physicians, which prompted me to consider how popular culture representations influence Black women's treatment in society and medicine today.[6]

It was in writing that dissertation that I landed on the word "misogynoir" to describe the particular venom directed at Black women through negative representations in media. How do you describe the ways that Black women are uniquely denigrated because of their gender and race? I played with a couple of terms before landing on "misogynoir." Initially, the term existed only in my dissertation until 2008, when I was invited to join the Crunk Feminist Collective (CFC), an online blogging community of feminists of color.

From 2008 to 2013, the CFC dominated the think piece blogosphere with insightful and pithy commentary on popular culture, primarily through the lens of hip hop feminism.[7] At its height, the CFC blog was home to fourteen Black and feminist of color bloggers who wrote about the news of the day, paying special attention to highlight the intersection of race and gender in their writing.[8] Founded by Black feminist scholars Brittney Cooper and Susana Morris, then graduate students at Emory University in Atlanta, the CFC bridged a seemingly contradictory love for crunk hip hop music that dominated the radio airwaves in the aughts and the feminist theory they were learning in grad school.[9]

The blog was a space for timely and incisive criticism, and my first post, "They Aren't Talking about Me . . . ," discussed my concern about my own apathetic response to "misogynoir" in music; it was the word's first appearance outside my dissertation.[10] Once I used the word, other members of the collective started to use the term and it appeared in more CFC posts. From there, some members of the blogosphere began to use it, but no one more compellingly than womanist blogger Trudy at her now sunsetted *Gradient Lair*.[11] Her work introduced online communities to the word, and she deftly articulated its utility. Her work and others helped the term reach a wide range of audiences, including an international one.

When I coined the term, I did not expect it to go viral. In addition to appearing in the *New York Times*, *Ebony*, *Essence*, and the *Washington Post*, "misogynoir" has its own Wikipedia entry, which receives thousands of views every day. It is also referenced in numerous scholarly journal articles and monographs. The adoption of the term and its wide reach in digital spaces make further theorization of its use important for gender, critical race, and cultural studies audiences outside the academy. I hope that, in addition to creating a term that is useful, I have created a book that is useful to the communities with which I study. I hope that future efforts similar to the successful campaigns and actions I describe here will further improve the lives of Black women and their communities.

Introduction

What Is Misogynoir?

"Misogynoir" (pronounced *mi-soj-uhn-nwar*) is a term I created in 2008 to describe the anti-Black racist misogyny that Black women experience, particularly in US visual and digital culture.[1] Misogynoir is not simply the racism that Black women encounter, nor is it the misogyny Black women negotiate. Misogynoir describes the uniquely co-constitutive racialized and sexist violence that befalls Black women as a result of their simultaneous and interlocking oppression at the intersection of racial and gender marginalization.

The term is a portmanteau of "misogyny," the hatred of women, and "noir," the French word for "black," which also carries a specific meaning in film and other media. French film critic Nino Frank coined the term "film noir" in 1946 to describe the gritty, cynical, and initially American movies that had unusually cruel themes for the time. The motion picture genre is characterized by its dark and sometimes sexually charged undercurrents; examples include films like *The Maltese Falcon* (1941) and *Sunset Boulevard* (1950). Like "film noir," "misogynoir" originally described American media but similarly grew to transcend borders to describe an unfortunately global phenomenon. Whether in film, television, or as I examine extensively in this book, digital media, misogynoir has found a home in each of the communication advancements of the last two centuries.

Misogynoir is perpetuated through popular media like cartoons, minstrel shows, yearbooks, television, movies, and even Facebook, the digital descendant of yearbooks.[2] Black feminist theory clearly articulates the power of the image to serve the hegemony of "white supremacist capitalist patriarchy" by controlling the way society views marginalized groups and how we view ourselves.[3] Black feminist theorist bell hooks discusses the importance of producing images that counter the normalizing force of stereotypes, but also exposes the danger of reactionary positive images that can constrain and confine. We need complex images that break the good/bad, white/Black dichotomy. As hooks offers in *Black Looks*, we should be "asking ourselves questions about what type of images subvert, pose critical alternatives, and transform our world views and move us away from dualistic thinking about good and bad."[4] Similarly, Patricia Hill Collins argues against "controlling images" that attempt to delimit the potential ways of being for Black women in the world.[5]

The media that circulate misogynoir help maintain white supremacy by offering tacit approval of the disparate treatment that Black women negotiate in society. Whether the Jezebel, mammy, Sapphire, and later the "welfare queen" or even the "strong Black woman" archetype, misogynoiristic portrayals of Black women shape their livelihoods and health. As media studies scholars attest, negative images and narratives do more than affect the self-esteem of the populations depicted. Misogynoiristic caricatures materially impact the lives of Black women by justifying poor treatment throughout all areas of society and throughout US history.

I use methods from a diverse number of fields, including Africana studies, women's, gender, and sexuality studies, digital humanities, and the social sciences to trace the ways that Black women transform misogynoir. Whether it is using the digital humanities tools Gephi and Voyant for network and text analysis, respectively, or the close reading of media texts in women's, gender, and sexuality studies and Africana studies, as well as the interview from sociology, this text draws on a variety of methodological traditions to tell the story of *Misogynoir Transformed*. Without a mixed-method approach, I would be unable to adequately convey the dynamic ways Black women are using social media as a form of health praxis.

Perceptions of Black women as animalistic, strong, and insatiable have had material consequences on their lives and bodies since Africans' nonconsensual arrival in the West. The 1810s display and public autopsy in Europe of the Khoi Khoi Sarah Baartman for her "abnormal" body, as described in the preface, is one of the earliest examples of misogynoir in media, as her exaggerated image was used in newspapers and advertisements to draw paying audiences to see her. Starting in the 1820s and lasting through the 1950s, minstrel representations that also exaggerated and mocked Blackness circulated widely through performances, postcards, and even radio plays. The humor attached to minstrel performances and representations attempted to assuage mounting racial and gender tensions in both the pre–Civil War and the post-slavery eras.

Antebellum constructions of the Black woman as the hypersexual Jezebel served the lecherous and capitalist intent of the white power structure, who profited off the children they forced these women to birth, often at a physical cost. The 1840s vaginal fistula operations without anesthesia that enslaved women Betsy, Anarcha, and Lucy were subjected to by J. Marion Sims, the so-called "father of gynecology," were engineered to repair Black women's bodies damaged during childbirth.[6] Once perfected on these women, who, as enslaved women, could not consent to treatment, the procedure was deemed safe for white women, who were not denied anesthesia since they were considered too delicate to endure the procedure without it. Enslaved Black women were simultaneously gendered and ungendered through the objectification of their anatomy, whether in the service of white women's health or being rendered as genderless laborers and property.[7] Black women were considered unrapeable and were understood in white society to be the lascivious and willing seductresses of white men. This imagining fueled the sexual violation of Black women during slavery as well as later Jim Crow sexual harassment and rapes.[8]

From the post–Civil War period to the Jim Crow era, the iconography used to support Black people's continued subservience morphed and expanded to make room for use of Black women as poorly paid domestics who reared white children. Since whites no longer needed to read Black women as exotic temptresses and breeders of an entire labor force, the mammy archetype promulgated an image of a sweet, caring, fat (i.e., undesirable) caregiver. Scholar Kimberly Wallace-Sanders's work on the mammy figure has exposed how caricatures and images are able to supersede reality. Wallace-Sanders describes how the images of the mammy in Harriet Beecher Stowe's classic abolitionist text *Uncle Tom's Cabin* became the definitive representation of the character, a big, dark-skinned Black woman with a checkered handkerchief on her head, when previous depictions of mammies showed women of different sizes and complexions who wore various styles of servant dress.[9] The real Black women who performed this domestic labor were obscured by a widely circulating representation of them that aided white supremacy by refiguring them as less threatening, asexual servants to the existing power structure.

The supposed good-natured warmth of the mammy figure is coupled with the indelible image of an asexual, happy yet sassy servant, an effective trope for white consumers that continues to live on contemporarily. Mammy is still used in the iconography of popular brands to this day.[10] For example, Aunt Jemima Pancake Mix and Syrup was sued in 2014 for failing to pay royalties to the alleged descendants of Anna Harrington, the Black woman whose likeness appears on the box and the purported original mastermind behind the recipe.[11] Only in June 2020 did Quaker Oats, the parent company of Aunt Jemima, acknowledge the damaging and enduring nature of this mammy iconography when it finally announced plans to remove the image and name from its products in the wake of criticism spurred by uprisings around the country in protest of anti-Black police brutality.[12] Mammy still serves as a mollifying myth that projects home and quality for white people, all the while obscuring the white male supremacist power structure's investment in and actual profit from this image that still hides their continued sexual abuse of Black women. Whether the Pine-Sol lady, the Popeye's Chicken lady, or a digital media meme of Hattie McDaniel from *Gone with the Wind* (1939), mammy remains an important archetype in all but name, and as such continues to weave misogynoir through Black women's lives and their health outcomes. The impact of cleaning chemicals, environmental racism, and fast food on the health of Black women is made a problem of Black women's poor choices rather than a predictable outcome linked to food deserts, brownfield lands, and limited access to healthcare.[13] In a culture that equates thinness with good health and desirability, fat Black women are demonized for their bodies even as their bodies are used to sell goods and rear white children.[14]

Fat Black women's bodies reinforce the idea that they are in service to others, whether through the reassuring support of a wide bosom on which to seek emotional comfort, their purported undesirability (which makes them available to others' needs), or their perceived slow pace (which keeps them tied to the domestic sphere). Despite important research that exposes the racial and gender biases embedded in the Body

Mass Index (BMI) used to determine relative health by calculating an ideal range of weight-to-height measurements, Black women are still considered to have the highest rates of obesity in the United States, with four out of five Black women considered obese.[15] Fat Black women even feel pressure to apologize for or justify their bodies because of how misogynoir makes them hypervisible in society. Memoirs by writer Roxane Gay and actor Gabourey Sidibe include extended discussions about why they are fat, with details of the trauma or genetic imprint that makes them look as they do.[16] Black women's bodies are never their own, resulting in a subtle pressure to not only be useful but explain oneself to others. This utility of the mammy archetype endures.

The sassy Black mammy evolved but did not disappear into the emasculating Sapphire, another stereotype used to mitigate a changing racial landscape where Black women's sexuality was no longer subsumed by ideas of reproductive capacity for slave labor.[17] Sapphire wasn't playfully vexed with her husband the way mammy was (though mammy's husband was rarely if ever seen); she was mean, ordering Black men to do her bidding and behave in ways she saw fit. This seeming gender role reversal—where Sapphire wore the pants in the family—became another enduring trope, still visible in the drag performed by Black male comedians and in the digital blackface and digital minstrelsy employed by white social media users for their own ends, as discussed in chapter 1 of this text.[18] Sapphire's emasculation and seeming hatred of Black men never ventured into the realm of sapphic sex or desire, ensuring that her representation remained a controlling image without a possible liberatory libidinal escape from heteronormativity.

Sapphire also appears as the sassy Black friend to white women protagonists in film and television, pulling on some of the threads of mammy, as she is never depicted as having a life of her own, forever in service to her thin white friends. She might also appear big in frame, having prominent muscles or big breasts and body, when compared to the white women and Black men near her. Sapphire's mean streak or sass is a source of comedy when directed at other Black people, a winning strategy for both the box office and Nielsen ratings. From Jennifer Hudson in *Sex and the City* (2008) to Alex Newell in *Zoey's Extraordinary Playlist* (2020), Sapphire provides the "magical Negro" balm of wit and wisdom, despite having no discernible life from which to have drawn these insights, given her deployment on-screen only in relation to her white friend.[19] The image of Black women can be distorted in ways that perpetuate misogynoir and ease the consciousness and line the pockets of everyone else. In other words, misogynoiristic representations allow Black women to be ignored in society without guilt and allow for people to profit from these enduring negative images at the expense of real Black women's lives.

Black women are caught at a vexing crossroads: hypervisible in media through misogynoir and invisible when in need of lifesaving attention. Misogynoir is the visual representation of anti-Black misogyny not only through caricature and false representations of Black women that inform how Black women are treated, but also through the omission of Black women and girls from view altogether.[20] The so-called "missing white woman syndrome," in which news media cover stories about missing white women and girls with a ferocity that is unmatched when women and girls of color go missing, continues to belie societal claims of growing racial equality.[21] Sixty-four thousand Black women and girls were missing in the United States in 2017. Amber alerts are not even issued for many of these girls because there is an assumption that Black girls run away. The lives of Black women are so devalued that there is little public outcry when we are violated or exploited.[22] When Black trans women are murdered, most often at the hands of men of color, there is no community outpouring of support for the victim or the victim's family. The life expectancy for trans women of color is just thirty-five years.[23] Initiatives like #SayHerName, discussed in chapter 2, and the Movement for Black Lives are trying to make the invisible visible, but it has been and continues to be an uphill battle. Whether it is through hypervisibility or complete erasure, Black women and girls are grappling with the negative consequences of misogynoir on their lives.

Misogynoir in Policy

During the 1940s, Black women who were in the hospital for any reason could be given hysterectomies without their consent or knowledge. This practice was so widespread in Mississippi it was dubbed a "Mississippi appendectomy."[24] Famed civil rights activist Fannie Lou Hamer was one of the women subjected to this practice, and the experience was a major

impetus for her activism.[25] Sterilization abuse as a tool of white supremacy exceeded the Jim Crow era and continued well into the 1970s with
victims like the young Relf sisters in Alabama, sterilized without their
knowledge or consent as teenagers.[26] These practices were supported by
media representations like Warner Brothers' *Coal Black and de Sebben
Dwarfs*, which portrayed Black women as sexually irresponsible and in
need of outside intervention.[27]

During the late 1970s and early 1980s, media outlets and political officials constructed the image of the "welfare queen" to justify federal
policy decisions that cut social services for millions of US Americans.[28]
Using the case of Linda Taylor, who in 1974 defrauded the welfare system
of $8,000 among other much more serious crimes, President Reagan
and his administration painted a picture of Black women willfully taking
advantage of governmental aid.[29] Despite the fact that the very rare oc-
casion of welfare fraud was generally committed by men (as former NFL
player Brett Favre's 2020 payments of over one million dollars in restitu-
tion to the Mississippi Temporary Assistance for Needy Families attests),
the representation of Black women as the culpable parties remains to this
day.[30] The welfare queen was depicted as an irresponsible Black woman
who was having kids and getting rich from government checks. She got
a "handout" for having lots of children and being unmarried. In a 1999
Harvard study on the impact of "welfare queen" imagery on participants'
ideas about welfare reform, "the most gender liberal white participants
appear to be most likely to implicitly blame African-Americans for the
plight of their racial peers, and there is early evidence to suggest that this
tendency is most pronounced among women."[31] Language and images
about the "welfare queen" were used to stoke misogynoiristic sentiment
that was leveraged into actual legislation. The Personal Responsibility
and Work Opportunity Act of 1996 was the culmination of years of Re-
publican efforts to reduce the number of people using government assistance; it overhauled the welfare system by creating time limits for the
use of assistance as well as work and marriage requirements, which were
all designed to re-engineer Black women's perceived dependence on the
welfare state. The circulation of the myth of the welfare queen negatively
impacted Black women by limiting federal resources that provided ben-
eficiaries access to food, money, and healthcare.[32] Black women's access
to the very means of life were curtailed for themselves and others be-

cause of the misogynoiristic image of the "welfare queen." Even though most welfare recipients were at that time and still are white, one Black woman's abuse of the system and the Moynihan Report were used by politicians to portray the Black family, particularly Black women, as pathological.

Daniel Patrick Moynihan, assistant secretary of labor in the Lyndon B. Johnson presidential administration, took it upon himself to investigate poverty in Black families. In his 1965 report, "The Negro Family: The Case for National Action," he noted that the major threat to racial equity was the deviant nature of the Black family, in which Black women often took on the role of head of household and primary breadwinner. Rather than address the structural impediments that made it difficult for Black men to find work, Moynihan pathologized the Black family, painting Black women's marginal success in finding work outside the home as a form of emasculation that further inhibited Black men's industry by making them depressed.[33] Rather than address the undergirding white supremacist, capitalistic, and heteronormative imperative implicit in the idealization of the nuclear family and man as the rightful money maker of the home, Moynihan demonized Black women. This Sapphiric representation of Black women as emasculating Black men and the welfare queen's continued circulation are examples of misogynoir's ability to create material consequences that harm Black women's health because these ideas informed and shaped public policy.

By the 1990s, anxieties around Black motherhood were further energized in the context of the burgeoning crack epidemic. An organization called CRACK (Children Requiring a Caring Kommunity) responded to the crisis by offering $200 to women of color using crack cocaine if they agreed to long-term or permanent birth control.[34] Instead of offering resources or assistance to help the women overcome their addictions, CRACK promoted sterilization through this small monetary incentive. Comparatively, the 2010s opioid crisis, which has disproportionately affected white communities, has not seen similar tactics designed to sterilize white women drug users. White users are not criminalized, and the crisis has been treated as a public health problem. In the 1990s, news media described the children of users as "crack babies," while media headlines in the 2010s discussed the plight of "opioid dependent newborns."[35] Black mothers are not afforded the same types of help or public compassion that white mothers are. As in the case of the "father of gynecology" or the 1940s sterilization abuses in North Carolina and Mississippi among other places, the supposed good intentions of these efforts are overshadowed by the misogynoirist foundations on which these projects were built.

What's Health Got to Do with It?

The emergence of the COVID-19 coronavirus pandemic in the United States in February 2020 reanimated conversations about disparities in healthcare. While not more likely to contract the virus, Black people were three times as likely to die of it.[36] Despite this reality, even trained medical professionals relied on dated stereotypes to make sense of the differences in outcomes. Ohio state senator Stephen Huffman, a medical doctor, said of the disproportionate number of Black people dying of complications from the virus, "Could it just be that African-Americans or the colored population do not wash their hands as well as other groups or wear a mask or do not socially distance themselves?"[37] Huffman's comments use both the antiquated racist language of "colored" and the completely unfounded stereotype of Black people as dirty. His logic depends on some of the longest-circulating racist imagery about Black people—that we are unclean, lazy, and not smart enough to follow public health guidelines amid a global pandemic. Ideas like his, held by healthcare providers, mean less effective care for Black people as they are being blamed for their health status as opposed to being treated as patients deserving of care.

The way that racism exacerbates care disparities and health outcomes has been discussed in a number of venues and has been championed by other healthcare professionals and practitioners as one of the "social determinates of health."[38] The popular PBS documentary series *Unnatural Causes* illustrates the way that racial disparities in health outcomes are connected to systemic discrimination.[39] Research by Black women health practitioners like Nadine Burke Harris and Lisa Cooper has shown the outsized impact of racist trauma on the bodies of Black people and the doctor-patient interaction, respectively.[40] Misogynoir contributes to Black women's experiences with healthcare by making them uniquely susceptible to abuse within the system.

The life of Henrietta Lacks offers an example of Black women's historical lack of agency in negotiating how representations of themselves are used. Lacks's biopsied cancer cells, later dubbed "HeLa cells," were the first to survive and grow outside the human body. They became the engine behind much of twentieth-century science and medical innovation, including the polio vaccine and some early investigations of humans' ability to survive in space. Yet Henrietta Lacks died at the young age of thirty-one, leaving a husband, children, and extended family who have never been able to fully access the mental and physical healthcare they need.[41] Moreover, neither Lacks nor her husband gave permission for her cells to be used for research purposes. Rebecca Skloot, author of *The Immortal Life of Henrietta Lacks*, which famously chronicles the story of HeLa, attempts to shed some light on the current situation of the family, but their reality is overshadowed by the success of the cells and Skloot's book itself. As in the case of Betsy, Anarcha, and Lucy before her, Henrietta Lacks's health needs mattered only insofar as they were connected to larger scientific needs, interests, and goals. Her image circulates on the cover of Skloot's book, but the book does not question the scientific racism and sexism that shaped her early death. Black women's bodies have been instrumental in the development of medical and scientific breakthroughs that have aided countless humans across the globe. However, the degree to which these advancements have helped the health and well-being of Black women remains unclear. This unsatisfying reality is misogynoir.

These historic abuses and others perpetrated by medical and political forces are now a part of a national narrative about Black people's troubled relationship to healthcare. They affect the willingness of Black patients to seek treatment and color how Black people, Black women in particular, are treated in society.[42] The sociocultural factors that helped engineer these systemic practices of mistreatment are beginning to be theorized, along with the activism of Black women that works to counteract them.[43] With the rise of social media, Black women are in an even better position to challenge the stereotypes that negatively impact their health and well-being. Black feminist theorists have hinted at the connections between representations and health for decades, calling for systemic changes in both media and medicine to ameliorate the disproportionate health burden Black women negotiate. Black feminist scholars Dorothy Roberts, Alondra Nelson, Harriet Washington, Imani Perry, Farah Griffin, Angela Davis, Sabrina Strings, and Rana Hogarth are just a few who have done the labor of putting into book form the cost of representation on the lives of Black women.[44] The path from stereotype to structural oppression, poor health outcomes, and ill treatment in society is still obscured.

In this book, I argue that Black women's digital resistance, through the creation of new content and digital practices, is a form of self-preservation and harm reduction that disrupts the onslaught of the problematic images that society perpetuates. Misogynoir impacts so many different facets of Black women's lives, but health—Black women's very right to life—is an essential vantage point from which to gauge its deleterious effects. While memes circulate through social media platforms such as YouTube, Facebook, Instagram, Tumblr, and others that depict Black women as more ugly, dirty, deficient, hypersexual, and unhealthy than their white or non-black women of color counterparts, Black women employ these same platforms in ways that subvert negative stereotypes through processes that can be their own health-affirming practice.[45] Simply put, both the process of creation and the material created are co-constitutive harm-reduction strategies. *Misogynoir Transformed* examines the social media activities of Black women as one way that they are attempting to redress the negative impact of stereotypes in their lives and on their health.

This book is not a history of misogynoir. Rather, I conceptualize the alternate representations created by Black women as counterpublic productions that trouble stereotypical depictions and as vehicles for processes that allow for other types of health interventions. I use multiple case studies that explore Black queer and trans women's digital resistance on social media platforms to illustrate the ways redefining representation empowers media creators to tell another story about their lives—one that is sometimes in reaction to mainstream narratives that distort their realities, but is also visionary in terms of evoking the kinds of realities they wish existed.

Misogynoir can be weaponized against Black women in ways that harm their health. The World Health Organization (WHO) defines *health* as "a state of complete physical, mental and social well-being and not merely the absence of disease or infirmity."[46] This definition has been criticized by disability studies theorists for making health unobtainable for those who do not have "complete physical, mental and social well-being." By definition, those who use wheelchairs, manage their depression with medication, or have mental and/or physical impairments, chronic illness, or disease fall outside the scope of "complete physical, mental and social well-being." As a scholar of disability, race, and gender studies, I also question how "complete physical, mental and social well-being" can be achieved if one lives in a neighborhood with little access to fresh food or ways to safely exercise. Race and gender not only play a role in the physical environment in which one lives but also impact the way one is perceived in society. Can a person achieve the WHO definition of health if they encounter racism, sexism, ableism, and other oppressions as part of their daily life in the world? The stress and material consequences of systemic oppression make it nearly impossible to have physical, mental, and social well-being in a white supremacist patriarchal country.

For the purposes of this book, I use the WHO definition of health to orient readers to the myriad ways misogynoir has material effects in the lives of Black women and expand our general thinking of health beyond statistical disparities. Misogynoir may impede Black women's health by negatively impacting their physical, mental, and social lives. As Color of Change senior campaign manager Brandi Collins acknowledges, "There's so much research out there showing that there are consequences for Black women when these stereotypes are allowed to rule the day. It's tied to diminished economic opportunities, less attention from doctors, stricter sentencing from judges."[47] As the first half of this introduction details, misogynoir also shaped US domestic policy, the buying and selling of goods, and even the development of healthcare procedures. The impact of misogynoir on the lives of Black women cannot be overstated.

Misogynoir through Media

There remains a belief that recognizing the misogynoir experienced by Black women detracts from efforts to support Black men and boys. In the wake of seasons of unarmed Black men being gunned down by police, instances of Black women's murders at the hands of the police have not evoked the same demands for police accountability.[48] The

Boston activist and 2020 poet laureate Porsha Olayiwola's poem "Rekia Boyd" asks the question why no one showed up for a rally in Boyd's honor following her slaying by off-duty police officer Dante Servin over an alleged noise complaint:

> Last night
> No one showed up to march for Rekia Boyd.
> Rekia was shot dead in the head by cops on Monday.
> A cook county judge acquitted Dante Servin, went jailbird free
> Rekia Boyd was a 22-year-old unarmed Black woman who had been living on the south side of Chicago and last night no one showed up to march at her rally.
> I guess all the protestors got tied up.
> I guess all the Black folks were busy making signs saying, "Stop killing our Black boys!"
> I guess no one hears the howling of a Black girl ghost in the night time.
> We stay unheard.
> Blotted out.
> Buried.
> Dead Black girls receive tombstones too soon and never any flowers to dress the grave so we fight alone.[49]

Olayiwola describes the disproportionate attention Black men and boys get when they are violated and the absence of similar demands for justice when a Black woman is killed. I argue that the silence and erasure of the violence Black women and girls endure are connected to society's inability to see them as worthwhile subjects deserving of respect and care, a sentiment exacerbated by misogynoir. Olayiwola's words echo the epigraph that animates this text, reminding us that since we as Black women "fight alone," "we must save ourselves."[50] Part of this saving includes the creation of representations that challenge the ways we are viewed.

Representations of Black women in popular culture help support and perhaps even bolster the harm they experience. In 2003, when fifteen-year-old Sakia Gunn and friends refused the street harassment of twenty-nine-year-old Richard McCullough and his friend by saying they were lesbians, McCullough got out of the car to retaliate. Mc-

Cullough stabbed Gunn and fled, and though she was rushed to the hospital, she died of her injuries. McCullough's sense of entitlement to Gunn's attention pushed him out of the car and into choking her friend and ultimately killing Gunn. His beliefs about her sexuality and his right to control and punish her for what he perceived as its misapplication have everything to do with the misogynoir that makes Black women and girls seem undeserving of their autonomy and lives. When Black women are only rendered visually as in service to men, their autonomy is not believed. Misogynoir can precipitate racist gendered violence that harms "social well-being" and impacts mental and physical health, and can even result in death, the direst of health outcomes.

Portrayals of Black women as straight and at the disposal of men who desire them shape our cultural landscape. When misogynoir paints all Black women as sexually available to men, Gunn's defiance is not only challenged but punished. Her health, her very life, is at stake when stereotypes materialize into justifications for deadly behaviors. In 2006, when another group of Black lesbian teens tried to defend themselves against a catcaller turned attacker, they were vilified in the news as a "wolf pack, an inhuman gang of animals."[51] Media's portrayal of the "New Jersey Four," as their group became known, led to them receiving longer and harsher prison sentences, despite the fact that the young women were trying to defend themselves against a man who tried to assault the smallest in their group.[52] This violence and these harsher sentences, as numerous studies have shown, are disproportionately visited upon Black women.[53]

While many studies have explored the physical health of Black women, few have considered premature death, mental health, physical well-being, housing, education, and access to pleasure as equally important health concerns that misogynoir negatively impacts. Beyond public health calls to address maternal mortality and the so-called "obesity epidemic" among Black women, there is a need to address Black women's health at a fundamental level that includes their quality of life beyond ableist metrics. Black women deserve to have accurate representations of themselves in popular culture. The images that circulate about them should support their well-being in society instead of negatively impacting their ability to live their lives. And, as in the quote that orients this entire text, Black women are doing that work themselves.[54]

Mitigating Misogynoir through Media Making

Black feminists' activist and scholarly interest in representation was born of these real concerns for the ways that misogynoir shapes Black women's daily treatment in the world. Like feminist legal scholar Kimberlé Crenshaw's term "intersectionality," "misogynoir" names a concept that Black feminists have discussed since our earliest preserved writings, speeches, and poetry.[55] In 1851, abolitionist Sojourner Truth revealed the ways womanhood is raced such that Black women are excluded from the category and therefore subject to abuses that white women are not.[56] Black studies scholar Hortense Spillers's classic text "Mama's Baby, Papa's Maybe: An American Grammar Book" explores the degendering of Black women in US slavery and their subsequent treatment as commodities of labor and breeding for white slaveholders.[57] Black women were not women, but their fertility was essential for the maintenance of slavery. Both Truth and Spillers describe the way that Black women are subjected to differential treatment in society based on their simultaneous marginalization along the lines of race and gender.

While initial challenges to misogynoirist representations of Black women in the early twentieth century involved some classist and moralizing sentiments about proving oneself in the public sphere, the digital age has made way for strategies that reject respectability in favor of more multifaceted representations of Black women in all of our complexities. Respectability is the idea that if marginalized groups comport themselves well, they may be able to be accepted into society. Whether through the activism of Black club women during the late nineteenth century through the 1920s, or the Black women's media renaissance of the 1980s and 1990s, Black women were creating the visions of themselves that they wished to see.[58] Black feminist thought has expanded to be more inclusive of Black women who are not interested in respectability because not only does it not produce different affective treatment of Black women in society, it delimits comportment and leads to intra-group policing that is more harmful than helpful. In every era, Black women have been at the forefront of creating media for themselves that challenge misogynoir, whether explicitly or implicitly.

These new digital dissensions follow a long history in the twentieth century of Black women transforming the way they were portrayed in popular culture. TV shows like *Living Single* (1993) and films like *Daughters of the Dust* (1991) gave Black women artists more opportunities to tell more stories about who they were from their own perspective. Current media projects attempt to bring forward alternative representations of Black women, but these efforts can be marginalized by the conglomeration of media companies, which makes it difficult for these dissident voices and images to find space. The digital skills built through social media use are being leveraged for more sustainable and generative media now and in the future.

Black Hollywood is producing images to counter the globe-circling archetypes that negatively portray our communities. Independent films like *Pariah* (2011) and the even earlier *Eve's Bayou* (1997) have received critical acclaim but have had limited circulation in mainstream venues. More popular and available Black films attempt to challenge some stereotypes while reinforcing others. In the process of creating these alternative/"positive" representations, cis male producers and writers may challenge depictions of Black men as weak, unemployed, or unintelligent while stereotypes about Black women are reified and reinscribed. Additionally, positive Black masculinity in these films is equated with the Black male character's ability to achieve the heteronormative, patriarchal, capitalistic American Dream. It is the acquisition of the assimilationist fantasy that provides the Hollywood ending. This goal is reached through the often-violent reassertion of hierarchal gender roles. Films popularized and written by Tyler Perry are consummate examples of this practice. Perry is in a category all his own, given his ability to finance his own productions and his popularity in Black markets, particularly among Black women. Yet his female protagonists are punished for their career ambition and assertive personalities through the contraction of HIV or humiliating chastising by a male paramour.[59] In his narratives, Black women are physically dragged back into their place or pushed out of the way by Black men.[60]

For example, in Perry's *Why Did I Get Married?* (2007), the character Marcus strangles his wife, Angela, when she reveals that his STI is courtesy of the man she was sleeping with, who passed it to her. Marcus's masculinity is presumably undermined by Angela's wine-induced,

Sapphire-inspired vitriol, in which she accuses him of cheating, which he (also) was. Her duplicitous intent for withholding her affair with Walter is presented as more egregious than his own deceit. His rage is justified by the reactions of his friends and the audiences viewing the film, while Angela's deception is not. As Marcus chokes her, we hear another man in the scene shout, "I hope you break her throat!" Marcus and his friend's support of physical violence against Angela does not elicit any reprimand from the other friends still seated around the dinner table. Though eventually pulled away from Angela, Marcus never faces consequences for his treatment of her, nor is Angela portrayed as someone who has just been assaulted.[61] The fact that the local sheriff is present but sees no need to do more than help pull the two apart further enforces the justifiable nature of Marcus's actions. The violence of the scene—Angela literally being choked—is set up as comic relief, with audiences prompted to laugh uproariously when Marcus finally loses his cool.

These acts of filmic violence are not coded as such. Violence against Black women is made normal, comic, and necessary for the attainment of a positive Black masculinity, making intraracial violence against Black women off-screen tolerable and unremarkable.[62] The poem "Brother" by Pat Parker addresses the violence Black women face in their own communities while trying to address systemic oppression:

> Brother
> I don't want to hear
> about
> how my real enemy
> is the system.
> i'm no genius,
> but i do know
> that system
> you hit me with
> is called
> a fist.[63]

Like Olayiwola, Parker identifies the ways Black women are supposed to ignore their own pain in service to a perceived greater threat outside the Black community. Black women are expected to sublimate their concerns for the good of their communities. Perry's scene also demonstrates an interdependency between gender role expressions, where proper "positive" Black masculinity can be obtained only through the subordination of Black femininity.[64] Perry's portrayals mirror Moynihan's damning report on the Black family, as Black men are often physically fighting to put Black women back into the imagined "correct" place in the gender hierarchy, with men at the top. Black women are publicly derided by other Black people—from ambivalent Black leaders to apathetic media moguls, Black comedians to hip hop stars—with little consequence.

While Black people were perhaps initially invested in a strategy of proving their humanity through self-policing behavior and comportment (like that of the turn-of-the-twentieth-century club women), the overwhelming evidence—in the form of continued disparate treatment—shows that these efforts did not mitigate misogynoir. The practice of displaying respectable representations of themselves in media as a strategy for uplift gave way to recognition that any secondary positive feelings white audiences had for Black people as a result of self-generated representation had little material purchase in their lives. Racial uplift in a white supremacist world remains a central theme in many media projects over the years; however, queer and trans Black women create cultural works that challenge intraracial misogynoir because of their liminal space within a community that is already marginalized. By crafting reflections of the racialized and gendered violence that happens in our own spaces because of colorism, homophobia, and trans antagonism, queer and trans Black women push for accountability within their own networks as opposed to without. It seems that Black women must continue to look to themselves for representations that affirm and expand who they are as human beings. *Misogynoir Transformed* endeavors to bring some of these practices to the fore.

Black Women ≠ Black Feminists

In writing this book, I struggled to come up with language that fully captured who is engaged with this transformation of misogynoir. The term "Black women" is often assumed to mean straight and cis, with queer and trans Black women identified explicitly because of this normative assumption. Additionally, the term "Black women" is not inclusive of nonbinary, agender, and gender-variant Black folks whose experiences of misogynoir are intimately connected with a misgendering of them. I struggled to reconcile my use of a term that is central to my definition of misogynoir yet excludes some of the people most invested in its transformation. For those of us on the margins of Black womanhood, "woman" is not what we name ourselves even as misogynoir colors our experiences of the world. As you will see in this text, it is often those of us in the shadow of "Black women" who are the most engaged in media projects that transform misogynoir. As we in the shadows are already limited by the frame of "Black womanhood," we become some of misogynoir's most vociferous opponents because it further diminishes our already limited light. When a hetero- and cis-normative understanding of Black woman is used, it obscures the realities of those of us in the shade.

I experimented with terms to describe those of us on the margins of the margins of Black womanhood as I experimented with terms before landing on "misogynoir."[65] Digital spaces are rife with words, phrases, and terms that attempt, sometimes awkwardly, to address the slippage between "women" and all who aren't cis men. One of these terms is "non-men," which centers men as it attempts to define those who are not. "Non-men" is used online as a catchall term, but its use recreates the exact erasure it wants to undo. "Womxn" seems a useful interlocutor with its roots in precolonial indigenous languages and contemporary decolonial lingual practices. The x in "womxn" intervenes in the racist colonial histories of English and Spanish while also attempting to solve the problem of genders beyond the man/woman binary. That is a lot of work for one letter to accomplish. However, even as "womxn" by definition includes gender nonbinary, agender, and gender-variant people who don't identify as women, reading the term in text does not make those communities readily apparent. As SA Smythe asks in their article on Black feminisms' slippages with the terms "feminists" and "women," "Who all over there in 'womxn'?"[66] When a term is created to encapsulate those outside or alongside the term "Black women," another erasure occurs.

The phrase "women and femmes" has also been used in social media spaces to make space for those who are not women but may find themselves hailed by the term "femme," which also has contested meanings.[67]

But "women and femmes" doesn't quite capture all the targets of misogynoir. There are masculine-of-center, agender, and nonbinary people who experience the deleterious effects of misogynoir and who may not identify as women or femmes, as Sakia Gunn's murder unfortunately illustrates. Similarly, not all nonbinary Black femmes experience misogynoir because they are not read as Black women in public. For some femmes, homophobia and femmephobia might be the lens through which they become targets of violence. Black femmephobia is an important form of oppression to discuss, but it is not a synonym for misogynoir. Misogynoir is deployed because of social beliefs about Black women, and those of us who are read as Black women—despite our self-identification—get caught in the crosshairs.

I appreciate my colleague Anima Adjepong's formulation of "Black women adjacent" (BWA) to signal members of the nonbinary, agender, gender-variant community who may still be interpellated by misogynoir. "BWA" signals the fact that these diverse groups of folks are neighbors of Black women on the gender block but are also living in their own communes and multi-family duplexes. "BWA" also extends a potential for solidarity in that "adjacent" means "alongside" and "near." While all neighbors are not neighborly, "adjacent" hints at possible coalitions that are worth imagining and fostering. But "BWA" as an acronym or written out does not make immediately clear who is being called forth.

"BWA" does not work for my purposes because it is opaque. The term opens possibilities of solidarity even as it makes the constituencies it serves more difficult to ascertain. Having already used my invented portmanteau "misogynoir" in the title and introducing a new framework of digital alchemy, I do not wish to overload this text with more new terms of which the reader needs to keep track.[68] I will write out "Black nonbinary, agender, and gender-variant folks" in this text when necessary to prevent the continued conflation and erasure of these members from our neighborhood.[69]

I challenge you, dear reader, as you read this text, to think of Black women first when you see the word "woman," to think of queer and trans women first when you read the term "Black women." When you read the term "Black feminists," do not assume that it is interchangeable with "Black women," for as this text and others I reference make clear, not all Black women are feminists and not all Black feminists are women. The projects and people I highlight in this text do not fit neatly into either category. Much like the media they create, these people are not easily slotted into a box labeled "feminist" or "women."

Many of the Black women and Black nonbinary, agender, and gender-variant people I discuss have a dynamic relationship to labels. There are feminist elements to their work though the work itself may not be feminist; they may have identified as a woman at some point but not at the time I examined their work. What they all do share, however, is that they create digital media that center and uplift the experiences of Black women and girls, trans and cis, as the primary targets of misogynoir. "Black women" in the title of this text affirms Black women's centrality to the project of transforming misogynoir, even when it is not Black women or Black feminists who engage in the production of transformative media. To say the same another way, not all these Black digital alchemists are women and not all of them are feminists.

Black nonbinary, agender, and gender-variant folks are often invisible in data-collection processes, making their realities marginal within the already liminal space of Black women's digital alchemy. Nearly all of the data collected for this book assume that the category "Black women" is capacious enough to address misogynoir, but as I will detail in chapter 4, Black nonbinary and gender-variant people are also on the frontlines of the Black feminist transformation of misogynoir. As you have read in this introduction, Black women have been the central targets of misogynoir since the settling and colonization of the Americas. That Black women would then be at the heart of digital alchemists organizing in this country and beyond follows logically. But as we continue to grow our understanding of gender beyond a binary, and our digital age helps new language travel, more and more Black people are articulating themselves beyond the bounds of "woman."

Over the course of writing this book, my collaborators—the folks about whom and with whom I write—have transformed themselves. Some have come to identify as Black feminists, having not understood themselves that way when this project began. Others reject feminism altogether in favor of womanism, or even create their own epistemic frames.[70] For some, womanhood is a central part of their identity, and for others, woman is a limit that their gender transgresses. And yet, it is the work of self-identified Black women that created the space, intentionally or not, for those of us beyond the binary to find our little bit of purchase on the planet. Black women anchor this book even as Black women can experience some relative privilege in relation to their Black nonbinary, agender, and gender-variant peers.

This project does not attempt to address this significant gap in the literature regarding Black nonbinary, agender, and gender-variant folks who still find their fate tied to the way society thinks about Black women. I am hopeful that as we acknowledge the need for our scholarship to become even more specific to ensure that all members of our community are not overlooked, more statistical data can become disaggregated to make those on the margins of the margins visible. Research by SA Smythe, Treva Carrie Ellison, and Kai Green, among others, is doing the careful work of reminding people to mind the gap.[71] Black women and Black nonbinary, agender, and gender-variant folks negotiate misogynoir in a myriad of ways, but as I explore in this book, they are able to achieve liberatory praxis through digital alchemy that can actually transform misogynoir into something useful.

Digital Alchemy

Digital popular culture includes all the images we see online, the conversations that happen on social media, and their circulation throughout society. As I have illustrated, negative representations of Black women existed for centuries before the digital age, but these representations have been able to circulate more quickly with the advent of the Internet. Communications scholar Safiya Noble's book *Algorithms of Oppression* traces the disturbing phenomena of early Google search engine results that equated any search for Black women and girls with a search for porn.[72] The first images that resulted from these searches are of websites that show Black women engaged in sexual activity. Conversely, a search for "women" or even "white women" did not engender pornographic results on the first or even second page of the search. Noble's findings challenge the widely held belief that the Internet is a democratizing force of good for all. The algorithms reflect the biases of our society and are not inoculated from them as initially postulated.

I argue that Black women and Black nonbinary, agender, and gender-variant folks' digital resistance through content creation that challenges these problematic representations is a form of self-production that disrupts the mainstream narrative that promulgates narrow and stereotypical visions of identity. Both the process of creation and the material created are co-constitutive harm-reduction strategies in that they don't eradicate the injury of misogynoir but they do help alleviate some of its painful impact. Harm reduction recognizes that some harm is inevitable given the current reality of society, but we can greatly reduce the impact of harm by taking appropriate actions. Black women and Black nonbinary, agender, and gender-variant folks are actively reimagining the world through digital content creation that challenges the misogynoir that negatively impacts their health, and minimizing the harm they experience in the process.

Twitter is a digital publishing medium with a low bar for entry. If you have access to a smartphone or a computer, you can make use of the platform to share your thoughts in 280 characters or less.[73] Hashtags—a metadata tool for linking similar content on social media—have been instrumental in raising awareness about important real-time events and have been successful in garnering near-immediate responses from entities that are normally slow to address constituents. As I will discuss in the chapters that follow, Black women, particularly Black queer and trans women, as well as Black nonbinary, agender, and gender-variant folks have used social media to create innovative stories that speak to their interests, to challenge oppressive actions in their communities, and to transform misogynoir by building powerful digital and real-world networks.

Black women and Black nonbinary, agender, and gender-variant folks have mobilized via Twitter hashtags to challenge their representation in American visual culture, carving out precious space for incubating restorative practices and projects digitally. While these efforts do not presume to disrupt the dominant ideology in mainstream culture that shrouds Black women, they do provide maroon landing sites of respite. Creatively manipulating and transforming social media platforms become means of harm reduction. Whether it is web series, websites, or witty hashtags, Black women and Black nonbinary, agender, and gender-variant folks are making room for themselves on digital platforms in ways that exceed what was ever intended by the engineers and corporations who designed and created these sites.

I build toward an understanding of *digital alchemy* as a praxis designed to create better representations for those most marginalized, through the implementation of networks of care beyond the boundaries of the digital from which it springs. Alchemy is the "science" of turning regular metals into gold. When I talk about *digital alchemy* I am thinking of the ways that women of color, Black women, and Black nonbinary, agender, and gender-variant folks in particular transform everyday digital media into valuable social justice media that recode the failed scripts that negatively impact their lives. Digital alchemy shifts our attention from the negative stereotypes in digital culture to the redefinition of representations Black women are creating that provide another way of viewing their worlds. I argue that this process of creating transformational images challenges the normative standards of bodily representation and health presented in popular and medical culture.

These Black women and Black nonbinary, agender, and gender-variant folks are carving out their own spaces rather than trying to make room for themselves within existing frameworks. These projects are born from their experiences as marginalized subjects but do more than suggest homonormative alternatives of class ascension to access needed resources. Instead of an attempt to appeal to people in power through persuasive media, much of what is created online is explicitly for their own communities, affirming their own values and beliefs outside a hierarchical mainstream. Representation still matters, but not solely or primarily as a means to educate those with privilege. This practice is digital alchemy in action.

Digital alchemy exists at multiple levels, with some enactments following a reactionary posture that seeks to address a presented problem, while other forms are more creative, emerging from a point of production for Black women. *Defensive digital alchemy* takes the form of responding and recalibrating against misogynoir, while *generative digital alchemy* moves independently, innovated because it speaks to a desire or want for new types of representation. Defensive digital alchemy can take a reactionary posture, with Black women and Black agender, nonbinary, and gender-variant people using the digital tools available to them to redress misogynoir. It typically takes the form of a one-to-one response—for example, #RuinABlackGirlsMonday is met with #RuinAnInsecureBlackMansTuesday, discussed in chapter 1. This tit for tat does not engender the kinds of transformation of misogynoir that leads to long-lasting change, but it does let the offensive content be called out as such. Conversely, generative digital alchemy is not concerned with responding directly to the misogynoir that might inspire its production. Generative digital alchemy is born of an interest in creating new media that appeals to the community from which they come. The hashtags, web shows, and Tumblrs I describe in chapters 2, 3, and 4, respectively, are all examples of generative digital alchemy in action.

Misogynoir without Borders

While the Internet has been celebrated for its ability to traverse national borders and make countries seem more porous through information exchange, social media platforms maintain demographic segregation that belies this perceived fluidity. I still find a US-centrism in the Black women's digital media I examined for this project. While some of the tweets, videos, and Tumblrs come from English speakers outside the United States, the vast majority of the content available is created by Black women and Black nonbinary, agender, and gender-variant folks in the United States.

Additionally, the history of misogynoir I trace is contextualized through US chattel slavery and its afterlife.[74] The examples of misogynoir I detail build on US history and inform the way misogynoir is manifest contemporarily in the digital spaces I examine. However, misogynoir's virulence does not heed geopolitical borders. I am awed and saddened by the term's uptake beyond the United States—awed that Black women and their supporters have found the word useful in a number of contexts and saddened that people find it necessary to use so frequently in all corners of the globe. I believe that those outside the United States are best positioned to speak about misogynoir—and hopefully its transformation—in their locations. I offer an invitation to readers to see this book as the first of many that address misogynoir in several arenas and locales, where I and other writers take on the unfortunate dynamism of this noxious reality. Trudy's blog entries on misogynoir helped the term move through Internet spaces. Academics and activists in Europe, South America, Africa, and even Australia have found utility in the term.[75] As recently as 2019, protests in Paris, France, and Johannesburg, South Africa, have included signs and chants decrying misogynoir.[76] These uses of misogynoir and the resultant mobilizations to curb its effect on Black women and Black nonbinary, agender, and gender-variant folks deserve the proper framing that only folks directly engaged in these organizing efforts can provide. I see my work in conversation with as opposed to supplanting or superseding other work on the term, and I look forward to more work that challenges the roots of misogynoir in other locations.

Even my work on misogynoir is complicated by the fact that within a US context, Blackness is not a monolith. The tensions between Black Americans descended from enslaved Africans, Caribbeans descended from enslaved Africans, and more recent African immigrants disrupt any fantasies of an easily achievable pan-African united front against misogynoir. These intraracial fault lines are frequently part of the discussion of how misogynoir manifests, and I look forward to work by other scholars and activists who can address these tensions.

Transformation

Energy is neither created nor destroyed. It can only be transformed from one form to another.
—Law of conservation of energy

I titled this book *Misogynoir Transformed* because I could not let misogynoir go unmodified. A book titled *Misogynoir* on its own does not represent an action or protest. I did not want to simply explain or rehearse examples of misogynoir in a book-length project. I, like trans advocate Janet Mock, wanted an action to animate misogynoir, to signal my interest in its destruction. I did not want to account for all the vile and deleterious hate that is misogynoir without making clear that there are those of us working to transform it. Chapter 1 does take on this necessary project but also highlights examples that extend the possibility of misogynoir's transformation. The idea of misogynoir being transformed, using that swirling mass of negative energy against itself to make something altogether different, inspires me.

"Embodied transformation," a concept from the practice of somatics as rearticulated by organizer and facilitator adrienne maree brown in her book *Pleasure Activism: The Politics of Feeling Good*, "'is foundational change that shows in our actions, ways of being, relating, and perceiving. It is transformation that sustains over time."[77] Transformation is achieved only when change is evident in the way we move through the world and how we continue to incorporate that change throughout time. When I talk of the transformation of misogynoir, I am interested in all of the ways that Black women and Black nonbinary, agender, and gender-variant folks work to transform the toxicity of these representations and images that cause them harm. While I hope for an eradication of misogynoir, I realize that a world without misogynoir requires more than the labor of Black women and Black nonbinary, agender, and gender-variant folks to be achieved. We can transform our relationship to misogynoir and transform the images and material consequences of misogynoir even as we are not the ones who create it. The transformation of misogynoir through the creation of new possibilities is an essential practice of the digital alchemy these communities engender. In the context of this book, I am looking at the digital tools that Black women and Black nonbinary, agender, and gender-variant folks employ to do this transformative work.

Transformation is also a key component of transformative justice, a liberatory approach to lessen harm and violence in society that does not center alienation or punishment as means of behavior modification. The now defunct social justice organization Generation Five, which described three essential elements of transformative justice, insisted that "the conditions that allow violence to occur must be transformed in order to achieve justice in individual instances of violence. Therefore, Transformative Justice is both a liberating politic and an approach for securing justice."[78] The transformation of misogynoir similarly requires a change in conditions, which includes the way that Black women are viewed in society.

What might seem difficult to understand is that my call for transformation is inclusive of those who cause harm by perpetuating misogynoir. Rather than punish or shame those who participate in the proliferation of misogynoir, transformation requires consequences for harmful actions. In the examples that follow, I go into detail about those who have used misogynoir to harm Black women and girls and Black nonbinary, agender, and gender-variant folks, but I do not wish to punish them or cause them harm in return. For those willing to learn and understand why their behavior was harmful, this text can serve as an opening, a place to learn why their behavior was harmful and hopefully start them on a path to transform their behavior.

The transformation of misogynoir occurs in the types of content that creators produce and in the lives of the people involved in the production through their participation in the process. On one level, Black women and Black nonbinary, agender, and gender-variant folks are transforming the misogynoir they experience in digital spaces by refashioning these very same tools for their own ends. Misogynoir is transformed through new content creation. And while new content is being created, the process itself produces opportunities and experiences that also challenge misogynoir. Black women and Black nonbinary, agender, and gender-variant folks can experience an embodied transformation through their participation in creating digital media. Content creation provides opportunities for unique self-care and group-care practices such as building interdependent relationships and sharing resources. This creative process transforms racist, homophobic, transphobic, and sexist mainstream imagery through the generation of new content, while simultaneously fostering conditions that allow creators to experiment with practices that support their "physical, mental, and social well-being" outside the purview of the Western biomedical-industrial complex.[79] While it may not be possible for Black nonbinary, agender, and gender-variant folks to eradicate misogynoir themselves, they can transform it and reduce the impact of its harmful effects in their lives through the digital alchemy they employ.

I see the digital alchemy that Black women engage on social media platforms as a form of harm reduction, given that this activism implicitly and explicitly challenges misogynoir. Harm reduction is an intervention strategy primarily associated with lowering the potential negative health outcomes of drug use, but the efficacy of the practice has led to its application in other contexts. It begins with the assumption that harm happens, but one can reduce harm by engaging in small transformative interventions. Black women's digital activism is a form of harm reduction because it does not stop misogynoir, but it mitigates its harm through the promotion of images and narratives Black women want to see. Black women can create their own networks with which to affirm one another, challenge unjust policies, and create the kinds of stories they wish were in the media, as well as transform the misogy-noir they experience by remixing it or creating something new entirely. Black women support their own health and well-being through what they create and the process through which they create it. *Misogynoir Transformed* examines both the creations and the process by which they are constructed, to illustrate the transformational ways that social media platforms can be used.

Overview

This book distinguishes itself from other critical work on stereotypes of Black women by privileging queer and trans Black women as well as Black nonbinary, agender, and gender-variant folks' work and voices. Rather than explaining how they differ from those of their heterosexual and cisgender counterparts, I focus on the representations created by queer and trans Black women as well as Black nonbinary, agender, and gender-variant folks for their communities. While Patricia Hill Collins, bell hooks, and Melissa Harris-Perry have critiqued what they call "controlling images," and scholars such as Paula Giddings, M. Bahati Kuumba, and Brittney Cooper have traced Black women's activist histories, none have centered queer and trans Black women's activism as pivotal to the creative strategies that have grown resistance movements.[80] My project troubles the assumed heteronormativity of the category "Black women" in other texts by speaking specifically to the realities of queer and trans women's lives and production. Building on the work of queer Black feminists like Cathy Cohen, Kara Keeling, Roderick Ferguson, and Sharon Holland, I argue that the radical queer politics of many of these content creators is an essential part of what makes their work compelling and unique, extending beyond reactionary alternatives into imaginative new realities.[81]

The digital resistance strategies deployed by the content creators I highlight utilize a queer framework that eschews respectability or a quest for "positive" counternarratives. I explore these ostensibly messy means that provide a much more nuanced way of imagining Black women's lives while simultaneously examining the links between the ways these images circulate and the material realities they engender for Black women as well as Black nonbinary, agender, and gender-variant folks' health. I conceptualize the alternate representations created by Black women as well as Black nonbinary, agender, and gender-variant folks as both counterpublic productions that trouble stereotypical depictions and vehicles for processes that allow for other types of interventions, such as network and resource building that far outlive the timeliness of the content produced. This reimagining through imagery may seem to serve only as an immaterial intervention, but as I argue throughout this text, representations are essential tools for fostering health on a physical, mental, and social level.

In the chapters that follow, I unpack misogynoir and Black women as well as Black nonbinary, agender, and gender-variant folks' critical digital resistance in the twenty-first century. Chapter 1, "Misogynoir Is a Drag," discusses the ubiquity of misogynoir in digital space, in the form of hashtags, memes, and videos that portray Black women through the lens of damaging stereotypes. I use the hashtag #RuinABlackGirlsMonday and the viral video *Shit Black Girls Say* to discuss the current landscape of misogynoir online. I explore how the hashtag and viral video have real-world consequences that negatively affect the health of the Black women dragged by these images—dragged by Black men's comedic drag performances, and also dragged by those who enforce punitive policies on Black women and girls. The defensive and generative digital alchemy that Black women enact in these situations is one way they can transform the misogynoir they experience even when they cannot stop it.

Chapter 2, "Transforming Misogynoir through Trans Advocacy," begins the section of the book featuring case studies that illustrate digital alchemy in action. I focus on Black trans women's use of social media as a lifesaving and health-affirming praxis that mitigates transmisogynoir. I argue that these practices extend our definitions of "health" beyond simple biomedical rubrics through the kind of generative digital alchemy enacted. I begin with trans advocate Janet Mock's wildly successful hashtag #GirlsLikeUs, which continues to be an important digital network for trans women to connect with each other. I discuss the evolution of the hashtag and its success in mitigating misogynoir by providing an outlet for Black trans women to build networks of care on and beyond the Internet. I discuss the digital campaign to #FreeCeCe McDonald, a Black trans woman incarcerated for the accidental death of one of her attackers during a racist transphobic incident. Her story was spread via YouTube videos and a support blog, all designed to re-frame the national media story that made her the perpetrator instead of a survivor who defended herself and lived. McDonald's story clearly illustrates the power of the digital to transform individual lives as well as spark the kinds of resistance strategies that persist even after a specific goal is achieved.

Chapter 3, "Web Show Worldbuilding Mitigates Misogynoir," investigates the proliferation of Black queer women's YouTube series and what messages are conveyed about health and well-being therein. *Skye's the Limit* best exemplifies the genre's concern with healthy relationships in queer community as it follows lead character Skye through her questionable professional and personal choices. Through close readings of scenes in the series' episodes, I argue that *Skye's the Limit*, *Between Women*, and *195 Lewis* address storylines concerning Black women's health that are not visible in mainstream media. Mental, physical, and sexual health along with pleasure are central explorations in these web shows, missing from mainstream television. Though these web series often have short runs due to the unpredictable nature of crowdsourced resources, I argue that ephemerality is actually a compelling quality of this digital media production that is not necessarily in contention with quality. By creating short cycles and seasons, casts and crews create a snapshot of the concerns of a moment in time as well as launch the creators into other platforms that allow for greater amplification of the messages from the small screen.

Chapter 4, "Alchemists in Action against Misogynoir," provides examples of where this transformative digital alchemy could be taking us. I interview two Black nonbinary femme Tumblr users about how they leveraged the platform to create and sustain a practice of care for themselves. I explore their engagement with the platform, their experiences of misogynoir on- and offline and how conversations through the platform helped them create a community for themselves that enabled them to transform misogynoir. In the book's conclusion, I end by suggesting what my line of inquiry opens for future research, including the potential impact of increased surveillance of digital media and feminist cultural productions and processes in digital spaces.

You will undoubtedly notice the lack of images in this text on Black women and Black nonbinary, agender, and gender-variant folks' creative digital resistance to the negative imagery that unfortunately shapes how they are treated in society. Given the graphic nature of some of these images, I have opted against including them in the text because I believe that we are already inundated with enough images of Black women's subjugation. If you want to see misogynoir in action you need only turn on the news, see a movie, watch television, or scroll your timeline. You will find examples of Black women being denied their humanity in ways that have a direct impact on their lives. But you will also, as I highlight in this text, find evidence of their resistance. And while this resistance offers up some beautiful imagery, I would do it a disservice to have it rendered here in black-and-white stills of dynamic—but often of limited production value—videos or screenshots of tweets with now broken links or missing images.[82] Instead, I opt for detailed description and encourage readers to find these gems in their natural habitat, in the digital sphere for which they were made.

While I initially endeavored to do a deep dive into the demographic data of the people who used these social media platforms to transform misogynoir, the information was difficult to access. Even the way I was able to access some of the tweets and videos I analyze in this text shifted over the course of writing the book, including the loss of accessible statistics regarding engagement with the digital media on different platforms. There are pieces of this project that I cannot replicate because of the changes in accessible data and the ever-increasing proprietary nature of these platforms' terms of service. As we note in my co-authored book #HashtagActivism: Networks of Race and Gender Justice, some aspects of this research would not be possible to undertake if we began writing any later than we did.[83] Similarly, Misogynoir Transformed has gone through its own transformation based on the changing nature of the data available.

You will also notice hyperlinks embedded in many of the tweets discussed. I decided not to provide active links to this content for both the users' privacy and the likely probability that these links would no longer work by the time of publication. As digital humanist Simone Browne notes, researchers must be suspicious of surveillance given its deeply anti-Black origins and development.[84] The line between accurately citing the social media content I procured and exposing the users who created that content to uninvited scrutiny is one I travel with care. The

URLs encountered here are evocative of the time at which these tweets were collected, before preview text and images that now accompany links in tweets were available to noncommercial users.

These Black women as well as Black nonbinary, agender, and gender-variant folks are carving out their own spaces rather than trying to make room for themselves within existing frameworks. To be sure, using social media to react to oppressive situations is not a long-term strategy for addressing the rampant misogynoir in our society, but the way Black women have enacted digital alchemy certainly creates opportunities for transformation.

1

Misogynoir Is a Drag

> Bars for years, niggas thought I did a bid,
> I'm draggin' these hoes like Harambe did the kid.
> —Nicki Minaj, "The Pinkprint Freestyle"

Nicki Minaj's verse in her song "The Pinkprint Freestyle" gives an example of how the term "drag" is used in Black vernacular English. Minaj boasts of her lyrical dexterity, referring to her rhymes as "bars" while simultaneously conjuring literal "bars" as though she has a long prison sentence. She follows this braggadocio with more, asserting that her superior wordplay is "draggin'" other rappers the way the gorilla Harambe did when he grabbed a three-year-old boy who fell into his zoo enclosure in 2016.[1] While referencing this physical dragging, Minaj claims that her rhyming prowess puts other rappers (i.e., hoes) to shame. Her own misogynoiristic dragging, by using the word "ho," signals both her superior abilities and the weakness of those who dare to challenge her on the mic. "Ho" has become such a ubiquitous insult, especially in the still imagined default masculine world of hip hop, that the misogynoir embedded in its roots might be difficult to see. However, "ho" has been reanimated in popular culture with the misogynoiristic slogan "Joe and the Hoe," referencing the 2020 Joe Biden and Kamala Harris Democratic Party presidential ticket.[2] But it is Minaj's lyrical use of "drag" and perhaps her hyperfeminine aesthetic that provide a glimpse into the figurative use of the term, which also has its own roots in drag queen and trans women of color 1980s New York City subculture.

When used as a verb, "to drag" is to "pull someone or something along forcefully, roughly, or with difficulty."[3] This verb usage has little to do with another meaning of "drag," which describes the practice of performative cross-dressing. "Drag" has multiple definitions, and the title of this chapter utilizes one of them. To say "misogynoir is a drag" is to say that misogynoir is tiresome and vexing, annoying and trying.

More than these, drag can be aggressive. It is this verb version of drag—coming from Old Norse English, meaning to draw or pull away—that informs the Black queer vernacular English use of "drag" that I discuss in this chapter. To drag in this context means to forcefully or roughly admonish someone verbally.

In the famed 1990 documentary about New York QTPOC ball culture *Paris Is Burning*, performance artist Dorian Corey describes *reading* as "the real artform of insult."[4] Reading is the directed and pointed castigation of a person with whom you have a problem. While reading is not dragging, they both share a deeper history in the Black cultural practice of *signifying*, a way of playing with words that blurs the line between derision and delight.[5] Signifying is at once jocular and needling. Dragging is not as refined or precise a form of insult as reading, but it is perhaps best described as its most extreme form. It is beyond the art of roasting or a good-natured ribbing, which are generally said in jest, with everyone, even the person being roasted, in on the jokes about their personality and behaviors. Dragging, however, is meant to verbally eviscerate the subject being dragged, to embarrass them publicly. Not one perceived fault of the person being dragged escapes the attention of the person doing the dragging. No one is laughing with you; they are most definitely laughing at you. To drag is to strongly and adroitly call out the problems and flaws of the person being dragged.

There is also a long tradition of Black men donning drag for laughs, making them the emasculating Sapphire caricatures of Black women. In this chapter, I also examine the way the digital has led to a proliferation of this drag that circulates misogynoir. "Drag" becomes a way to both describe the practice of men donning dresses to behave as women for comic effect and evoke the resultant negative screed that often accompanies these portrayals of Black women. Sonic and sartorial drag can be forms of misogynoir and transmisogynoir, which I unpack through the YouTube viral video *Shit Black Girls Say*. I explore the viral spread of the hashtag #RuinABlackGirlsMonday as another example of digital drag and digital blackface that spread misogynoir online and begin to surface Black women's resistance to such characterizations.

I explore the *dragging* of Black women and girls both literally and figuratively through digital platforms as misogynoir. Though dragging Black women and girls predates the Internet, the speed with which digital devices move misogynoir makes for an unparalleled urgency in addressing its effects. Like the term itself, the dragging of Black women and girls occurs on multiple levels, resulting in harm that includes the circulation of digital caricatures that misrepresent them, which in turn fuel their physical mistreatment by multiple institutions, including the government and schools. I examine the proliferation of videos of the violent assaults, the physical dragging of Black girls in public spaces that circulate the material impact of misogynoir on their bodies and health. Here, only barely surfaced is Black girls' resistance to these tactics through defensive digital alchemy, their own efforts to combat misogynoir in their lives. By navigating these facets of the digital spread of misogynoir, I provide the context for why Black women and girls desire to see misogynoir transformed.

Dragging in Drag

[Billy] Sorrells's dramatic, obnoxious black woman character seemed more like the butt of the joke than someone who was laughing along with it. There were also a few casual quips about domestic violence, as if that could ever possibly be funny.

Today, I know the vocabulary word to explain exactly why "Shit Black Girls Say" made me uncomfortable: misogynoir. The term, coined by activist Moya Bailey, describes the unique interplay of racism and sexism that black women face. Sorrells was drawing on an all-too-familiar trope: Black male comedians like Tyler Perry and Eddie Murphy donning drag and regurgitating the same racist stereotypes that white supremacy uses to oppress black women. These portrayals paint us as loud, angry, aggressive, hysterical, overly sexual, neck-swerving, gum-popping clichés who scream, "Oh, no, he didn't!" on loop. While these tropes persist all over modern media like Instagram, YouTube, Vine (RIP), and film and television, they're not too different from the mammy and Jezebel stereotypes promoted by Jim Crow–era advertisements and cartoons.[6]

The *Shit Black Girls Say* YouTube video is a perfect example of misogynoir in digital public space. Building on the 2011 *Shit Girls Say* viral video created by white comedian Kyle Humphrey, in which he performs in drag, making fun of the way girls (read: white girls) talk, comedian

Billy Sorrells's iteration repackages Humphrey's gender stereotypes with an overtly named Black twist. Written by Black queer woman creative Lena Waithe, the two-minute and forty-eight-second video features Sorrells in a wig portraying "Peaches," a cis straight Black every-girl who loves wine, the *Basketball Wives* franchise, and yelling at her man.[7] Waithe wrote Peaches as a self-loathing social climber, with none of her dialogue able to pass the Bechdel Test.[8]

In her 2018 memoir *Well, That Escalated Quickly*, which describes her meteoric rise to fame as a YouTube star, Franchesca Ramsey explains why Sorrells's comedy fell flat for her. Ramsey's description of finding misogynoir a helpful frame for understanding the way Black women were being negatively portrayed in Sorrells's *Shit Black Girls Say* video captures both the proliferation of these problematic portrayals on the Internet and the viral spread of the term. "Misogynoir" describes the uniquely co-constitutive racialized and sexist violence that befalls Black women as a result of their simultaneous and interlocking oppression at the intersection of racial and gender marginalization. Black women experience racism and sexism not as discrete or separate forms of prejudice but as an inseparable amalgamation of toxicity. As I discussed in the introduction, misogynoir takes many forms, the roots of which have their genesis in ideas of Black women's inherent inferiority. Stereotypes about Black women's supposed lack of femininity, undesirability, and unintelligence show up in the Internet memes and digital content of today but are the descendants of the minstrel show and movie fodder of days past. Sorrells's portrayal of Peaches mirrors the minstrel era character of Sapphire, and he is simply the latest in a long line of comedians to use Black women as vehicles for comedic success. Ramsey acknowledges both the mammy and Jezebel stereotypes, but the less discussed and later developed Sapphire stereotype is essential for understanding the way Black women are represented in digital culture.

First introduced on the minstrel radio show *Amos 'n' Andy* in 1928, Sapphire didn't have a voice and was talked about by the white radio actors Freeman Gosden and Charles Correll, who voiced the Black titular characters Amos and Andy, as well as Sapphire's husband, Kingfish Stevens. Sapphire was described as an emasculating ballbuster who berated Kingfish for being a failure at securing and keeping a job. In the later days of the radio show, after it had grown in popularity and changed to a longer syndicated format, Correll and Gosden decided to hire actresses to voice their female characters. The white radio actress Elinor Harriot was the first to voice Mrs. Stevens. Ernestine Wade, a Black woman actress and singer, was hired to give Sapphire a permanent voice and later a face when the show moved to television.[9]

Sapphire was a loud and angry Black woman, impossible to satisfy, irrational with rage, and completely outside appropriate (read: white) femininity.[10] She voiced white animus toward Black men through her snide remarks and derisive comments to Kingfish and his friends. This heterosexual dis-ease between the characters helped bolster widely circulating ideas about Black familial pathology. The radio show and then the television show were immensely popular, though they faced condemnation from Black organizations like the NAACP for promoting damaging stereotypes about Black life. Wade defended her portrayal of Sapphire, saying that the character was loved by many and opened doors for Black women on the radio and screen. But Sapphire's origin and defining characteristics remain steeped in the white minstrel imagination, auditory blackface, and gender drag even in absentia.

Sapphires portrayed through drag have appeared throughout television history, before finding a home online. Flip Wilson's 1970s Geraldine along with the 1990s-era Wanda by Jamie Foxx and Shenehneh by Martin Lawrence are caricatures of Black women performed by ostensibly straight cis Black men donning drag both sartorially and auditorily for laughs. In the quote that opens this section, Ramsey laments this drag used by Sorrells to make his character Peaches come alive, noting the history of Black male comedians using drag to "regurgitat[e] the same racist stereotypes that white supremacy uses to oppress black women."[11] An essential element of this supposed humor is the obvious masculinity of the straight Black man that lies just beneath the makeup and wig, a not-so-subtle critique of Black women's perceived femininity. These caricatures also amused audiences because of their insistence on their physical beauty despite their masculine features and usually dark skin, the complete opposite traits of desirability and beauty in a white supremacist culture. Their insistence on their own attractiveness despite the ways that the audience is supposed to read them as unattractive reinforces a delusional confidence that is supposed to be funny. Whether Geraldine's off-key singing or Shenehneh's insistence that Martin is hitting on her, these "women" know no shame when viewers believe they should. White and Black audiences have been laughing at these misogynoirist portrayals on television for decades, and with the advent of digital platforms like the short-lived Vine and the increasingly ever-present YouTube, these depictions seem here to stay.

Like Humphrey's "girl," Peaches does not really know how to use her computer. She is even confused by the Apple logo on her MacBook. She just wants to watch TV and eat snacks. Unsure of her relationship, she questions whether her male partner (whose face we never see) loves her. She also voices that she "can't stand [him]!" to her friends and directly to her never fully visible paramour.[12] The scene that directly follows is one of the most startling segments of the video. Peaches cries emotionally after an unseen physical assault by her boyfriend as she threatens said partner with her brother's retaliation. Audiences are prompted to laugh at this outburst of emotion, given her earlier disgust, disinterest, and insecurity regarding her relationship. As Ramsey comments, it is unclear what the humor is in this moment except perhaps for the loud dramatic nature of Peaches's admonishment of the man off-screen. Together, these clips paint Peaches as unintelligent, vapid, emotional, and ridiculous.

As the title of the video suggests, Peaches's words are not just those of an individual character but reflective of the shit Black girls (plural) say. Peaches and Black women are infantilized as girls and their interests made trivial through this diminution in the title. While Humphrey's girl is ditzy, she is not the subject of intimate partner violence, nor is she constantly discussing or fighting with her man. Humphrey's girl is presented as carefree with little to worry about besides what to wear and asking her boyfriend to turn the music down. Sorrells's portrayal of Peaches is supposed to be funny because of its projected universality. He paints Peaches with a class brush as well, labeling her "ghetto," or unsophisticated with her choice in television and snacks. The jokes hinge on the assumed familiarity viewers have with this representation of Black girls, which lampoons both their physical appearance and their purported preferences. Sorrells builds on Peaches's presumed universality by utilizing another well-worn trope: a Black man in a dress.

His visible facial hair adds to the comedic performance by reminding viewers that he is a man pretending to be a woman. By being obvious men in wigs, Sorrells and Humphrey pull nonbinary folks and trans women into their punch lines. Portrayals like theirs have the tangible effect of making trans women and nonbinary folks who have stubble or hairy faces laughable, and participate in the erroneous yet pernicious idea that trans women are not women. As trans women have become more visible, the stakes of this classic comedic trope of a man in a dress are higher. Trans women are already disciplined for being outside cultural gender expectations, and these caricatures add fuel to an already raging fire. More than being the butt of jokes, trans women are targets of life-threatening violence and discrimination. As actress and writer Jen Richards offers in the 2020 Netflix documentary *Disclosure: Trans Lives on Screen*, cis men playing women—cis or trans—call forth the possibility for violence against trans women:

> The public thinks of trans women as men with really good hair and makeup in costume. And that's reinforced every time we see a man who's played a trans woman off-screen. . . . Having cis men play trans women, in my mind, is a direct link to the violence against trans women. And in my mind, part of the reason men end up killing trans women out of fear other men will think that they're gay for having been with trans women is that the friends, the men whose judgment they are in fear of, only know trans women from media, and the people who are playing trans women are the men that they know. This doesn't happen when a trans woman plays a trans woman. Laverne Cox is just as beautiful and glamourous off-screen as she is on-screen. As is Jazzmun, as is Trace Lysette, and Alexandra Billings and Angelica Ross and so on. When you see these women off-screen as women, it completely deflates this idea that they're somehow men in disguise.[13]

For Richards, transphobic violence gets activated through homophobic fears perpetuated in media by the idea that trans women are not women but men in dresses. When Hollywood reinforces this trope by lauding male actors for their portrayals of trans women, the "man in a dress" trope is further concretized. Real trans women get embroiled in ideas about transformative cinematic performances even though they live their lives every day and are not acting. Sorrells's rendering of Black women as caricature by being an ostensibly straight cis Black man in a dress does not just evoke misogynoir but also evokes this trans antagonism that is rarely named.

When Black women are made girls who care about inconsequential topics and display unjustified anger by evoking the Sapphire trope, Black men comedians reify an image that denigrates Black women, cis and trans alike.[14] There is clearly a power in the digital medium that is furthering a tradition that dates back to minstrelsy. Geraldine, Wanda, Shenehneh, and Peaches all represent intraracial cis heterosexual class tensions that go under-addressed in Black communities. Black men express their dislike of the sexual economy of the community by portraying Black women as money-hungry and manipulative. Laughing at Black women through the artifice of drag provides a socially acceptable outlet for misogynoir and for the entertainers who utilize the medium, a proven path to more visibility and success. Misogynoir is on display through representations of Black women as contemptible and laughable, undeserving of consideration or care. The audience laughs at these caricatures, not with them, much like the difference between dragging and a good-natured ribbing. By being made other, Black women become disposable, and this comedic rendering circulates in ways that produce harmful material effects in Black women's lives—namely, the murders of Black women.

Despite the generally histrionic portrayals of the Black woman as Sapphire, Black media makers have tried to recoup widely circulating damning imagery of Black life and Black men in particular. In her analysis of heteronormative ideologies expressed through fictional Black characters in novels, Candice Jenkins critiques the "salvific wish" that informs the "recurrent black drive toward a patriarchal 'family romance.'"[15] The salvific wish is the desire to "rescue the black community from white racist accusations of sexual and domestic pathology, through the embrace of conventional bourgeois propriety."[16] Filmmaker Tyler Perry's work, particularly his drag character Madea, is a quintessential example of Black women being dragged by drag for the purpose of racial uplift at their expense.

Though Perry outwardly expresses a desire to challenge stereotypical depictions of Black men through his stage plays and films, his character Madea does the exact opposite for Black women. Madea embodies all the elements of the Sapphire with the mammy thrown in. Madea is a loud, pistol-toting, fat, elderly Black woman. The audience is instructed to laugh at her outrageous persona, but also find humor in the fact that she is obviously Tyler Perry in drag. Whereas Sorrells and Humphrey use visible facial hair to disrupt their drag performances, Tyler Perry "rips off his wig, appears onstage baring his fat suit, or drops his voice really low to expose the fact that he is really a male underneath the dress."[17] Even in film, Madea is only made real through the constant framing of Tyler Perry, as in the film title *Tyler Perry's Madea's Family Reunion* (2006). Perry still wants his audience to know that he is a man playing a woman for laughs.

Madea also serves other purposes in the plays and films in which she is featured. Madea, like Sapphire, gets to voice the thoughts of the dominant group, which in this case is Black men, through the relative safety or cover of drag. As my frequent collaborator and cultural critic Whitney Peoples attests, "Perry appropriates the body of black women and the cultural mythology that surrounds that body as yet another mechanism to legitimize his ability to speak to and about black women."[18] Madea lectures Black women about how they should behave as an in-group member, just as Sapphire lectures Kingfish about how he should behave as a fellow Black person. The comedic relief that characters like Madea, Sapphire, and Peaches provide is predicated on a misogynoir that dictates how women ought to be, even if that behavior is made laughably ridiculous. Whether it is the big screen or small, Black men in drag are able to use their portrayals of Black women as a source of fatphobic, transphobic, homophobic, misogynoiristic, and classist comedy that ultimately serves to discipline Black women.

Unfortunately, *Shit Black Girls Say* is one of many viral videos that feature cis and ostensibly straight Black men pretending to be Black women for comedic effect online. Calling himself "the Instafamous Modern Madea Comedian taking the world by storm," YouTube and Instagram star Kwaylon Rogers, also known as BlameItOnKway, dons bright pink lipstick, retains his moustache, and wears a teal wig as he plays the loud and always ready-to-fight Titi.[19] With 4.5 million Instagram followers in 2019, BlameItOnKway tapped into a viable market of people interested in the day-to-day musings of his misogynoirist character. Initially going viral in 2015 for a video in which he portrayed a disgruntled Black woman *America's Next Top Model* contestant arguing with a spliced-in

Tyra Banks, who hosts the show, BlameItOnKway established himself as a YouTube comedian who specialized in portraying Black women who think they are beautiful when they are not. He harnessed the widely circulating clip of Banks's emotional diatribe at a contestant, manipulating digital technology for misogynoiristic success. Like Perry and the others before him, Rogers built his success on the misogynoir that animates his portrayal of Titi.

Titi believes that she is beautiful despite being dark-skinned and masculine with a moustache. She is the antithesis of the white beauty standard of fair-skinned, hairless femininity. As in comedian Amy Schumer's 2018 film *I Feel Pretty*, viewers are supposed to laugh at this obviously unattractive woman's confidence in her appearance. Whereas Schumer's beauty is made laughable because of her perceived fatness, Titi has multiple strikes against her—race, color, masculine features— and yet she still understands herself to be beautiful. In contrast to the men interacting with Wanda, Shenehneh, and Madea, Titi's male suitors are not repulsed by her; rather, they are eager to get her attention. The hackneyed joke of her suitors' repulsion is slightly revamped through a realism that is a direct product of reality TV culture, where Titi narrates to the camera and video visibly supports her contention that she is desirable.

Her clothing, hair, and makeup choices all introduce a level of class antagonism that goes unspoken. Her bright turquoise hair and pink lipstick along with her tube tops and short skirts project an aesthetic that is also made comical because it does not match the luxurious environment in which she is situated. In the short-lived Zeus Media online reality TV show *Titi Do You Love Me*, Rogers portrays his titular character in a bachelorette situation where multiple men and one lesbian vie for Titi's affection while "staying" in a palatial home.[20]

Through online visibility, Titi caught the attention of many celebrities, including Tyler Perry, who invited Titi to Madea's Farewell Stage-Play Tour throughout the United States. Comedian Tiffany Haddish and international pop star Janet Jackson are just a few of the famous Black women who have worked with Titi on-screen, inadvertently furthering the notion that these misogynoirist depictions of Black women are not only mainstream but also harmless. If famous Black women support Titi, what's the problem?

The problem with Titi and caricatures like her is that they create a flat, one-dimensional view of Black women, so much so that other images of Black women remain out of frame. When Titi or Peaches becomes the default characterization of Black women, real Black women's lives are erased. The caricature becomes the truth and real Black women are the exceptions to the newly established rule. Real Black women are expected to be as sexual, loud, and uncouth as these caricatures. For Black women who travel from the United States to Europe and other parts of the world, these stereotypes become people's point of reference for who they are. In a 2015 article on Black women's study abroad experiences, researcher Tasha Willis found that Black girls experienced gender and racialized harassment that their white peers did not experience. Their race and gender made them particularly susceptible to catcalls, sexual harassment, and the assumption that they were sex workers in the places they traveled.[21]

Similarly, social media has made it all too easy for videos like those of Titi to circulate, adding to the misogynoir that Black women must negotiate while moving through the world. Whereas radio and television used to be the primary vectors of ideas about Black women, digital media can spread these images so much farther and faster. Additionally, with the advent of smartphones with cameras that can capture and produce video, production is eased, allowing videos to circulate even more quickly. People with no radio or film experience can become producers in minutes, and with the proliferation of video sites and apps like Vimeo, TikTok, and YouTube, it is a simple process to start building an audience.

YouTube stars like Jay Versace exist in an interesting space where their perceived queer sexuality gives them more license to play with drag performance and not be accused of the same types of violent trans antagonism or misogynoir as their ostensibly straight counterparts. There is a way that queer identity gives them room to play with drag as members "of" the community and not "outside" it. Versace and NotKarltonBanks lip sync and impersonate Black women in ways that seem to be in the spirit of laughing *with* as opposed to *at* Black women. Whether it's Versace's minute-long homage to Erykah Badu's classic song "On & On," or NotKarltonBanks's portrayal of Black women serving food to fellow parishioners after church service, their videos rely on the viewers' knowledge of these cultural touchstones and do not seek to render the Black women as caricatures.[22] These subtle differences in portrayal are sometimes hard to bring into complete relief, and these images continue to blur the line between impersonation and caricature.[23]

The fact that *Shit Black Girls Say* was written by Lena Waithe, who has risen to prominence for her nuanced creation of Black queer characters on shows like *Master of None* and her own Showtime vehicle *The Chi*, may seem surprising. But if one is attentive to the clout gained by getting one's foot in the proverbial door of Hollywood, a "by any means necessary" approach that includes shitting on Black women is not a revelation. To assume that Black women, particularly Black queer women, would not participate in the very misogynoir that can be turned on them is to miss the ways that masculinity can cohere across gender identity.

As I articulated in the introduction, Black women and Black feminists are not synonymous. A long-practiced stigma-management strategy by those multiply marginalized is to deflect negativity away from themselves by admonishing others. In crafting a legible female masculinity, Waithe seems to employ the same "bros before hoes" mentality rampant among cishet men.[24] Through the denigrating character of Peaches and her initial reluctance to address the sexual harassment of two Black women on *The Chi*, Waithe casts her lot with the boys.[25] It should be no surprise that toxic masculinity does not need a man to do its bidding. This defensive and toxic masculinity has also been discussed as "protest-hypermasculinity" by scholar Laura Lane-Steele. She reads the misogynoir enacted through toxic masculinity by masculine-of-center women as a means to escape the generally lower social position of Black lesbians in a heteropatriarchal society.[26] Waithe and other masculine lesbians in the entertainment industry like R&B singer Syd or the rapper Young M.A. take on a "bro" persona, effectively distancing themselves from the misogynoir that would otherwise be sent in their direction. This assertion is not meant to imply that the masculinity that these queer women wield is any more performative than anyone else's, but it is to say that masculinity in a patriarchal world means protection.

Syd of the Afrofuturist hip hop groups Odd Future and The Internet has successfully deflected attention away from her gender by reinforcing a gender binary and hierarchy that she is able to benefit from as a more masculine-presenting woman.[27] In a 2011 *MTV News* interview with the group, Syd recounts a conversation with her father about being the only cis woman in the group, saying, "When I first started fucking with Odd Future heavy, my dad was like, 'Really? Like, they talk about, like, some crazy shit and you're, as a female, like, you're slapping a lot of other females in the face.' I'm like, 'That's what I do. I slap bitches, Dad.'"[28] She and her Odd Future bandmates dissolve into laughter. Her words prove that she is one of the boys and not one of the girls because she "slaps bitches" and does not get slapped. Whether this violence is real or figurative is not the point, as her laughter and the laughter of her bandmates solidify their bond. Her belonging is connected to her gender presentation, which is aligned with her male friends through a masculinity that is antagonistic to women; she is not the hypothetical woman getting slapped. Laughing at and potentially hitting women make Syd one of the boys, which supports her position in the group. I am reminded of Syd's commentary when I think of Lena Waithe's role in making *Shit Black Girls Say* a viral success. By distancing themselves from Black women by making other Black women the punch line of their jokes, Syd and Waithe are both able to move in the world with the slight advantage their masculinity affords, sparing them the deadly consequence that befell their masculine-of-center sister Sakia Gunn. But part of shoring up that masculinity requires the sacrifice of fellow Black women.[29] The internalized misogynoir of these queer women is expressed through their denigration of their more feminine peers.

Waithe has effectively distanced herself from this early writing, refashioning herself as pro-woman in her writing and deeds. Tyler Perry's decision in 2019 to stop performing as Madea might reflect a similar such transition.[30] Perry's ascension to billionaire status and opening of a 330-acre studio lot outside Atlanta, which will purportedly have housing for Black women and girls, nonbinary and gender-variant folks as well as LGBTQ youth, are seen to close the chapter on his misogynoiristic portrayals of Black women in his production projects.[31] It is relatively easy and very effective to put down Black women toward your own ends and then reject that path to success later. As I describe in the preface, the rapper Nelly saw no irony in asking the students of the historically Black women's institution Spelman College to register to donate bone marrow after depicting Black women as hypersexual in his videos. In the effort to get ahead in film and television, getting clicks and video views by stepping on or dragging Black women is the quickest way to get a boost up the ladder of fame.

Black women are the unpaid and exploited labor behind the success of many comedians and entertainers, mules that drag their drivers to new heights. But these attempts to ride Black women to success and digital fame are not always so successful. In the section that follows, I examine the hashtag #RuinABlackGirlsMonday, a hashtag that was designed to disturb Black women but mostly failed. The hashtag did not evoke the sentiment that its creator hoped in Black women, but it did provide examples of Black women's reactionary resilience in the face of such a troubling attempt to attack them.

#RuinABlackGirlsMonday

On Monday, July 21, 2014, the hashtag #RuinABlackGirlsMonday began to trend on Twitter.[32] Though it was used in fewer than ten thousand tweets, the hashtag still managed to capture the attention of Twitter algorithms and ended up in the day's "trending topics." User @DInHer-Friends led tweeters of the hashtag to post images of white women with round butts, ample chests, and long hair, suggesting that these images would ruin a Black girl's day because these white women had features that Black women seemingly solely possessed. These physical features were portrayed as more desirable to men when paired with white skin. Many of the images and language in the hashtag perpetuated age-old stereotypes of Black women's supposed unattractiveness and hypersexual nature, while promoting white womanhood and femininity as especially desirable when mixed with stereotypically Black women's physical features. These tweeters imagined that Black women would be hurt by these images of white and other non-Black women with physical characteristics that are presumed desirable by Black men. In addition to these images, Twitter users also used the hashtag to say hateful things to and about Black women, including one Twitter user who wrote, "I don't participate in #ruinablackgirlsmonday cause I'm against animal abuse."[33] This tweet and the nearly six thousand others like it were designed to stoke misogynoirist ideas about Black women, but their actual ability to ruin a Black girl's Monday was questionable. Black women enacted a defensive digital alchemy to address the hashtag.

Black women did indeed respond to the hashtag and accompanying imagery, but in no way did the Black women commenting on the hashtag describe their day as ruined by it. Black women Twitter users expressed annoyance and sadness at the faulty premise that these images should upset them. User @gabrielleSTORM_ tweeted, "wtf is this ? Why is another bitches ass going to ruin my Monday?"[34] Echoing her sentiment was another Black woman Twitter user, @Scream_GeGe, who noted that it was the same few pictures of white women being reposted over and over, so how was that supposed to ruin her day? User @emptysovl simply posted a picture of a Black woman rolling her eyes in response to the hashtag, an expression of annoyance rather than anger or distress.[35] User @trillosophy got to the heart of the matter by tweeting, "#ruinablackgirlsmonday ?? Why would you disrespect a black woman when you came from a black woman? The self hate is so real tonight!"[36] Her tweet was retweeted 130 times, making it the second most popular tweet using the hashtag. Her astute assessment of the underlying self-hate evoked by the hashtag users demonstrates that Black women's concern about the hashtag was not rooted in feeling undesirable. The internalized racism and sexism of the Black men behind the trending hashtag were far more evident than Black women's supposed anger or sense of a ruined day. Black women consistently questioned why these images were supposed to ruin their day and exposed the faulty and corrosive logic in the hashtag's premise.

Not all the responses by Black women to the hashtag fully challenged the underlying anti-Black misogyny it presented. Defensive digital alchemy was a strategy employed by these hashtag interlopers. While it did not trend, the reactionary hashtag #RuinAnInsecureBlackMansTuesday was an attempt to challenge the negativity of #RuinABlackGirlsMonday. User Taylor J suggested that Black women flood the Twitter timeline with beautiful pictures of themselves accompanied by her remixed hashtag. User @maryamayusuf posted a picture of herself with the caption, "#ruinablackgirlsmonday how could my Monday be ruined when I look in the mirror and see this?"[37] She is a thin Black woman with light skin, curly hair, and hazel eyes. The image and caption received 123 likes and 37 retweets. While her decision to post a picture of herself to affirm her own beauty is noteworthy, her physical features (perhaps inadvertently) play into in-group politics around desirability.

Being thin and light-skinned with curly as opposed to tightly curled hair allows @maryamayusuf to fall into some of the internalized standards of beauty that align with the white supremacy the hashtag embraces. No dark-skinned or fat Black women took the approach of posting an image of themselves to challenge the hashtag, perhaps because they knew they would not receive a similar positive response.

My commentary is not meant to chastise @maryamayusuf for her decision to post an image of herself but to discuss how her choice to do so unintentionally may have reinforced some of the problems presented by the hashtag itself. Her tweet exemplifies the limits of a defensive digital alchemy. Because she is the kind of Black woman who may still be seen as desirable because of her features, @maryamayusuf's rebuttal may not have been as powerful as she thought. It unfortunately opened her up to critiques as well. While the comments to her picture were overwhelmingly positive, a few Black men chose to critique her body, commenting on the size of her forehead and whether they thought she was attractive. Her attempt to disarm the hashtag by asserting herself as beautiful ended up reinforcing hierarchical and heterosexist notions of attractiveness. @maryamayusuf took a risk by literally putting herself out there to be judged in the thread of the hashtag, but other Black women took the approach of diminishing the hashtag's significance.

Black women in the thread talked about the asinine nature of the original hashtag and encouraged other women to ignore it. Some also called out the message behind the hashtag that "the only thing black women are is a big ass & if other girls have it then they're nothing."[38] A few (three) Black women users opted to downplay the hashtag completely. Queer Black woman user @jiinandtonic wrote, "#ruinablackgirlsmonday is top 5 dumbest hashtags I've ever seen on this website to date. Lol." She went on to reply to another user, "@ArchieTheBaker It's just white girls with cakes. Like . . . my skinny black ass will bag her before you niggas can. My Monday is fine lol."[39] Her comment discredits the hashtag by pointing out that these are just images of white women with ample butts. She goes on to assert her own sexual prowess over the men posting these images by saying she could date one of these women before they could. She closes by reiterating that she is unfazed by the hashtag.

Another user tried to provoke @jiinandtonic by calling her a roach, a derogatory term used for dark-skinned women. To this, she responded,

"@KusUmikLeBeau, A roach that'll fuck ya girl better than you can," once again asserting her sexual prowess as a queer woman over and above the men who are using the hashtag. This tactic has its own sexist implications, with the women in the pictures and attached to these men becoming objects of sexual conquest to be volleyed over, but the refusal to acquiesce to a position of injury by the hashtag is significant. @jiinandtonic's tweets exemplify the nonfeminist response to misogynoir I discuss in the introduction. She uses her queerness to out-macho the men, inadvertently participating in the objectification of the women pictured as well.

Black woman user @arlettearts wanted to redirect the negative energy of the hashtag, tweeting, "#ruinablackgirlsmonday is a stupid and pointless hashtag when we have deeper issues going on like #GazaUnderAttack and #RIPEricGarner."[40] @arlettearts's tweet is evocative of the emotional labor that Black women performed in relation to the hashtag and also provides an example of the transformation of misogynoir. Rather than lament the ill-informed nature of #RuinABlackGirlsMonday, she redirects those following the hashtag to two other more pressing concerns, the attacks on Gaza following anti-war protests and the murder of Eric Garner, an unarmed Black man choked to death by New York City police. By engaging the hashtag with a mention of two other hashtags with political import, @arlettearts transforms a misogynoirist conversation into a space for potential activism around US imperialism and anti-Black police brutality.

User @HEYBONITA just wanted the hashtag users to really think about what their posts meant for Black women: absolutely nothing. "#ruinablackgirlsmonday do y'all not realize tweeting girls of other races w fat asses does not effect or take away ours?"[41] Her tweet addressed the material reality of the hashtag and its inability to change Black women's bodies such that they would lose their features. Her literalism challenged the premise of the hashtag itself by reminding users that Black women will continue to have the features they have regardless of what other women's bodies look like. Implicit in her tweet is the rejection of a perceived concern on Black women's part about the bodies of other non-Black women. The equation of stress with the power of the image of a white woman's body to ruin her and other Black women's day is thwarted.

Other retaliatory hashtags like #RTToMakeABlackBoyMad, #Ashy-Larrys, and #AshyMandigos had mixed success. The #AshyLarrys hashtag predates #RuinABlackGirlsMonday, as it was derived from the character of the same name on comedian Dave Chapelle's self-titled show on Comedy Central. As such, #AshyLarrys continues to be used to describe Black men who project misogynoirist views on Twitter. These hashtags turned the focus back on the creators and promulgators of #RuinABlackGirlsMonday and in so doing, highlighted the undesirability of the Black men who deem Black women undesirable.

For the Twitter users who embraced the hashtag, to assume that Black women were threatened or concerned about curvy white women builds on some of the oldest misogynoiristic tropes. One implication embedded in the hashtag is that Black women are only as useful or desirable as their bodies are to the Black men who participated in the hashtag. It does not acknowledge Black women's ideas for themselves about who they desire or even what they find desirable about themselves. The hashtag assumes that Black women are inordinately concerned with their desirability to Black men and that the knowledge of other women being portrayed as more desirable than them would ruin their day. Further, this narrative insists on a heterosexual relationship among Black men and women, where Black men are arbiters of Black women's value, which user @jiinandtonic's comments disrupt.

Moreover, the reduction of Black women's desirability to physical traits is telling. To suggest that Black women will be overlooked because white women have physical traits that men find desirable reduces Black women to body parts, not unlike the way they are reduced to parts by the showmen who displayed Sarah Baartman or the medical experimentation of J. Marion Sims. As user @_Beckaah put it, "So the only value to a black girl is a big bum?? #ruinablackgirlsmonday."[42] Misogynoir sets Black women up to be seen as undesirable, which can lead to Black women's participation in dangerous cosmetic surgery. Butt injections and other procedures designed to accentuate the body have had disastrous repercussions for the Black women who pursued them.[43]

Black women asserted that they are more than their desirability to straight Black men. Tactics of ignoring and expressing an unbothered attitude in the wake of the hashtag were employed by Black women to challenge the narrative that was being asserted about them. By responding to ludicrous assertions made by those tweeting using the hashtag, Black women had entered the fray and shifted the conversation. Black women's deployment of defensive digital alchemy transformed a misogynoiristic screed designed to make them "feel bad" and demonstrated a variety of tactics that could be used to neutralize a negative situation. Black women protected their mental and emotional health by ignoring, responding to, and transforming the misogynoir of the hashtag.

#RuinABlackGirlsMonday further illustrates the ubiquity of misogynoir. That a Black man would spontaneously decide to launch this hashtag and find willing users of the hashtag who were other Black men, white women, and white men shows that misogynoir can be perpetuated by anyone. The Black woman's body once again becomes a measuring stick and rubric by which white women's bodies are judged and deemed superior, though this time for their approximation to the desirable traits of Black women's physiology. The internalized anti-Blackness and sexism that animate the logics of this hashtag are replicated in the ways Black women and girls are treated in society.

Physical and Digital Dragging of Black Girls

Unfortunately, the dragging of Black women and girls is not limited to impersonation through drag or even the drag of seeing physical features ridiculed on your body and then praised when attached to someone else. But the potential impact of misogynoir on the physical and psychic health of Black women and girls remains largely outside the purview or locus of concern for those who perpetuate misogynoir. In the introduction I talked about misogynoir being utilized to shape public policy that harms Black women, but other institutions also use misogynoir to shape their disciplinary logics. Law enforcement is weaponized against Black women and girls at an alarming rate, and misogynoir unfortunately shapes the nature of these interactions, putting them at risk for physical and emotional harm.

Black girls are subject to a disproportionate amount of physical violence by the state when compared to their white girl counterparts. Not only do these physical assaults hurt Black girls physically, these girls are then dragged through the mud of social media as YouTube commenters debate the merit of their claims, enacting mental trauma that is impossible to quantify. Black girls are portrayed as more mature than they are, a process of adultification that leads to a disproportionate amount of discipline and punishment when compared to both their Black boy and white girl peers.

Dajerria Becton

On June 5, 2015, fifteen-year-old Dajerria Becton attended a pool party in her community of McKinney, Texas. According to party attendees, a white woman adult started a kerfuffle by yelling at and attempting to fight one of the young Black women organizers of the pool party. When police arrived, Becton was thrown forcefully to the ground by Corporal Eric Casebolt, who then sat on her tiny hundred-pound frame to keep her from moving. Brandon Brooks, also a fifteen-year-old but a white boy attending the party, captured and posted video of the violent police behavior to YouTube the following day. His video amassed nearly thirteen million views and showed Casebolt dragging Becton by her braids in her bikini and then sitting on her body as she cried and pleaded for help. The seven-minute and nineteen-second footage shocked viewers because of Casebolt's aggression toward a visibly vulnerable Becton; he threw her easily and with great force.

This incident caught the attention of mainstream news media because of Brooks's video. His capturing of Casebolt's actions made clear the disproportionate force directed at Becton when compared with the other pool party attendees. The video's popularity helped to bring the literal dragging of a Black girl into the spotlight, but in so doing, commentators on the video felt compelled to address the merit of the resulting outrage. That Brooks was a white boy capturing this video footage seemed to elicit a sense among commenters of empathy for Becton. I wanted to explore the comments more fully to analyze my initial appraisal of the reaction to the video.

I used the open-source Java script tool YouTube Comment Scraper, created by Philip Klostermann, to collect all of the comments from the video uploaded to YouTube by Brandon Brooks.[44] I then used the text-mining tool Voyant to analyze the content of the extracted comments to find patterns in the way commenters responded to the video. One of the functions of Voyant allows researchers to understand the relative frequency of the words used in a corpus. In the comments from Brandon Brooks's YouTube video, the words "officer," "cops," "cop," and "police" were used more than any other words. The frequency of these words is not surprising, given the dramatic nature of the police presence in the video. In truth, the police are the reason Brooks started filming in the first place. But the recurrence of these words in the comments makes clear that viewers are grappling with the role the police play in the video. The police and their actions overtake the screen, causing commenters to question why they are present in the first place, given the general responsiveness of the teens to their instructions to move along. We do not see the teens in frame behaving in a way that seems to warrant police presence, as they listen to the officers' instructions, though some linger and talk in groups.

After words related to the police, the words "black" and "white" were used 4,871 and 4,278 times, respectively. Commenters used these words to debate the role that race played in the forceful police behavior directed at Becton. Less frequently—3,566 times—but still significant was the appearance of the word "girl" in the corpus of comments. As I explore later in this chapter, Black girls are often adultified, made older than they are, and their girlhood is erased. It seems that at least in this comment thread there was a sense that Becton was a girl, but as a Black girl, she was judged more harshly than her white peers.

Several commenters argued that Becton and her friends, a group of Black girls, were "pestering" the officer, as their group stood talking, near where Casebolt and the other officers had detained Black boys by forcing them to sit on the grass. Casebolt told the girls to stop "running their mouths," even though there were other groups of kids, white and Black boys and white girls, standing in view and talking while in the street. Casebolt directs his attention to the group of Black girls despite being parallel to the other groups of talking teens.

User NRobbi42 has the most-liked comment on the video for using timestamps to acknowledge the differential treatment of the white and Black children by the police. The user writes, "0:52 White kid with towel told to sit down. 1:19 White kid gets up 2:13 White kid nowhere to be found Please, continue to tell me that race has nothing to do with this."[45] By identifying the exact moments on the video where the one white kid, a boy, was told to sit down and then defies the order, user NRobbi42 provides evidence of differential treatment. It is clear that Black boys, white boys, and white girls are all being treated differently than Becton and her Black girl friends.

The Black boys are forced to sit and are handcuffed while the white girls are allowed to pass by, unmolested by the police. One white girl even tries to explain to an officer that the Black boys are part of the group and should not be sitting on the ground or be handcuffed. However, it is the Black girls who are told to stop "running their mouths" and leave, though it is only Becton who is thrown to the ground. The way that Becton is singled out despite the numerous other teens present is startling, especially since she appears to be walking away when Casebolt grabs her. The contrast of her small frame in a bikini bathing suit makes her all the more vulnerable, as Casebolt is fully clothed in his uniform and "twenty pounds of gear."[46] For most commenters, race is the issue that provoked the incident, not the synergistic force of misogynoir that singled out Becton among her Black and white peers.

Black girls, because of misogynoir, are viewed differently than their white girl and Black boy peers. Becton is deemed a threat that deserves excess force despite being nearly nude and much smaller than the officer on top of her. Her pleas for help are ignored and the attempt by others to intervene on her behalf are rebuffed as well. Her Blackness and her *girlness* come together to make her a target, one that is easily and—in the officer's mind—justifiably detained. There is nothing about her behavior that signals a threat to anyone around her, but the idea that Black girls are angry, animalistic, and strong beyond their size results in the officer's outsized reaction to her.

Casebolt and the other officers give different instructions and with different intensities to the groups of teens present, and the only discernible differences between the groups are their race and gender. The aggressive way that Casebolt barks at the Black girls to leave and forces the Black boys to the ground is in stark contrast to the calm discussion he and fellow officers have with white girls who try to explain what has happened or his slightly more emphatic call to Brooks to stop filming. These Black boys prefer deference to explanation and submit to the cops' wishes without hesitation. Casebolt and his fellow officers do not ensure that Brooks stop filming, nor do they force the white teens to the ground or make them stay put, but when some of the seated Black boys speak up in Becton's defense, Casebolt draws his gun while still pinning Becton with his knee in her back.

Brooks, who is never touched by the police present despite filming the incident, thought that the force used by Casebolt was excessive and racially motivated. In response to the McKinney chief of police, who claimed, "The McKinney Police Department is committed to treating all persons fairly under the law," Brooks said, "They're just going to discriminate against them because they're black. What if that was your kid getting slung to the ground? Would you still be talking about them in the way that you are?"[47] Brooks does not specifically acknowledge Becton's gender in his comments, and yet it is clear that there was a unique level of animus directed at her by Casebolt because of her race and gender. Casebolt's focus on Becton seems disproportionate given the number of young people who are milling about right in front of him, talking and otherwise ignoring his requests.

That Brooks's video was viewed nearly thirteen million times and generated nearly thirty thousand comments begs the question, Who is watching this literal dragging of a Black girl by a police officer and why? How has the physical violence directed at Black women and girls become a viral sensation? While Becton was physically dragged by Casebolt only once, the viral video of the incident results in a continued, infinite, digital dragging that is still taking place. With every view of the video, with every comment, Becton's dragging is performed again and again.

Becton's actions are questioned, along with the officer's, but the emotional and social impact on both of their lives is different. Becton and her family won a small settlement from the city, but Casebolt was able to resign and was never criminally indicted. Becton's relationship to pools and swimming has been forever transformed, as she has refrained from swimming since the incident, returning to the water only when her lawyer threw her a pool party for her birthday.[48] Her reluctance—no doubt the result of this traumatic experience—also conjures the fraught history of Black people and the segregation of public swimming pools.[49]

Brooks achieved some positive praise for being a white person who captured the misogynoiristic event in process and for acknowledging the racial motivation (if not the gendered one) behind Casebolt's actions. Brooks's video undoubtedly helped Becton in her legal pursuit of justice, but her $148,850 settlement does not make amends for an emotionally devastating attack that lives on in the Internet forever. The continued dissection of the video and her horrific experience captured in it are still being debated by YouTube commentators at the time of publication.

The defensive digital alchemy of recording Casebolt's manhandling of Becton was actually enacted by a white boy. Brandon Brooks's video is treated as more objective because of his whiteness even as commentators debate Becton's culpability in her own assault. Misogynoir is somewhat tempered by Brooks's being behind the camera, but the immediate violence that Becton experienced and the residual harm the incident caused her are not transformed by the incident being captured on camera.

"Shakara" and Niya Kenny

Five months later, on October 26, 2015, at Spring Valley High School in South Carolina, a Black sophomore girl identified only by her first name, Shakara, was instructed by her math teacher to put away her cell phone. Shakara did not act quickly enough, prompting her teacher to demand that she leave class. When she remained seated, her teacher called the vice principal and the resource officer, Ben Fields, to the classroom. All three men demanded she leave. When she continued to silently refuse, Fields flipped Shakara out of her chair and physically dragged her out of the classroom. In an ironic twist, the incident was captured on the also prohibited cell phones of the other students in the class.

Led by Niya Kenny, another Black girl in the classroom, students began to record the incident. Kenny and her classmates participated in the growing practice of documenting racist and sexist interactions with authority figures. Kenny was shocked by what Fields was doing to her classmate, saying later, "'Oh, my God. Is this really happening?' I was crying and screaming. 'This is crazy. Is this really happening? Is nobody going to help her?' Then I started telling people, 'Record! Record!'" The viral videos taken by Kenny and her classmates recorded Fields physically forcing Shakara out of her chair and threatening to return for Kenny. Once Shakara was moved out of the classroom, Fields came back in to handcuff and remove Kenny for her digital and verbal defense of her classmate. Both girls were arrested, taken to jail, and charged with the misdemeanor of "disturbing a school," which can carry a "$1000 fine and up to 90 days in jail."[50]

Kenny was clear that she felt that gender and race played a role in the events that unfolded in the class that day, as well as her decision to speak up when her teacher and vice principal did not. "Me, personally, I feel like they were two grown men. I felt like they could've stepped in, tried to say, 'Whoa, whoa, whoa.' Even a simple, 'Whoa, whoa, whoa,' would've worked. Like, 'No, that's not how we handle situations here.' You're working in a school, that's not how you handle kids," said Kenny.[51] Kenny wanted and deserved more from the adult men, her teacher and administrator, who watched Shakara, a young Black girl, being forcibly removed from the classroom. Kenny questions why these men did not use their masculinity to help Shakara, rather than collude with the safety officer. That she, a fellow student, was the one to offer support to her classmate exemplifies a disproportionate care for others that Black girls have for each other. Kenny exhibits a maturity and sense of justice that one would hope to see in the grown men who ultimately escalated the situation by calling the resource officer.

On her own experience of being arrested by Fields for orchestrating the recording of digital evidence in defense of her classmate, Kenny said, "Maybe [Fields] felt like, 'Oh, she's trying to challenge my authority as well, so I'm going to take her to jail.' I had no clue what was going through his head, honestly."[52] That Fields would choose to retaliate against a Black girl for trying to support another in a trying situation further exposes a bias in treatment. Though Kenny did lead the digital protest in asking her classmates to record the events unfolding in the classroom, she was not the only student who captured the events on her phone. Black girls are often targeted within schools for behaving in ways that do not match the racialized and gender expectations of white girls and Black boys. It is Black girls who are disproportionately punished for violating behavior norms for which other students are not disciplined. Both Kenny and Shakara were made examples of, which follows this pattern of extra scrutiny directed at Black girls.

The videos Kenny and her classmates captured got millions of views, and, as with Dajerria Becton's case, commenters debated the merit of Shakara's choice to stay seated. The most-liked comment on a *Wall Street Journal* clip, the one surviving clip of the incident on the Internet, received nearly 500,000 views on YouTube; it reads, "i don't see anything wrong with this," with 348 people showing support for that sentiment by giving the comment a digital thumbs-up.[53] Similar comments like "welcome the 'no spanking' generation. How's that working out," "wtf the officer supposed to do.....ask with pretty please......," and "the suspect did not cooperate. lol" all put the onus on Shakara to have behaved differently. Labeling Shakara a "suspect" while sitting in her seat in class makes her behavior seem criminal. While there are many comments that push back on the framing of Shakara as the aggressor, despite sitting passively and silently in her chair, most blame her for the violence she experienced. In examining all 1,161 YouTube comments, I found that an overwhelming majority of comments supported the officer.

Commentators debated whether race was a contributing factor in the escalation of the tactics used to remove Shakara from her seat. Unlike with the video Brooks captured of Casebolt's excessive force on Becton, most of these commenters were adults who felt that Shakara should have listened to Fields and because she did not, she deserved what she got. These comments reflect a view that Fields was provoked and incited to act because of Shakara's unwillingness to follow directions. Among these comments, words like "police" and "officer" were among the most used, as was the case for Brooks's video. Shakara was referred to as a student more than she was referred to as a "girl." Her behavior was read as incongruent with the way a student should behave. Her being identified as a student became a source of blame as commenters accused her of not behaving properly at school. Her quiet, passive behavior was read as insolence in the context of the classroom. Commenters used words like "leave" and "force" to debate the merits of Shakara's choice to stay seated despite the instructions of her teacher, vice principal, and safety officer. User Sean Thomas said, "She was asked to leave the classroom several times by her teacher and assistant principal. She refused and got what she asked for. She brought this on herself." User Fola Hurlingham pondered,

> I understand that the Cop was using excessive force, nevertheless there's no other videos that shows everything that happen before. All of this could be avoid if the student would comply with the school regulations and leave her cell alone she was ask many times to put it away. Her attor-

ney said that she wanted to stay in class to learn. Really? if that's the case why she was on her cell ignoring the teacher? I wounder [*sic*] if all of this would come out in the news if the Cop was Black or the student white?[54]

Hurlingham's question about race role reversal is an interesting one, given the swift punishment of officers of color in situations like these. When Sheriff's Deputy Willard Miller, a Black man, slammed a white fifteen-year-old girl to the ground, he was suspended without pay and charged with one count of child abuse.[55] It seems that rather than be spared national media attention, a Black officer is more likely to be charged and convicted of using excessive force than his white counterparts.[56]

Shakara was initially so shut down, she could not speak about the incident. Kenny noted that when the girls met in their lawyer's office, Shakara was "shaken up. She's traumatized."[57] After the arrests, Kenny decided not to go back to school, opting to get her GED instead. She experienced her own PTSD from the incident, telling *Education Week*,

> Police officers made me really uncomfortable after that situation. I don't know if that was anxiety or what it was, but it just, that whole situation really did traumatize me, because I could not be around police officers after that, like at all. If a police officer tried to come to my register [at my job], I would just kind of say, "Hold on I have to get somebody else to take your order," because I just couldn't do it. I would get shaky and it was just bad.[58]

The trauma that both girls continued to feel after the incident impacted their choices and abilities to move through their communities. Fear of the police and feeling silenced are a few of the long-term side effects of the misogynoir they encountered in the classroom on that fateful day in October 2015.

Kenny enacted defensive digital alchemy when she spoke up on behalf of her classmate and instructed her classmates to record the events of the classroom. By recasting the banned cell phone as a video camera, Kenny was able to capture Fields's excessive force. Unfortunately, many of those who watched the video did not agree with Kenny's frame, further complicating the way we understand the utility of the practice. That she, another Black girl, had the courage to intervene when two adult men, a teacher and an administrator, did not, is evocative of the quote I used to begin this book. In the words of Student Nonviolent Coordinating Committee's Black Women's Liberation Committee member Mary Ann Weathers, "We cannot sit on our behinds waiting for someone to do it for us. We must save ourselves."[59]

Kenny repurposed her cell phone and those of the other students in the class to document the harm caused to Shakara. Kenny continued in the struggle, saving more than the students in her school from "Officer Slam."[60] She joined other South Carolina students as the named defendant in an ACLU class action lawsuit against the state's education system for the "disturbing schools" charge, which is disproportionately leveraged against Black students, Black girls particularly, in the state. Kenny's advocacy led to the repeal of "challenged provisions of the law," effectively making it impossible for any other child to be charged with this crime.[61] By connecting the issue of Fields's excessive force to the larger statewide concern of Black students being charged with "disturbing schools," Kenny helped change an unjust law—generative digital alchemy in action.

Voyant revealed similarities between the comments on both Brooks's and Kenny's videos as users asserted the need for the kids to let the cops do their jobs, irrespective of the physical and mental harm they caused the Black girls in frame. For Black girls, there is no assumption of innocence. Both girls were subject to a brutal dragging both physically by these officers and then again in the comments of these viral videos that attempted to blame them for their pain. Becton may have been served by the fact that it was Brandon Brooks, a white boy, who captured the footage, perhaps engendering a sense of fairness that a Black girl can never give to the story of a fellow Black girl.

I highlight these two cases of Becton as well as Shakara and Kenny as examples of a wider phenomenon of viral videos that capture officers' disproportionate rage directed at Black girls. In her illuminating 2016 book *Pushout: The Criminalization of Black Girls in Schools*, scholar Monique Morris discusses the way Black girls are disproportionately disciplined for behavior or "attitude" infractions when compared to their white girl and Black boy counterparts. Morris writes, "Black girls are

16 percent of the female student population, but nearly one-third of all girls referred to law enforcement and more than one-third of all female school-based arrests."[62] That Casebolt would read Becton's retreat as hostile or that Fields would see Shakara's silence as a threat suggests that both men see these Black girls as out of line and deserving punishment. As mentioned earlier in this chapter, the Sapphire trope is ascribed to Black women, marking them as tough, angry, and hypermasculine. That this trope would also be assigned to Black girls is part of another insidious element of misogynoir: the adultification of Black girls.

In a landmark 2017 study by Georgetown School of Law's Center on Poverty and Inequality, researchers found that Black girls were routinely perceived as older than their white peers. This adultification bias started early, evident as early as birth through age four. Adultification bias manifested in Black girls being seen as needing less nurturing, comfort, support, and protection, coupled with expectations for them to be more independent and know more about adult topics, including sex.[63] This study was followed by another in 2019 in which the same researchers conducted focus groups with Black girls about how adultification bias showed up in their lives. Black girls described being treated like women and being subject to inappropriate treatment as a result.

One respondent described "a traffic stop in which a police officer did not believe her when she told him she was 15 years old, and handcuffed and fingerprinted her because he insisted that she was too old not to carry identification."[64] Another girl described being blacklisted by a school she had hoped to transfer to because of an assault and battery charge on her record from her current school. The assault and battery charge resulted from an errant ball hitting another girl in the face during recess.[65] What would be understood as youthful negligence or an unfortunate playground incident if the girls were white, transmute into crimes to be disciplined when Black girls are involved. Other research supports the subsequent notion that the harshness of the punishment is directly proportional to the color of the so-called perpetrator. Researcher Jill Viglione and colleagues found that Black women defendants with light skin received lighter sentences than their dark-skinned counterparts.[66]

The Georgetown researchers also found that stereotypes like Sapphire and Jezebel contributed to the adultification of Black girls:

We described two dominant paradigms of Black femininity in white culture that reach far back in our country's history and that emerged as relevant to our focus groups' discussions of adultification bias: the stereotype of the angry, aggressive Black woman ("Sapphire" caricature) and the hypersexualized Black woman ("Jezebel" caricature). By interpreting Black girls' behavior as consistent with stereotypes of Black women, adults effectively erase the distinction between adulthood and childhood.[67]

Black girls described being told by adults that they were "angry" and "bad" for disagreeing with them. Teachers were likely to say that Black girls, even kindergartners, were "sassy, disrespectful, and threatening."[68] Black girls described being subject to the Jezebel stereotype, which translated into adults assuming that they were sexually active even when the girls themselves felt that they were too young to be engaging in sexual activity. One respondent described an incident with the school nurse:

> In . . . sixth grade, . . . the school nurse, like, ask[ed] my aunt if I was sexually active. . . . And I was, like, at the time, like, what? Like, what? Nobody has sex. Like, I didn't know anyone that had sex. And it was so crazy to me. And then just thinking, like, she would never think to ask my [white] friend that.[69]

This disparate treatment of Black girls and white girls in the sixth grade exemplifies both the adultification of Black girls and the material effects of the Jezebel stereotype on a young Black girl. Black girls are read as adults when their white counterparts are not and are already negotiating the real-world impact of negative stereotypes in their lives. Whether it is the kind of punishment they receive or expectations that they know more about sex, Black girls are negotiating the part of misogynoir that is adultification bias.

Becton, Shakara, and Kenny were treated as older than they were by officers. They were not treated as girls but were roughly handled as though they were adult Black women, or even Black men. White girls are not subject to the type of excessive violence that is visible in these viral videos. For Black girls, an interaction with the police can be just as traumatic as it is for Black men. The rampant extrajudicial killings of Black mothers, girls, and trans women all support this odious conclusion that Black women and girls are not afforded the slim protection that gender provides their white counterparts.

When K.P. came home from a sixth-grade school camping trip in the spring of 2016 with a rope burn around her neck, her mother was appalled. K.P., as she is described in court documents, was just twelve years old at the time she said that three white students tied a rope around her neck and pulled, dragging her to the ground. As her mother described the injury, "It looked like somebody ripped my daughter's neck off and stitched it back together."[70] The private school administrators at K.P.'s school denied claims that the incident was the result of bullying or that the failure to contact K.P.'s parents had anything to do with her race. But her lawyer disagreed. "If it had been a little white girl [the school] would have been on the phone with her mother within the hour," he said.[71] That K.P.'s mother wasn't aware of what had happened to her daughter until she saw the rope burns on her neck seemed to suggest a lack of care or at worst a cover-up on the part of the school. The school's insistence that the rope burn on K.P.'s neck was an accident did not convince jurors, and the case was settled for $68,000.[72] This paltry sum does not come close to accounting for the duration of the bullying, the permanent disfigurement of her neck, or K.P.'s need to transfer schools for her own protection. Like Becton, before her, K.P. received a settlement that was but a band-aid on the ongoing emotional and mental trauma that still lives on from the event. While not a viral video, the Instagram and Facebook posts of K.P.'s injuries spread and made the school's assertion that the rope "accidently" hit her in the neck all the more implausible.[73] If Black girls aren't safe at school or in their communities, where are they safe?

Misogynoir animated this attack on K.P., making her the victim of an almost lynching at just twelve years old. Her classmates had already learned the lesson that her life was less valuable and that she was less deserving of care than they were. The adultification of K.P. by her peers illustrates the insidious nature of this aspect of misogynoir. That it takes root in elementary school children is to say that the lessons of a racist sexist world are learned early. Before hitting puberty, K.P.'s classmates were sent a message of her vulnerability and expendability, a message they wrote into her flesh. It seems ludicrous to have to type the sentence "Black girls should not have to face the kind of retaliatory violence that they do in school and in their neighborhoods," but as the experiences of Becton, Shakara, Kenny, and K.P. show, this idea is not a foregone conclusion. The defensive digital alchemy of recording videos highlighting the disproportionate violence that Black girls encounter can have some rehabilitory results, such as the financial compensation and policy changes that were the end results of these incidents. But these conciliatory outcomes are not the systemic types of changes required to transform misogynoir's negative impact on Black girls' health and lives.

Black women and girls are getting dragged by drag, whether by Black men, white women, or white men. On the big and small screens of US media, Black women are being portrayed as caricatures, which have real-world consequences on their lives. The dynamics of representation can perpetuate a risk to their mental, physical, and social health through the way they are treated by police, school resource officers, and even other folks online. Hashtags, police interactions, and school discipline all become methods through which Black women and girls are dragged and treated differently than both their white women and Black men counterparts. Actual physical dragging of Black women and girls is captured on camera and spreads virally on the Internet, making the proliferation of these images even more difficult to manage.

For Black women and girls and Black nonbinary, agender, and gender-variant folks' healthcare disparities to be ameliorated, society must change the way these communities are viewed. As the *Combahee River Collective Statement* articulates, "if Black women were free, it would mean that everyone else would have to be free since our freedom would necessitate the destruction of all the systems of oppression."[74] Creating these conditions requires work toward the freedom the Collective articulates and requires action beyond the current purview of the medical-industrial complex. As Black women and girls and Black nonbinary, agender, and gender-variant folks work toward freedom, sophisticated critiques of popular media have shifted to include the production of the images and subsequent networks that support the changes we wish to see. In the chapter that follows, I explore how Black trans women use social media to transform misogynoir, enacting digital alchemy to create healthy images that are outside the mainstream.

2

Transforming Misogynoir through Trans Advocacy

In an online video chat via Google Hangout with other trans women who read her first memoir, writer and trans advocate Janet Mock discussed her decision to retitle her 2014 book *Redefining Realness: My Journey to Womanhood*.[1] The book was initially structured as a very personal and singular journey of Mock's unfolding relationship to her identity as a Black trans woman, but in the process of writing, she realized that she wanted to animate her narrative and make it something that other trans women could find useful as well. She said, "I felt like I needed an action, so the act of redefining realness . . . allowed me to share the very complicated, nuanced idea of trans girls of color in a very emotional experience for me as a trans woman of color."[2] She also articulated her desire to use language that hailed the transgender community, citing *realness* as an homage to the 1990 film *Paris Is Burning*, which first made trans women of color visible to a mainstream audience.

Realness is the way that trans and queer people of color describe aesthetic and sartorial choices that make them indistinguishable from cis and straight people. As Judith Butler and other feminists argue, gender is performative, meaning that gender is something we enact through the repetition of behavioral and sartorial choices.[3] This representation is performative, though not a performance in a way that implies acting. Here, Butler means performative in that gender is something you do, that the behaviors, clothes, and mannerisms you choose to repeat "consolidate an impression of being a man or being a woman."[4]

In the Ball scene—queer of color community, dance, and actual performance spaces—participants compete in categories like "school boy realness," in which they are judged for their ability to appear as real or as much like an ostensibly straight cis school boy as possible. In the 1990 documentary film *Paris Is Burning*, trans women and gay men revel in their ability to "serve realness," or "consolidate an impression of being" these genders better than their cis and straight counterparts, effectively achieving the look and mannerisms the category describes. Ball culture brings these implicit practices of choosing clothes, mannerisms, and so forth to the foreground while playing with the notion of performativity in a literal way as participants walk different categories and are judged on how successfully they execute the look.

Mock expounds on the importance of realness in the book, stating, "To embody 'realness' rather than performing or competing 'realness' enables trans women to enter spaces with a lower level of risk of being rebutted or questioned, policed or attacked."[5] For Mock, gender performativity that is "unclockable," or unable to be detected by cis people, can potentially mean safety in a transphobic world. "Embodying realness" becomes a way for trans women to move outside the relative safety of the Ball scene. However, this safety remains elusive for trans women, as being undetectable still means being subject to the violence that cis women experience regularly. According to the LGBTQ advocacy group Human Rights Campaign, 91 percent of all trans women murdered in 2019 were Black women. Cis Black women have the highest murder rate among cis women in the United States, at a rate of 4.4 murders for every 100,000 Black women.[6] The statistic for Black trans women is even more sobering, with 1 murder for every 2,600 Black trans women.[7] While perhaps offering a small reprieve from the disproportionate violence they receive as being identifiable trans women, "passing"—the idea that trans women are deceiving people by expressing their womanhood—provides only a conditional safety. Realness is both theatrical and practical, essential for creative expression and potentially the ability to live one's life without being subject to the extra violence that transphobia elicits. Realness both reifies and troubles the gender binary by adhering to a normative gender expression for safety even as it may be mocked and playfully chided in Ball categories.

Referencing this world of realness is important for acknowledging the queer and trans people of color genealogy from which Mock descends, but her desire for realness transcends the boundaries of this community. Whereas early Ball performers engaged realness on glamourous imaginary runways in ways that sometimes mocked and made clear the performative nature of cishet embodiment, Mock wants a realness steeped in the everyday. By redefining realness in her book, she shifts attention away from realness as spectacle, or even realness as subtlety for safety's sake, to a realness redefined by an acceptance of self and embrace of one's desired expression outside social expectations. For Mock, this looks like a "consolidation of an impression of being a woman," while for others it may not. The call for "realness" is a call for a performative gender of your choosing that does not require an attention to choices that facilitate safety because they adhere to established precedents. Realness is redefined to mean authenticity or choosing performative gender that is her truth as a Black woman independent of what others might wish for her gender expression or identity. Rather than realness being used as a metaphor for passing, realness transcends a performative goal and focuses more on a realness that aligns with self. As Mock puts it, "Self-definition is a responsibility I've wholeheartedly taken on as mine."[8] For Mock, this self-definition is facilitated by her ability to meet traditional beauty standards and her ability to be perceived easily inside the bounds of the gender binary. Other Black women as well as Black nonbinary, agender, and gender-variant folks may not have the same ease with achieving self-definition as the world exists now.

For Mock, *Redefining Realness* involves her documentation of her own transformation into the person she is today, but also her creation of a touchstone work for other trans women of color on their own journeys. The catharsis that came through the process of writing her book is part of the reason she chose the medium. Despite being an avid YouTube, Twitter, and Tumblr user, Mock used the comparatively old technology of the book to tell her story. Mock talked of the importance of getting her book to incarcerated trans women and making sure there were copies in local libraries so that anyone who needed her words could find them. Books have a comparative permanence and portability that lend them weight in society, as they are material artifacts of history. Books have a longevity and accessibility that might be undervalued by some in this digital epoch. Not everyone can access social media, and its impermanence can make it difficult to return to ideas and concepts years or even days later.

However, the ephemeral nature of social media serves the real-time concerns of the present in ways books do not. By employing a multimedia platform press plan that included the use of social media, Mock ensured that many demographics would know about her work. In additional promotional YouTube videos for the book, Mock discussed different concepts and experiences that appear in the text, such as passing, sex work, and identity. The immediacy of the platform allows for dynamic, real-time engagement that the book itself cannot provide. By deftly using YouTube, Twitter, and Tumblr to spread the book through the hashtagification of the book title, #RedefiningRealness was able to reach a lot of people. The book debuted at number 19 on the *New York Times* best seller list.[9]

Mock's book launched her down the path of celebrity as a visible trans advocate. Mock's narration of her own story marks a practice of Black women's media production that can challenge problematic mainstream representations of marginalized communities. From the films of Black women filmmakers like Cheryl Dunye's *The Watermelon Woman* (1996) or Aisha Shahidah Simmons's *No! The Rape Documentary* (2004), to Audre Lorde's biomythography *Zami: A New Spelling of My Name* and June Jordan's autobiography *Soldier*, Black women have been telling their stories through media in ways that challenge the limiting script society projects about who we are.[10] Each of these works, like Mock's, helps to bring the reality of Black women's lives to the fore on their own terms.

Mock's book is her own form of harm reduction, a way of mitigating the trauma of her young life by retelling her stories. By writing a memoir, Mock can release and reinterpret the events of her life. Mock unpacks her depression, dysphoria, and relationships to her family, all of which significantly impacted her health and sense of safety. While she is not able to change the trauma she has already experienced, she is able, through writing, to transform her narrative about those events in light of adult wisdom. By sharing her personal narrative, Mock gives what her friend and fellow trans advocate Laverne Cox might say is a "possibility model" for other Black women. A possibility model is not a role model, not someone you wish to emulate, but someone who provides a vision of what life could be. By discussing her participation in group therapy, access to hormones through an accommodating doctor, and thoughts of self-harm, Mock provides a vivid picture of the health realities Black trans women must navigate. Mock grants access to her interior life and the material conditions that helped her become the woman she is today, creating a vision of possibility for other trans and Black girls.[11]

While few would deny the popularity of social media sites, their significance as digital media platforms for activism is only beginning to be understood. In the last chapter I explored the ways that viral videos can invoke empathy for Black girls through the documentation of the misogynoir they experience. YouTube itself started because one of its founders had difficulty finding video of pop icon Janet Jackson's 2004 Super Bowl halftime show wardrobe malfunction caused by Justin Timberlake.[12] That the unintentional baring of a Black woman's breast, for which she was assigned the blame (or Nipplegate, as it came to be called), was the impetus for YouTube speaks to the embedded nature of misogynoir in social media. YouTube was and is a repository for video but now includes original content uploaded just for the site. Twitter began as a platform for small group communication and has grown from a default 140 characters (to match the length of text messages) to 280 characters in 2017.[13] Tumblr, a microblogging platform that allowed users to curate and reblog each others' content, launched in 2007 and was at its height in 2013 before being sold to Yahoo!, the Internet search engine. YouTube, Twitter, and Tumblr are marshaled to build networks of information and support by people multiply marginalized in society in ways that impact health and well-being beyond traditional health-seeking behaviors like seeing a doctor. These activities include Black women using Twitter to build networks of support that provide real, everyday solutions for problems that are not being adequately addressed by the institutions that should help, a process that values crowdsourced knowledge and the creation of images that subvert dominant representations of their communities.

Black women are repurposing the capitalist tools of social media into tools that allow them to grow community, share resources, and even advocate for each other's safety and health. This chapter explores Janet Mock's and other Black trans women's use of digital media platforms to create redefined representations of themselves outside the problematic lens of transmisogynoir.[14] These images and texts counter negative stereotypes about the community in media through a process that addresses health and healing beyond the WHO definition of health. The creation of the hashtag #GirlsLikeUs by Janet Mock and the proliferation of other hashtags for trans women, including #TWOC and #FreeCeCe, are examples of how Black trans women transform social media into social justice magic that advocates for their lives.

#GirlsLikeUs and #FreeCeCe are hashtags that helped to share resources, distribute articles, and create connections that helped Black women survive and even thrive in a world that disproportionately roots for their destruction. Misogynoir is transformed through the everyday digital alchemy of those who use these hashtags to build community and advocate for change. I examine #GirlsLikeUs and #FreeCeCe as examples of hashtags that did more than create community. Both of these hashtags were instrumental in real-world transformations that include the creation of new media projects on- and offline that challenge stereotypes about Black trans women as well as a successful prison support campaign that fomented an activist career, all acts that mitigated misogynoir and led to better health outcomes for Black women.

#GirlsLikeUs

In March 2012, when writer and editor Janet Mock learned that Jenna Talackova—a multiracial trans woman contestant for Miss Universe—was being denied access to the pageant because Talackova was trans, Mock worked quickly to bolster a collective response. Mock wanted to show her support and called on her Twitter followers to send theirs when she tweeted, "Please sign & share this women's rights petition in support of transgender beauty queen Jenna Talackova & #girlslikeus: https://www.change.org/93-miss-universe-canada-donald-trump-reverse-the-unfair-disqualification-of-jenna-talackova."[15] The linked petition explained that Talackova was one of sixty-five finalists for the Miss Canada competition, the winner of which would advance to the global Miss Universe Pageant. When pageant officials learned that Talackova was assigned male at birth, they removed her from the finalist pool and took her photo off the pageant website. Mock's tweet helped the petition rack up nearly twenty-two thousand signatures of support for Talackova, ultimately resulting in her reinstatement as a finalist. Talackova made it to the top twelve in the competition before being eliminated.

Mock framed her support of Talackova as an act of solidarity for women's rights, but lending support to a woman who wants to participate in a beauty pageant begs the question, Is this feminist online organizing? Should a beauty pageant's discriminatory policies be the subject of a feminist campaign? It's not easy to classify this call for support as feminist given the inherently anti-feminist practices of traditional beauty pageants, particularly one owned by Donald Trump, who is known for his sexist and violent interactions with women.[16] Pageant contestants are expected to meet a white, Western, able-bodied, and (though previously unarticulated) cis standard of beauty, conforming to the very performative norms that Ball culture transforms. While some communities marginalized by these aesthetic preferences elect to create their own pageants where beauty can be redefined, they, like Talackova, should not be summarily dismissed before even having the opportunity to participate in a traditional pageant.[17]

For women who are often denied social legitimacy as women, a win in one of the most gender-binary and normative spaces humans have created could be a move in a positive direction. It exemplifies the defensive digital alchemy that was employed by Black women responding to #RuinABlackGirlsMonday. A crown atop the head of a trans woman contestant conveys the message that trans women are women and there are a panel of ostensibly cis judges, viewers, and fellow contestants who support this assertion through their participation in the pageant. But trans women's participation in beauty pageants also sets the stage for an ideal trans woman, a trans woman who must uphold the same circumscribed beauty standards cis women must possess to win. But as actress Jen Richards argues in *Disclosure: Trans Lives on Screen* (2020), "A lot of people will look at trans women's performance of femininity and see it as somehow reinforcing the worst patriarchal stereotypes of women, and it's really unfair and ahistorical to foist that same perspective on people who are just trying to survive."[18] The performativity of the pageant expanding to include those who have traditionally been excluded does not change the social script of the importance of women's beauty. Would a woman—cis or trans—who challenged the gender binary make it to the top twelve or receive the same support that Talackova did? But, as Richards asks, would a trans woman who did survive?

Talackova's removal from the pageant and the subsequent support she received from trans and cis folks alike harken back to a point I made in the introduction. It is not easy to classify all the digital alchemy that Black women creators are working to achieve as feminist, but that does not mean that it is not still transformative. Not all challenges to transphobia or heterosexism are feminist, but that does not mean that the work is not a necessary part of creating a more just world. Talackova's digital petition as well as Mock's support of it pushed boundaries and made space for those who would otherwise be denied entry to the elite club that is "woman." But access for one to an already exclusionary party also raises the question of whether this is the party to which we wish to gain access. I see the #GirlsLikeUs hashtag helping a community create what it needs for itself, without seeking this sort of external validation.

As Mock describes it, her initial use of the hashtag #GirlsLikeUs was not a particularly calculated launch and was not specifically for Black women:

> I didn't think it over, it wasn't a major push, but #girlslikeus felt right. Remarkably a few more women—some well-known, others not—shared the petition and began sharing their stories of being deemed un-real, being called out, working it, fighting for what's right, wanting to transition, dreaming to do this, accomplishing that. . . . #girlslikeus soon grew beyond me. . . . My dream came true: #girlslikeus was used on its own without my @janetmock handle in it. It had a life of its own.[19]

Mock thought of the hashtag and immediately saw its utility in attracting people to sign the petition in support of Talackova. What she did not foresee was its continued utility as she and then others started to use the hashtag for all sorts of conversations among girls like her. From beauty to safety, from health to harassment, the hashtag became an invaluable channel for women, particularly Black women, to find community and care.

Women deploy the hashtag #GirlsLikeUs in discussions of specific desires to medically transition, the banality of everyday living, and dreams of success, as well as the more general threats and realities of the violence related to being outed in unsafe situations. The hashtag crosses strict lines separating private and public spheres of concern. Furthermore, because trans women generally are not born into families where conversations regarding their health and social needs are addressed— unlike conversations about other types of identity, such as race—the use of hashtags like #GirlsLikeUs allows for a network where information can be shared, communities formed, even with anonymity. #GirlsLikeUs can signal other trans women without necessarily making it clear that it is for trans women in the hashtag, an important feat given the deadly violence that trans women face. #GirlsLikeUs becomes a safe space through which a dissection of the misogynoir Black women endure can be discussed.

Computational scientist Alan Mislove created a database that collected a random 10 percent of all tweets tweeted since Twitter began.[20] With the help of computer science graduate student Devin Gaffney's script that gathered all instances of the hashtag #GirlsLikeUs within this database, I examined all publicly accessible tweets using #GirlsLikeUs between Mock's first uses in March 2012 through October 2014. With over eleven thousand tweets in this 10 percent sample dataset that used the hashtag, I had enough tweets to begin to unpack how users were deploying it. I utilized the visualization software Gephi—an open-source platform that visually renders the connections between data points—to chart the network of people using #GirlsLikeUs. Because Gephi also generates nodes that correlate with the number of interactions between Twitter users and their proximity to other users, I was able to determine the most prolific users of the hashtag and their levels of interconnection. It is not surprising that Janet Mock and her friend Laverne Cox, actress on the Netflix hit series *Orange Is the New Black* (2013–2019), are primary users of the hashtag whose growing celebrity helps propel the hashtag to new constituencies. Their Twitter handles appear with the greatest frequency in the corpus of tweets after one other user. Cami, a self-described "politically incorrect conservative t[rans] girl," had her own network of followers who do not interact with Mock or Cox. Cami is a visible outlier in the network because of her conservative politics and her prolific tweeting.

Cami and her more famous white conservative peer, Caitlyn Jenner, have actively cultivated or been thrust into the spotlight as spokespersons for trans community. However, their political beliefs result in their continual distancing from the majority of the trans community. Cami and Caitlyn's conservatism is an important reminder that gender marginalization doesn't always translate into a transformative politic. While Talackova may have been the impetus for #GirlsLikeUs and while Cami was a prolific user of the hashtag, the content of the tweets tagged with #GirlsLikeUs reflects the racial and gender justice politics of trans women of color on the left of the political spectrum.

The networks being built around #GirlsLikeUs are along lines of affinity and not only ones of identity—along lines of shared analyses of power or felt kinship rather than simply gender. Within the #Girls-LikeUs network, "like us" also means a left politic that is supportive and affirming of progressive stances regarding issues of race, sexuality, class, and of course gender. Rather than invoking cis women as the reference point of its discussions, the #GirlsLikeUs network places trans women's experiences at the center of the conversation. Thus, #GirlsLikeUs does not function like other slogans of Black struggles for self-representation.

For instance, the iconic Freedom Struggle–era images of Black Memphis sanitation workers holding placards that read "I AM A MAN" were an attempt to reach the people who did not hold that truth to be self-evident. Historian Steve Estes writes that the phrase "I am a man" "represents a demand for recognition and respect of Black manhood and Black humanity" in the face of a white supremacist paternalism in southern mayoral politics.[21] This marked a shift from the abolition-era question of "Am I not a man and a brother?" and a question generally attributed to Sojourner Truth, "Ain't I a woman?" that fully brings Black women's marginalization into view. The evolution from question to declaration is significant, but so too is the turn away from a white authorial gaze to which such inquisitions and demands are made. The conversations tagged with #GirlsLikeUs are most often between trans women and about issues that concern the community. It calls community forward by using "us" as opposed to "me." #GirlsLikeUs signals a conversation that is for, by, and about trans women.

I used Voyant, a web-based textual analysis tool, to generate word visualizations and measure the frequency and occurrence of words in the corpus of the collected tweets as I did with the YouTube comments in chapter 1. The most popular hashtags used with the hashtag #Girls-LikeUs were other words of identity affirmation, including #Trans, #Transgender, and #TWOC (trans women of color).[22] Not surprisingly, "trans" was the most popular word in the corpus of tweets, occurring more than 2,600 times in the sample. Following far behind were "Transgender" and "LGBT," with over 1,000 and 500 occurrences, respectively. The second most popular co-occurring hashtag was #TWOC. Occurring nearly 600 times, #TWOC signaled a mix of both affirming tweets and tweets designed to bring attention to the disproportionate amounts of violence and health concerns trans women of color face. I highlight the 600 times #TWOC is used to show that even though #GirlsLikeUs is for all trans women, the concerns of TWOC are central to the Twitter conversation. I examine the themes these hashtags and words highlight in the network, underscoring their ability to build connections both on- and offline.

Janet Mock used the hashtag #TWOC in conjunction with #Girls-LikeUs to amplify the voices and needs of other Black women and to celebrate the time she spent with other trans women of color. In May 2013, Mock tweeted a link to the GoFundMe for Egyptt, a Black woman who had dedicated her life to trans advocacy but now "needs resources to get back into housing, to replace lost possessions, and to cover outstanding healthcare costs."[23] Because Mock's Twitter presence was still nascent at this time, her tweet received only fifteen retweets. Egyptt's virtual passing of the hat raised $3,125, nearly $7,000 short of her $10,000 goal. Trans women and trans women of color struggle to find work and when they do, it often does not pay a living wage. The practice of using crowd-fundraisers to support the necessary expenses of life is an all too common and unsustainable occurrence in the community.

For Black women, misogynoir and transphobia lurk in the background, informing their ability to successfully crowdfund and find gainful employment. According to the 2019 analysis of the 2009 National Center for Transgender Equality (NCTE) and National LGBTQ Task Force data on the unique challenges faced by Black trans people, "Black transgender and gender non-conforming people had an extremely high unemployment rate at 26%, . . . over three times the rate of the general population (7%) at the time the survey was fielded."[24] The survey results also revealed that nearly half of Black trans respondents were denied a job because of their trans or gender nonconforming identity. With these realities in the workplace, it is no surprise that Egyptt's call to her community could not net much. When everyone is struggling, there is only so much to go around. With a third of Black trans and gender nonconforming people living in extreme poverty, #GirlsLikeUs crowdfunding has real limits. Despite not reaching the monetary goal, Egyptt's Go-FundMe exemplifies the kinds of material support the community who uses the hashtag is able to provide to Black women. This act of solidarity was echoed by other Twitter users as several other crowdsourced fund-raisers for #TWOC were shared with the hashtag.

But crowdfunding is not only used for the day-to-day survival of individuals like Egyptt. The hashtag #TWOC was also used alongside #GirlsLikeUs to raise funds for a documentary about the Black trans elder Miss Major. A popularly retweeted tweet from the project's Twitter account stated, "@theMAJORdoc: 5 days and $6759 left to tell #Miss-Major's story. We can do this with your help! http://t.co/GDJfhBkFhC #girlslikeus #twoc."[25] Here, #TWOC is used to let potential supporters know a bit about who Miss Major is and who might also be interested in supporting her story. By tagging the tweet with these hashtags, the film-makers are hailing a receptive—and hopefully financially supportive—audience. The filmmakers use these two hashtags to draw in the communities with which they are associated and provide an opportunity for these community members to support projects that speak to their interests. The documentary was successfully funded and has toured the United States and beyond on the film festival circuit in addition to being distributed by Amazon Prime Video.[26] This digital alchemy of crowd-funding a documentary is a tactic that Black indie creators perfected. The successful crowdfunding of the second season of the web series *The Misadventures of Awkward Black Girl*, written by and starring Issa Rae, led to her successful transition into mainstream television, becoming a possibility model in her own way for Black creators who couldn't get studio backing. The success of the Miss Major crowdfunding campaign and the documentary itself offer more self-produced representation of Black women in popular culture.

The hashtag #TWOC was used by other users to celebrate #TWOC connections within the hashtag community of #GirlsLikeUs. In July 2013 Janet Mock tweeted, "Spent the day this far engaged in revelatory conversations with my dear sister [@tourmaliiine]. Blessed to know you. #twoc #GirlsLikeUs."[27] Mock consistently posted pictures and tweets while out with her #TWOC friends. Similarly, trans advocate Cecilia Chung posted a picture of her with Laverne Cox and Bamby Salcedo while attending the 2013 Philly Trans Health Conference, with the caption, "See you next time ladies! @translatinbamby @Lavercox #twoc #sisterhood #girlslikeus #pthc."[28] While easily dismissed as self-congratulatory tweets, these public displays of affection among trans women of color illustrate a solidarity that is being built both on- and offline. The ability to connect virtually and then in person builds the network in ways that belie dismissals of online activism as armchair activism or slacktivism. Community is being formed online, but it is also nurtured in real life (IRL). In a heterosexist world that wants to paint women as each other's competition, the real connections and sisterhood being developed challenge that limiting perspective.

Just three months earlier, however, #TWOC was used to amplify the tragic death of Ms. Cemia "Ce Ce" Acoff, a Black trans woman murdered in Olmstead, Ohio. Initial reporting in the local paper, the *Plain Dealer*, used Acoff's legal name, misgendered her, and also highlighted previous unrelated arrests. User @Cisnormativity tweeted, "Criminalizing the body of a trans woman of colour. This day must be ending with a y. #MsAcoffRIP #girlslikeus #twoc #nolessvalid."[29] Cisnormativity acknowledged the ubiquity of violence and unjust treatment trans women of color experience as a daily occurrence. The *Plain Dealer* implied that Acoff was responsible for her own murder because she was trans. The paper painted her as someone unworthy of sympathy because of her past interactions with the law. The diversity in the way the hashtag #TWOC was used speaks to a vibrant community experimenting with and exploring what the net can net in terms of tangible support. #TWOC signals both the joys of connection and the sadness of loss. For #GirlsLikeUs and specifically #TWOC, joy and sorrow are enmeshed, with one never too far from the other. #TWOC and #GirlsLikeUs make for a powerful pair that center trans women of color's efforts to support one another in life and the all-too-frequent instance of death.

After the hashtag #TWOC, another popular word within the corpus of tweets I analyzed was "love." Used 504 times (four more times than "LGBT"), "love" is used in a myriad of ways to show support to members of the network. In another tweet from Janet Mock to trans artist and activist Tourmaline, Mock wrote, "[@tourmaliiine] thanks sis—the signal boost + love means a lot to me. #girlslikeus." Mock also lifted fellow hashtag super-user Laverne Cox, writing, "@Lavernecox Love you, Laverne. I was so elated to 'plug' you + #OITNB on #huffpostlive today ;-) http://t.co/i7ZQmWcXvb #girlslikeus."[30] These tweets from Mock are representative of many of the tweets within the network, where words of affirmation signal solidarity and support among users. Other users loved other #GirlsLikeUs tweeters' pictures, outfits, and hair. Users tweeted about their love for the supportive nature of the network. Laverne Cox even offered a twist on Black gay activist Joseph Beam's quote turned tagline for fellow Black gay activist Marlon Riggs's *Tongues Untied* (1989), "Black men loving Black men is the revolutionary act," with "thanks for the love. Loving trans people is a revolutionary act #girlslikeus."[31]

#Love also brings to the fore discussions of romantic love and partnership, a sometimes dangerous proposition for trans women. According to a 2017 *ABC News* article about the murder of twenty-two-year-old Tracey Williams at the hands of her boyfriend, "A 2015 study by UCLA's Williams Institute on Sexual Orientation and Gender Identity Law found that between 31% and 50% of transgender people have experienced dating violence at some point in their lives, compared to between 28% and 33% of the general population."[32] A 2017 study by the Arcus Foundation examining intimate partner violence in LGBTQ communities found that "transgender women were three times more likely to report experiencing sexual violence and financial violence than survivors who did not identify as transgender women."[33] Of the LGBTQ homicides for that year, 46 percent of the victims were trans women, all of whom were women of color, 60 percent of whom were Black.

Given these realities, Laverne Cox also used the #GirlsLikeUs network to ask a vulnerable question that is an issue for many trans women: "For those trans women who are in healthy relationships with men, how did you meet him? Suggestions? #girlslikeus #transchat #bfsearch."[34] The tweet started a Twitter thread in which trans women shared both heartwarming and cautionary tales of relationships. Users discussed the pros and cons of telling potential partners they are trans up front, places where they met their boyfriends, and even their reluctance to date because of the violence they might face. The Human Rights Campaign's 2018 Anti-Trans Violence report noted that 54 percent of trans people report having experienced intimate partner violence, while one in six murders of trans people are suspected to have been committed by intimate partners.[35] Dating while trans is not only difficult but can also be dangerous and deadly.

One user even used Twitter to help identify an attacker, tweeting, "This is the guy who attacked me, can you help identify him? Please share . . . #Brighton #girlslikeus http://t.co/PTLQqmn1MJ." The link connected to a police website with a sketch of the alleged attacker. The tweet was shared 403 times and was accompanied by words of encouragement, though it was not clear whether the attacker was ever identified. By using the hashtag in this manner, the user expanded the initial utility of #GirlsLikeUs even further and hopefully helped some other women stay safe. Amplifying this tweet is a form of defensive digital alchemy in that it allows concerned community members to act collectively to identify someone who had caused harm in their area, a form of harm reduction. #GirlsLikeUs is transformed into an outlet for accountability and activism for the trans community.

On June 11, 2012, an episode of the TLC show *Cake Boss* aired in which an employee of the Cake Boss was to flirt with Carmen Carrera, unaware that she was trans. *Cake Boss* is a popular reality TV show that follows Buddy Valastro and his family-owned bakery as they make incredible cakes for high-end events. Carrera agreed to participate after talking to producers about appropriate language and what would make the prank insensitive. Despite these conversations, producers still elected to film the encounter and include a framing that implied that Carrera was "really a man." Calling trans women men in dresses contributes to a culture of deadly violence. Carrera and her supporters along with GLAAD created a Change.org petition that was tweeted alongside #GirlsLikeUs, and by June 13, Carrera received an apology from the Cake Boss and TLC, and the show did not re-air the episode. The hashtag amplified the story internationally because of its global reach, making the Cake Boss's behavior not only a national but international scandal for TLC. Again, the amplification of the story through Twitter, and specifically the hashtag #GirlsLikeUs, forced TLC to change its tune.

#GirlsLikeUs exemplifies the magic of generative digital alchemy through this practice of shifting from margin to center, utilizing established mediums to create literally transformative realities. Other Black trans activists, like Tourmaline, are using the Internet not to appeal to mainstream media about their humanity but to support and push for a community for themselves that promotes their own well-being and survival.[36] The added benefit of creating this community online is that it is visible to out-group members and does the work of humanizing inadvertently and without draining energy from the more important work of supporting each other. However, this visibility cuts both ways. In the book *Trap Door: Trans Cultural Production and the Politics of Visibility*, Tourmaline and fellow editors and contributors make the sobering point that visibility can also lead to violence.[37] People are using digital media to create and support a network of connection among communities that have traditionally had trouble finding each other, let alone reaching a larger audience. By doing the work of community building online, groups are leveraging both visibility and education at once, while also risking exposure. Women are telling their own stories but in the process are forcing more recognition for their identities in mainstream publics.

Before Janet Mock and Laverne Cox, Black trans women's experiences were not very visible in mainstream media. The popular media trope of trans identity as a form of deception is iconized in the 1992 film *The Crying Game*, which shows a man throw up when he realizes that the Black woman he loves is trans. As Nick Adams, GLAAD director of Trans Media and Representation, notes, "In the same way that *Psycho* created this ripple-effect of cross-dressing psychopathic serial killers [in film], *The Crying Game* created a ripple effect of men reacting with vomiting when they see a transgender woman."[38] Additional representations of Black trans women were limited to daytime talk shows where trans identity was made spectacular and salacious.[39] *Paris Is Burning* (1990) is one of the few vehicles for Black trans women's representation prior to the wave that Mock and Cox helped to usher in. The advent of social media and other digital spaces has allowed for more "real" representations of trans life, including the vibrant community reflected in the hashtag #GirlsLikeUs.

But the real beauty of the hashtag #GirlsLikeUs is in the networks that formed on- and offline. #GirlsLikeUs helped expand and nuance conversations that had failed to take stock of the unique impact of certain policies on trans women's lives. Health topics like the introduction of the Affordable Care Act (ACA), street harassment, and the dearth of resources for the health and well-being of trans women were popular subjects in the compendium of tweets. I explore some representative tweets related to these topics and how they indicate a network that is better able to address the healthcare needs of trans women than what is generally available elsewhere in the public sphere.

The Health of #GirlsLikeUs

How are members of the hashtag network using and talking about health and healthcare in their tweets? I wanted to examine how issues of health and well-being were discussed in the Twitter corpus generated using #GirlsLikeUs. Not surprisingly, these tweets offered a complex and multivalent representation regarding trans women's relation to health and well-being. Health was used to raise awareness about the physical and mental health concerns within trans community, while also highlighting the unique challenges Black women face regarding health. Twitter users adroitly made connections between transphobia, health outcomes, and early death that trans women face, making pointed connections between media outlets' negative portrayals and the health of their community. Anti-trans violence is a health issue because it leads to stress, which community members often respond to with self-medication, using illicit drugs and alcohol, and the violence itself can cause death. Trans women have more trouble navigating the world when negative tropes circulate about them, making housing, employment, and healthcare discrimination much more of a reality.

When Fox News used a photo of Robin Williams dressed in drag as his character Mrs. Doubtfire to illustrate a story about trans healthcare, one immediately begins to understand the life-and-death stakes of trans (mis)representation. Janet Mock tweeted, "Guess who used 'Mrs. Doubtfire' to illustrate a story on trans healthcare. http://t.co/W2SQzw7k #girlslikeus."[40] The tweet links to an article by TakePart Press that reports on the photo and its subsequent impact, citing Mock in the process. Mock is quoted as saying,

> Trans people are not wearing a costume. Our lives and struggles are not jokes, and using such an image spreads damaging stereotypes that who we are is put on, entertainment and fictional. It's those same misconceptions and stereotypes that allow trans people to be discriminated against when it comes to access to housing, employment and healthcare.[41]

Mock's words indicate the importance of images in the real-world health outcomes for trans women. In the same 2011 National LGBTQ Task Force study of Black trans and gender nonconforming people,

"41% of Black respondents said they had experienced homelessness at some point in their lives, more than five times the rate of the general U.S. population."[42] Fox News reduced trans women's lives to a fictional movie character who dons a wig and padding to be able to interact with his children. Robin Williams's drag is portrayed as funny because the audience knows he is a man. Much like the *Shit Girls Say* and *Shit Black Girls Say* videos discussed in chapter 1, the gag relies on the trope that a man in a dress is ridiculous and therefore comical. Society's willingness to connect men in drag to trans women impacts the way trans women move through the world. It makes their real issues a source of comedy and their lives something to be made fun of and not taken seriously. When such images are used to illustrate a story on trans healthcare, trans women's lives are made ridiculous by association and their health made trivial. When trans women go out in public they are at risk of life-ending violence. When trans women seek medical care, they are at risk of negative encounters with medical professionals because of the bias engendered by the trope of a man in a dress. The use of a picture of Williams as Mrs. Doubtfire results in the legitimacy of trans health concerns being called into question. If transness is only drag, then why would gender affirmation surgery be medically necessary? While it's not clear how many people saw this article on the Fox News website, the Fox News Channel has maintained the highest watch rates of all basic cable channels from 2013 to 2018, a sobering statistic given this type of dangerously misleading and transphobic content.

This problematic representation of trans women is not limited to explicitly straight or conservative publications, as mainstream LG(BT) media coverage often neglects and undermines trans women as well. Janet Mock tweeted a 2012 article from the *Daily Beast* that acknowledged the ways that violence against trans women of color is ignored.[43] Mock wrote, "@thedailybeast challenges media & 'mainstream gay community' as to why CeCe, Paige & Brandy were ignored http://t.co/7QKF4b1s #girlslikeus."[44] The tweeted article describes the arrest and trial of CeCe McDonald, a Black trans woman charged with second-degree murder and incarcerated for defending herself against neo-Nazi attackers; Paige Clay, a Black trans woman from Chicago found murdered in a park; and Brandy Martell, another Black trans woman murdered and shot in the genitals and chest by the men who initially hit on her.[45] The article reports that, "while [McDonald's] sentence has sparked outrage in some circles, it has gone virtually unnoticed by the mainstream media, as well as in the mainstream gay community, which has been consumed by the same-sex-marriage debate," among other issues.[46] These murders and the incarceration of McDonald have been central to Twitter conversations using the hashtag #GirlsLikeUs. Trans women are made both hypervisible, with their bodies measured against cis expectations, and invisible, with their lives and deaths absent from even queer community news.

With the implementation of US president Barack Obama's Affordable Care Act (ACA) on the horizon, LGBTQ activists worked to educate community members about the plan and its potential benefits and shortcomings throughout 2012 and 2013. The organization Out2Enroll galvanized LGBTQ organizations to make healthcare coverage and the provisions of the ACA a community issue. However, as was evident in the dearth of reporting in mainstream queer publications about the murders of Paige Clay and Brandy Martell, as well as the incarceration of CeCe McDonald, trans women's unique experiences were overlooked by the organization. One user implored the organization to pay attention to the unique needs of trans people prior to the 2014 enrollment deadline, tweeting, "#out2Enroll please mention the continued use of #trans specific exclusions in health care plans denying trans people coverage. #girlslikeus."[47] When trans people sign up for healthcare coverage, medically necessary treatment is often illegally denied because of provider and insurance company bias. As a result of this public digital activism, Out2Enroll now has a dedicated webpage that provides trans insurance guidance that is broken down by state and plan.[48]

Twitter user and trans advocate Cecilia Chung continued to carry this message of trans healthcare concerns, tweeting, "We want trans-competent health care that is also gender responsive. #srhr #aids2014 #transgender #girlslikeus #trans," demanding care that also allows trans people of all genders to receive the care they need.[49] The type of care trans patients are trying to access is the same care that cis people take for granted; access to hormones and surgery that are medically necessary is routinely denied despite the state and federal mandates that prohibit such discrimination. Chung's use of the hashtag #GirlsLikeUs alongside #SRHR (Sexual and Reproductive Health and Rights) and #AIDS2014 created a connection between activist communities that might not automatically see the resonance between themselves. One tweet of less than 140 characters is demonstrating the link between trans healthcare, HIV, and sexual health. Beyond the question of access to medically necessary treatment, this tweet is calling for trans health to be inclusive of trans sex lives.

The hashtag #GirlsLikeUs also made connections to other digital platforms. For example, the Google Hangout platform, referenced at the beginning of this chapter, was also used to address issues of health. A live Google Hangout called "Transgender Health: An Evolution to Understanding" was open and available for anyone with the link to watch, and a recording makes the video accessible to this day.[50] In addition, transitioning "vlogs" (video blogs) uploaded to YouTube provide recommendations for specific trans-friendly doctors and depictions of the bodily changes experienced during transitioning.[51] Where some parts of the medical community have been slow to acknowledge the growing demand for gender affirmation services and publicly accessible transition documents, trans women are using such online networks to get what they need from receptive providers. Other YouTube videos identified with the #GirlsLikeUs hashtag include videos by TWOC discussing important issues, including the spread of HIV in the community and the challenges for trans women to simply live their lives unmolested. By sharing this information via the hashtag #GirlsLikeUs on Twitter, YouTube, and various other outlets, Mock has developed a new media network through which a message generally reserved for members of the transgender community can reach beyond its immediate context.

Another user of the hashtag discussed the challenges of "being trans in the UK where getting a doctor's letter mentioning '. . . dressed & presented well in female attire' is a thing :-/ #GirlsLikeUs."[52] This tweet illustrates the patronizing attitudes and potential humiliation that women endure when doctors are in a position to assess how they present as women for them to be able to access necessary healthcare. The sad perplexed emoticon at the end of the tweet is a commentary on the unease the Twitter user feels with doctors being able to decide that she is or is not performing her sex and gender well. Realness is again being managed by cis people's expectations of how trans women should perform gender to be regarded as real. This sentiment was shared by another user, who proclaimed, "Who I am is not decided by any doctor, country nor school. #GirlsLikeUs."[53] These tweets provide a window into the way doctors are gatekeepers to trans women's health and experience. In the United Kingdom, "'84% of doctors think NHS funds shouldn't be used 2 treat GD as it's a lifestyle choice' (gires). Ignorance or prejudice? #girlslikeus."[54] Doctors' thoughts are not simply individual biased opinions with no consequence. If doctors think that gender dysphoria is a lifestyle choice, the barriers to treatment for trans patients remain.

When trans people have difficulty finding accepting healthcare providers, their health suffers in other ways as well. According to a 2018 study by the Fenway Health organization for LGBT care in Boston, "HIV prevalence is as high as 50% for Latina transgender women and 48% for Black transgender women, compared to 4% among White non-Hispanic transgender women in the US."[55] An important contributing factor to trans women's reluctance to seek care is the negative attitudes of healthcare professionals they encounter. Even healthcare centers built specifically to serve women can be essentialist in that undertaking. A tweet from a disgruntled potential patient read, "If you missed it: 'Open letter to Feminist Women's Health Center on its refusal to treat trans women' #girlslikeus," which links to the author's detailed experience of being denied care and access.[56] The Fenway Health study mentioned earlier concluded,

> The 2015 national transgender survey found that one-third of its 27,715 respondents reported experiencing at least one negative event in a healthcare setting as the result of their gender identity. Additionally, an earlier version of the survey found that 28% of participants reported being harassed in medical setting and 2% reported being subjected to violence in a healthcare provider's office. Overall, transgender women report fewer positive interactions with healthcare providers and have less confidence in their abilities to integrate HIV-treatment into their lives.[57]

If women do not feel comfortable going to the doctor because of disparate treatment, how are patients' health outcomes to improve?

Stereotypes about trans healthcare are apparent in the responses of doctors who don't think that trans care should be covered by the national health service and in the tendency to conflate trans healthcare with cosmetic or elective surgery.[58] Hormones, blockers, and gender affirmation surgeries are not unlike healthcare services cis people receive regularly, but when trans people seek these same services, they are understood as asking for more than they deserve. Cis women are prescribed hormones for menstrual regulation, birth control, and menopause, and they receive hysterectomies for various reasons. For trans people, having access to the medical services they need impacts not only physical health but mental and social health as well. Access to healthcare, particularly care that is gender affirmative, reduces stress for people. A 2017 study by researchers at Georgia State University found "a significant association between delaying healthcare because of fear of discrimination and worse general and mental health among transgender adults."[59]

Having no confidence in healthcare providers can lead to women taking matters into their own hands. Janet Mock posted a 2012 article from the *Los Angeles Times* about the dangerous realities for trans women wanting gender affirmation surgery, not being able to afford it, and subsequently submitting to unsafe treatments by nonmedical personnel. Mock writes, "Stop obsessing over our bodies. Start reporting on our lack of healthcare coverage: http://t.co/kqcIscMc #girlslikeus."[60] In the linked article, author Laura Nelson mistakenly identifies people receiving silicone injections as trans men as opposed to trans women, further signaling the disconnect between cis journalists and trans people's lives.[61] The article does not contextualize the desire for butt injections with social expectations of women's bodies to be curvy in certain places, nor does Nelson acknowledge cis women's interest in these enhancements as well. Nelson describes a trans woman's desire to fill out her jeans but doesn't connect that longing to added safety or the embodied realness that Mock describes in her book. Realness, once again, is in the eyes of the cis beholder.

Nelson is not alone in her prurient interest in trans women's bodies. The 2012 murder of Lorena Escalara was reported in the *New York Times* with a first sentence that read in part, "she often drew admiring glances in the gritty Brooklyn neighborhood where she was known to invite men for visits to her apartment."[62] One Twitter user posted a link to an alternative news website that critiqued this "sleazy" depiction of Escalara and called on the media to do a better job of representing women like her. Mainstream media maligned Escalara, subtly framing her death as her fault by suggesting that her sex appeal ultimately attracted the kind of men who would set her on fire and leave her to die. Similarly, Black girls are blamed for unwanted attention from men and blamed for the violence they experience at the hands of the police. The fear of this type of violence, the resultant stress from this fear, and subsequent raised cortisol levels have made the already precarious lives of many women of color that much more difficult to manage. Nearly constant reminders of the dangers of living in a cis heterosexist world are made more real with the announcement of another trans girl's murder. Escalara did not make it to her twenty-sixth birthday.

In one of the rare tweets that discussed trans and health in a positive light, the late Black trans Twitter user Monica Roberts used the word *doctor* to describe the contributions trans women have made to society. Roberts tweeted, "#Girlslikeus rock & we have much to be proud of. We have doctors, lawyers, writers, artists, educators & beauty queens in our ranks."[63] Another user mentioned a doctor who was doing right by trans kids, highlighting the work of Dr. Spack to ensure that kids are able to access blockers that delay puberty and/or get the hormones they need. "So many tears at how Dr. Spack has brought hope . . . & life! . . . to so many #trans kids & their families. http://t.co/mohHfrcX #girlslikeus," the user tweeted.[64] The linked article goes on to describe how Spack's direct and routine treatment expanded to become a standard of care embraced by the doctors he mentored and trained. Celebratory tweets like "Vermont Requires Insurers to cover transgender healthcare! http://t.co/jbOtd5KOqG #girlslikeus @transadvocate" are rare but important.[65] They highlight years of on-the-ground advocacy that led to actual policy changes that should improve health outcomes for trans communities across the country. Unfortunately, more common are tweets that show the differential treatment that Black trans (and cis) women experience as a result of policies that are not equally enforced.

Twitter users' health concerns are also made visible in the hashtag through the discussion of the violence that Black trans women encounter in the world. User @Cisnormativity posted an infographic with the tweet, "Who is protected by 'Stand Your Ground'? http://t.co/5YAbDCEi7P h/t @ThessalianHarp #girlslikeus #cwoc #twoc #racism #Trayvon," calling out the way that trans women of color are outside the realm of people who can successfully "stand their ground."[66] "Stand your ground" laws give people the right to defend themselves, even with lethal force, if they are threatened, but as the infographic makes clear, Black women are not afforded that right. Three columns show Marissa Alexander, CeCe McDonald, and George Zimmerman with facts about their respective legal cases below their pictures. Marissa Alexander's column includes that she was "—Abused by husband while pregnant.— Fired warning shot at a wall to defend herself in her own home.— Didn't hit/harm anyone.—Prosecuted by the same attorney as George Zimmerman.—Told she should have run out of her home, not 'stand her ground.' 20 Years Prison." CeCe McDonald's column reads that she was "–Chased down the road by drunk neo-Nazis who were high on meth, shouting racist and transphobic slurs at her.—Slashed in face w/ bottle requiring 11 stitches.—Defended self w/ scissors as last resort. 41 Months Prison." The three-column image ends with George Zimmerman who "—Stalked an unarmed child who was simply walking home to his family, even after being directly told not to by 9-1-1 dispatcher.— Murdered child.—Received donations to cover legal fees.—Used 'stand your ground' legal defense. FREE."[67] Neither McDonald nor Alexander were able to "stand their ground" successfully, as both were incarcerated for their acts of self-defense, while George Zimmerman was found not guilty for the murder of Trayvon Martin. That Zimmerman and Alexander were tried in the same state by the same prosecutor heightens the outrage regarding their disproportionate treatment within the legal system. The juxtaposition of these three photos and narratives speaks to the ways that Black women are held to different standards and are routinely punished with far greater severity than others who commit more egregious acts.

Both hashtags #TWOC and #CWOC (cis women of color), which accompany the image of Alexander, McDonald, and Zimmerman, show that both trans and cis Black women find themselves outside the realm of believability when it comes to "stand your ground." Misogynoir is at work when Black women are unable to successfully defend themselves against attackers. Both Alexander and McDonald were punished for their survival of altercations that could have led to their deaths. Both have been able to garner support from activists across the country and world and further their own activism despite their unjust incarcerations. In what follows, I examine the #FreeCeCe campaign that helped to support CeCe

McDonald before, during, and after her incarceration. #FreeCeCe is a testament to the power of online and offline networks working in tandem to support trans women of color, and would not have been possible without the proto-scaffolding of the #GirlsLikeUs network as a model.

#FreeCeCe

Free CeCe began as a local organizing effort called Support CeCe in CeCe McDonald's community of Minneapolis, Minnesota, in 2011. On June 5 of that year, McDonald and her friends were verbally and then physically accosted by racist, homophobic, and transphobic neo-Nazis as the friends walked by a bar on their way to a grocery store. McDonald kept a pair of fabric scissors in her purse for her own protection and was forced to use them during the attack, fatally injuring one of the men in the neo-Nazi group. McDonald was charged with two counts of second-degree murder, which carries up to a forty-year prison sentence.

McDonald and her lawyers decided to forgo a jury trial despite what many read as an obvious act of self-defense on her part. Her lawyers were unable to get the judge to allow into evidence the deceased's swastika tattoo emblazoned across his chest or the toxicology reports of the illicit drugs in his system at the time of the attack. His previous arrests for domestic violence and other violent crimes were inadmissible, while McDonald's previous conviction for writing a single bad check was admissible because the judge felt that it spoke to her character. McDonald was not permitted to have expert witnesses speak to the ways that transphobia and misogynoir impact her life as a Black trans woman, nor were her supporters, who were growing in number, allowed to show up with shirts or signs of support reading, "#FreeCeCe."[68] Expert testimony could have illuminated the statistics that realities in the #GirlsLikeUs hashtag bear out. As noted in the introduction, the average life expectancy for trans women of color is only thirty-five years. Additionally, Black women, young women, and lesbian and bisexual women report the highest frequency of sexual harassment, with more than a third of each group reporting being harassed in the six months prior to the release of the collaborative National Study on Sexual Harassment and Assault.[69] That her attackers used misogynoirist and transphobic slurs to begin the altercation was not considered by the jury. For McDonald, a young Black trans woman, these realities made her survival of the attack extraordinary.

Black women are never the "appropriate" victim.[70] The hashtag #Say-HerName, created by Black feminist legal theorist Kimberlé Crenshaw's African American Policy Forum, has been used to bring much-needed attention to the extrajudicial killings of Black cis and trans women. While hundreds of thousands of people around the country rallied in reaction to Trayvon Martin's murder, much smaller gatherings were held in support of McDonald. Martin was shot by a vigilante, he was not armed, he was a good student, and he had some class privilege. He was doing something mundane, simply returning from buying Skittles and iced tea. He was "innocent" and was killed in cold blood. McDonald, as a working-class Black trans woman, was never innocent in the eyes of the law nor the eyes of a potential jury. Her legal team knew that her survival would be held against her. I point out the differences between Martin and McDonald not to pit their situations against each other but to illustrate the way that misogynoir operates to further disadvantage Black women when they survive it.

Supporters of McDonald were undeterred. Thirty friends, family, and community members showed up for the pretrial motions where these trial decisions were made. Using the FreeCeCe Tumblr page and the Support CeCe WordPress website, Support CeCe members indicated that they would shift their sartorial support from explicit messages of "Free CeCe" to wearing purple, McDonald's favorite color. This inspired pivot did not come to pass, as McDonald decided to accept a plea deal, but purple remains the background color for both the Free CeCe Tumblr page and the Support CeCe WordPress website as well as a color utilized in #FreeCeCe mobilizations. That her support team listened and adapted its strategy to best suit CeCe's needs is a model for how true solidarity works.

Support CeCe was started by members of the Minneapolis trans community, including Billy Navarro, who helped found the group. Navarro was clear that McDonald's fate was not unique, stating, "This could have been any of us," as any trans person could find themselves subject to the kind of violence that would force a defense that would make them the villain in their own story of survival.[71] What Navarro's statement misses is the anti-Black and sexist aspects of the attack that McDonald faced as a Black woman. McDonald's gender and race together are what made the situation dangerous; racialized and gendered slurs were hurled at her. As a Black woman, McDonald was uniquely punished for her survival of a misogynoirist incident. The sense of solidarity and support for CeCe among the trans community rippled beyond Minneapolis, and as more people heard McDonald's story, a wider network developed. When Janet Mock tweeted the #FreeCeCe petition in April 2012, it had 9,514 signatures. It would grow to nearly 20,000 by the month's end.

Popular YouTubers, like HARTBeat, used their channels to express their dismay that McDonald was essentially being charged for surviving an assault. They created a video message to the governor of Minnesota asking that McDonald be pardoned and released.[72] And though the plea deal did require McDonald to serve time for her defense of herself, the external support that she received lessened the time she served; McDonald served nineteen months in jail for the death, despite being sentenced to forty-one months. Thanks to a different online petition that was circulated through this digital activism, the Minnesota Department of Corrections agreed to administer the full regimen of hormones McDonald needed, though she remained quartered with men despite a transfer to a second facility.[73] Online activism shortened her sentence, ensured that she received hormones while incarcerated, and enabled her continued healing once released.

McDonald chronicled her thoughts and feelings while incarcerated through blog entries on the Support CeCe website. During the nineteen months of CeCe McDonald's incarceration, blog entries on Support CeCe demonstrate her developing political education via the books and shows she had access to in prison. Blogging gave McDonald the opportunity to share her thinking while incarcerated by giving her space to publicly process her feelings in a supportive digital environment. The blog drew people to it who were empathetic to McDonald's position, creating the type of space where McDonald felt comfortable telling her truth. Blogs are part of the digital women of color feminist story as they serve as a space for building connection and understanding through the digital word. For McDonald, blogging chronicled transformation, especially her rejection of internalized misogynoir.

She was just shy of her twenty-third birthday when the attack occurred. It is a remarkable archive of her shifting sense of self as she is buoyed by texts and experiences that complicate previous narratives she held around identity and survival. In McDonald's first post on the blog, she struggled with her incarceration for merely surviving. She writes,

> I am truly sorry for the loss of a person who also was involved in the incident, but how would my mom and family feel if she heard that I was killed by a group of racist, homophobic/transphobic people only for walking to the store and being at the wrong place at the wrong time, which luckily I wasn't by myself. Or even looking at it in different aspects, would the situation have been the same. Would they have taken the same lengths to prosecute him if he had killed me?[74]

McDonald asks the question that her supporters answer with their limited numbers. Her transness, her queerness, and—though not stated—her Blackness set her up to be an unsympathetic survivor. The man who died trying to kill her would not have been prosecuted the way she was. In the same entry, McDonald discusses the impact on her body and spirit as a result of the attack: "Now I have to deal with the repercussions of other people's hateful actions. To deal with the nightmares, the stress, and the PTSD. To feeling paranoid that someone might try to kill me, or my family. To be unsure of where my future lies."[75] This fear and stress are the result of her surviving this misogynoiristic violence. As was the case with other Black trans women before her, McDonald's survival is not without cost to her health and well-being. She does not get to enjoy or process her saving of her own life but must deal with the repercussions of her defense of herself in her body and in prison. The trauma that so many women experience as a result of the misogynoiristic violence they have suffered goes unremarked upon and unaddressed, contributing to chronic health problems like depression, PTSD, and more.

In the same blog entry, she describes her family's negative reaction to reading a note she had written to a boy she was "talking to" in school. Her uncle threw her to the ground and choked her. Like Black lesbian poet Pat Parker, McDonald encountered the pain of intraracial violence. McDonald describes knowing that "my family would not be supportive of me in my life decisions, especially dealing with my sexuality."[76] For McDonald's family, her transness was legible as aberrant queerness. Her desires were policed before she was even old enough to act on them or

truly articulate them. McDonald connects the gender and sexuality policing she experienced as a child to the reluctance of men to identify as
gay. She acknowledges that the harassment she experienced in the home
and at school was both physical and emotional abuse. In her own family,
at school, and on a sidewalk in Minneapolis, other people felt the need
to discipline McDonald for her gender. This violence at home and out in
the world makes it difficult to know where or how to find safety. Despite
this difficult content, which includes the violence that she suffered at the
hands of family, classmates, and the neo-Nazis she survived, McDonald
titled the entry "Pursuit of Happiness." She describes the events of her
life, and her pending trial, as loops and deep dives that will not deter her
from her pursuit of happiness. How others feel about her also will not
derail her from what is possible for her life.

In this first entry, McDonald's articulation of her sexuality and gender
are discussed through the binary frames of man and woman, gay and
straight. She troubles those binaries in a later post, moved to do so in
part by an episode of HBO's *Sex and the City* (1998–2004). In the episode, the sexually aggressive Samantha talks about having sex with two
gay men at the same time. For McDonald, this storyline became a possibility model that allowed her to reconsider her own sexuality. She writes,
"I found myself saying I can't like girls, that that ship has sailed and the
attraction wasn't there. That was until I became more experienced in
the world, and learning about femininity and masculinity. The more I
understood about myself the more I realized what it was I was actually
attracted to."[77] McDonald goes on to write that she realized what she
was really attracted to was masculinity and that she could be and was
attracted to masculine women. This episode-turned-possibility-model
opened the door for her to consider sexuality beyond a straight/gay binary and embrace the identity of pansexual. Later, McDonald would
reclaim bisexual as attraction to more than one gender as opposed to the
dimorphic definition that "bi" implies to people skeptical of the identity.
In chapter 3, I examine the term "bi" in the context of one of the web
shows I analyze.

Even while incarcerated, McDonald was participating in lifesaving
generative digital alchemy that helped other women like herself survive.
McDonald's thought processes about her life and the state of the world
through the Support CeCe blog offer a special insight into the types of

pop culture and politics she was consuming and making sense of while inside. In wanting to pay forward some of the support she received, she created a "31 days of giving" list that included nonprofit organizations followers could donate to beyond the GoFundMe started in her honor. She uplifted other women of color, including Sage Smith, who went missing in November 2012 before being presumed murdered four years later in 2016.[78] McDonald posted a request to support a woman identified only as Estrellita, who was described as trying to seek asylum in the United States, only to be detained in Arizona by border patrol. McDonald asked supporters to donate funds in support of her bond so that she could leave the detention center.[79] McDonald's organizing from prison was facilitated by the generative digital alchemy through social media platforms like her blog and the GoFundMes she supported.

While dealing with the PTSD of the attack and the bureaucracy of the Department of Corrections, McDonald was able to express her frustration with other seemingly less important pop culture situations. During rapper Snoop Dogg's brief rebranding as Snoop Lion, he offered the opinion that gay rappers would never make it in the rap industry because rap is such a masculine arena. McDonald used her blog to offer a two-part rebuttal:

> For one, it just goes to show that people still have a stereotypical idea of what "gay" is and that there is no possibility of masculine, or even hyper-masculine, gay and bisexual men in the world. Well, guess what? . . . THEY EXIST! For two, to say that "rap is a masculine arena" is an underhanded insult to both masculine gay and bisexual men and also to feminine men, trans, GNC (gender non-conforming) and cissexual women who are rappers. It's clear that women are just as much of a force in the rap industry just as any man is, so why is it so unfathomable that someone that is QLGBT-GNC can't be such a force in an "arena" that really have no gender "boundaries" or "guidelines"? How can one just say that a person can't do something because of their sexual identity and/or orientation. That's like saying we can't have a black president. Well, you see how that turned out. Twice![80]

McDonald lays out two important fallacies in Snoop's logic: that queer people cannot be masculine and that rappers can only be masculine.

The meteoric rise of out gay Black rapper Lil' Nas X and his hit "Old Town Road" belie Snoop's assertion. Rappers like Nicki Minaj and more recently Megan Thee Stallion further disprove his point with lyrics that celebrate and tease bisexuality. But at the time of McDonald's critique, these realities were not as readily apparent. And still, McDonald used Snoop's limited imagination to expose a broader truth about our social expectations of gender.

This same April 30, 2013, entry also features an acknowledgment of climate change in which McDonald laments that it is still snowing in Minnesota and that people need to change their behavior if we want the planet to still care for us. She connects global warming to the energy expenditures in prisons:

> At any jail or prison I've been to I've noticed that they leave lights on 24/7! Now think about all the other jails, prisons, juvenile centers, etc., etc. around the world that does exactly the same thing. Now think about how much energy could be saved without them, hmmm . . . see where I'm coming from? We could save a lot of resources, actually, with abolishing prisons.[81]

McDonald deftly makes the end of incarceration a green initiative that could help save the planet. Her intimate knowledge of the prison-industrial complex provides insights that could push more dynamic collaborations between environmentalists and abolitionists.

McDonald's blog is a journey through her evolving perspective, and one can see her move from her individual feelings of guilt to global concerns for those incarcerated. McDonald transforms from someone who accepts her punishment with guilt and shame, to an international prison abolitionist. McDonald's blog posts vary widely, but they all signal a Black woman making sense of the many arrows being slung her way, whether directly because of her identities or indirectly as someone with little individual power in the world. However, McDonald's experience of communal support speaks to the power of just a few people working together to affect change. In pleasure activist adrienne maree brown's book *Emergent Strategy: Shaping Change, Changing Worlds*, she describes nine principles that inform her belief in organizing. Principle number seven calls for people to "focus on critical connections more than critical mass—build the resilience by building the relationships."[82] McDonald and her supporters were able to do exactly that by addressing potential allies through digital platforms such as Twitter, Tumblr, and the Support CeCe website. These platforms fostered critical connections that provided the sustained support that allowed folks to remain committed despite an unsuccessful petition to get McDonald freed or pardoned.

The Support CeCe Minnesota chapter organized a monthly book club in concert with what McDonald was reading. When McDonald began reading *The Hunger Games* by Suzanne Collins on April 2, supporters made it the book of the month for April. The book club continued, and a separate list of books McDonald was reading while incarcerated was published on the Support CeCe website. These texts included *The Autobiography of Malcom X as Told to Alex Haley*, *The New Jim Crow* by Michelle Alexander, and *Abolition Democracy: Beyond Empire, Prisons, and Torture* by Angela Davis.[83] While some might read the sci-fi dystopia of *The Hunger Games* as altogether different from the call to end prisons in *Abolition Democracy*, I would argue that these texts actually work well together. Collins exposes the evils of a fascist state as Davis calls forth the world we want by showing us a way out.[84] As Mock's own practice of producing her book shows, books have the ability to travel in ways some other digital forms cannot. These texts speak to McDonald's developing political consciousness and the way she understood her incarceration.

The Free CeCe campaign organized letter writing and book deliveries for McDonald. Still visible on the Support CeCe website is the exact address to which to send books to CeCe in the prison where she served the last of her nineteen months. In the foreword to the book *Captive Genders: Trans Embodiment and the Prison Industrial Complex*, McDonald describes wanting to create curriculum for incarcerated folks that opens up the false history of the United States that is taught through public education. McDonald goes on to critique the idea that this work is done only in isolation or through the Internet. She writes of folks who call themselves activists, advocates, or allies, "If you showed up to a meeting once and spend your day online, that's not activism."[85] For McDonald, good words are paired with continued actions, which was the true alchemy of the Free CeCe movement, which sustained an organizing effort through McDonald's trial, release, and beyond.

The hashtag #FreeCeCe moved digitally to support work on the ground in Minneapolis and other parts of the world. #FreeCeCe announced rallies and protest marches in support of McDonald and other trans women caught in the crosshairs of transphobia and misogynoir. When Paige Clay, a Black trans woman in Chicago, was found murdered on April 16, 2012, Twitter users like Janet Mock called for more support for McDonald, stressing that Clay's murder was potentially McDonald's fate had she not defended herself. As Mock put it on Twitter, "We can't bring Paige back, but we can save CeCe. Please sign, share & RT this #freeCeCe petition: http://ow.ly/1LoXlc #girlslikeus."[86] At the May Day 2012 protests in support of workers' rights, activists carried signs in remembrance of Clay and in support of McDonald. The late trans activist and author Leslie Feinberg visited McDonald in jail and was later arrested for support actions in Minneapolis, which included tagging the jail with "Free CeCe" in purple spray paint.[87] #FreeCeCe was used to announce Facebook events of local Support CeCe chapters that organized letter-writing campaigns and workshops.

#FreeCeCe also enabled practical support at the local level. In addition to imploring people to write to McDonald in prison, Support CeCe organizers used the #FreeCeCe hashtag to fundraise for bus passes for McDonald's family members so they could visit her in prison. The hashtag also carried the petition asking the Minnesota governor to pardon McDonald following her sentencing. When it became clear that the prison was in violation of court orders to allow McDonald her medically necessary hormones, yet a third petition was drafted and shared via #FreeCeCe. Over the course of her nearly two-year incarceration, #FreeCeCe kept the community aware and responsive to McDonald's needs.

Not only did Support CeCe inspire digital activism, including a Go-FundMe campaign that went directly to supporting McDonald and the letter-writing and book-sending campaign, the group also transformed how McDonald was discussed and who took up her story in mainstream media outlets. While the early #FreeCeCe tweets were from Black and non-Black trans women, by the time of McDonald's incarceration, mainstream Black publications like *Ebony* began to tell her story. Award-winning journalist Akiba Solomon's piece for the digital edition of the magazine, titled "CeCe McDonald: Attacked for Her Identity, Incarcerated for Surviving," laid out the context of McDonald's survival and the way her gender led to her subsequent incarceration. "If she weren't a Black transgender woman, she wouldn't be expected to stand for that kind of abuse. Actually, she would be considered a survivor," Solomon wrote.[88] Just a month later, scholar Marc Lamont Hill wrote an article in support of McDonald in *Ebony* as well, titled, "Why Aren't We Fighting for CeCe McDonald?"[89] Hill called on Black organizations like the NAACP and Urban League to take up the effort to rally for McDonald as they had done for Trayvon Martin. These explicit calls for Black support in a Black publication opened dialogue about who is a member of the Black community. While the goals of this activism are not to appeal to those with comparatively more privilege, visibility in alternate circles helps to foster the type of solidarity necessary to move institutions to behave differently. Days later, on June 17, a silent march on Father's Day to protest stop-and-frisk policies brought together activists in the Black community and LGBTQ youth workers who recognized the disproportionate police attention given to Black men and LGBTQ youth of color. The NAACP, GLAAD, and other LGBTQ organizations began working in concert to uplift these concerns, making misogynoir an important issue to address when addressing police violence.[90]

Free CeCe grew relationships among Minnesota activists who wanted to support McDonald but had not previously worked together. The local collective was then able to access its multiple networks to leverage digital spaces to bring international awareness to McDonald's situation. Digital pictures captured Free CeCe protest signs at progressive protests around the United States and the globe, including Canada, England, India, and Germany.[91] On both the local and international levels, McDonald's disparate treatment galvanized communities to actively resist the transphobic and misogynoiristic message that she and other Black trans women do not deserve to fight for their lives.

Though McDonald was released on January 13, 2014, the advocacy networks built to support her while she was incarcerated persist. Laverne Cox teamed up with McDonald to create a documentary about her time in and after prison. The *#FreeCeCe* documentary was named one of the best LGBT documentaries of 2016 by the *Advocate*. McDonald has become an outspoken advocate in the prison abolition and gender justice movements. She joined fellow Black trans activist Joshua Allen for the #BlackExcellenceTour, taking full advantage of hashtag activism in the promotion of their speakers' series. The Tumblr-powered website that organized support for McDonald while she was incarcerated remains and is an incredible archive of the work they supported and helped blossom. #FreeCeCe became a model campaign for how to support someone who is incarcerated and spawned numerous #FreeCeCe chapters as well as new support campaigns for others.

Whether through #FreeCeCe or #GirlsLikeUs, Black trans women were able to mobilize Twitter and other social media to support themselves but also created the digital networks that supported others. Janet Mock's #GirlsLikeUs became a vehicle for amplifying #FreeCeCe, and #FreeCeCe led to the documentary produced by Laverne Cox as well as a new career for McDonald. McDonald is now a highly sought-after speaker on prison abolition. In September 2019, McDonald was awarded a Soros Justice Fellowship to support her work in developing a curriculum "for grassroots education that builds community support and power for transgender women, particularly transgender women of color."[92] #FreeCeCe's legacy includes the political activation of people who wanted to support McDonald, but grew to wanting to support prison abolition. McDonald herself is an abolitionist fighting for the end of prisons, not just reform that would make them "safer" for Black trans women. #FreeCeCe shows the permeability between online and offline activism, through a digital alchemy that moved organizers to use strategies in multiple arenas to aid their activism.

As Janet Mock's star continues to rise, so does the reach of #GirlsLikeUs. Mock went on to publish her second book, *Surpassing Certainty: What My Twenties Taught Me*. She also had a short-lived digital web show with MSNBC called *So POPular* (2014), where she tackled the latest celebrity happenings as well as important issues within marginalized communities in a few minutes at a time. Just a decade earlier, such representation seemed impossible; by building a digital audience, Mock made herself—and the stories of her communities—marketable to the mainstream. In 2018 she began to write and direct for the FX television show *Pose* (2018), which chronicles the lives of Black and Latinx trans women and gay men involved in the Ball scene of late 1980s New York City. The show is unprecedented, with trans characters played by trans actors and a majority cast of color. Mock has also inked the first overall deal with Netflix by a trans person, allowing her to green-light and produce the stories that matter to her and her communities.[93] Formerly marginalized, trans of color media is moving to the center. Mock's commitment to storytelling and narrative reiterates the power of media to transform the world around us.

Twitter and Tumblr are two social media platforms that have facilitated organizing and exchange for Black trans women who might not otherwise be able to connect. Twitter enabled both Mock and McDonald to achieve greater visibility, thus propelling their work into new markets. And yet this visibility is a double-edged sword: As much as we want to celebrate the successes of trans women of color in the public sphere, that excitement is tempered with the deadly reality of trans women of color's lives being cut short by violence. Visibility also means that Black trans women's health is at risk when they are unfairly discriminated against when trying to secure and maintain housing, healthcare, and employment.

Social media is not limited to Twitter or hashtags. Queer web shows on platforms like Vimeo and YouTube allow creative content producers to build audiences that sometimes translate into traditional platforms. Whether it is the web success of a show like *The Misadventures of Awkward Black Girl* (2011) transforming into the hit HBO series *Insecure* (2017–), there is something to be said for the specific kind of incubation that the web makes possible. Janet Mock was able to translate her web savvy into contributing to a groundbreaking television series and an unprecedented deal with the leading digital streaming service. For queer and trans people of color, these web projects are not solely for incubation, but they may be where projects live. In the next chapter, I explore queer Black women's web shows and their proliferation in the last ten years.

3

Web Show Worldbuilding Mitigates Misogynoir

As Janet Mock sought to redefine realness, other Black queer and trans people redefine representations through their own creative processes. It is by attending to self that Mock makes room for other trans women. Similarly, Black queer and trans artists have sought to write themselves into places where they were not represented. Building on queer of color media production and artistic movements from the 1970s, 1980s, and 1990s, younger voices are creating innovative web series, visibility projects, and funding initiatives that reimagine mainstream narratives about their identities. The successful crowdsourced campaign to turn writer and director Dee Rees's short film *Pariah* (2011) into a feature-length film is an example of Black queer media products enabled by digital technologies. Rees intentionally reached out to Black and queer web communities like Quirky Black Girls and Beyond Stud, which were Facebook-like niche sites for people to connect around these identities. Hosting thousands of members between them, the sites and their members generated enough votes to push *Pariah* into the winner's circle.

Web shows became a popular venue for Black creators because of the difficulty they had accessing mainstream outlets. Before the viral success of *The Misadventures of Awkward Black Girl* (2011–2013) encouraged many other Black creators to begin to see the web in a new light, Black queer creators were building audiences online.[1] A queer favorite and the first with an all-woman cast, *Lovers and Friends* (2008–2010) followed a group of Black lesbian friends and all of their drama in late aughts Miami.[2] Despite poor production values and stilted acting, the show built on its YouTube success with a spinoff series and in-person events at Queer Prides across the country. *Lovers and Friends* proved that there was a Black queer women's audience hungry for digital content.

As digital cameras got smaller and cheaper, a virtual explosion of Black queer web shows found their way to YouTube. Each show reflects the community in which it was produced, with visual and articulated references to the cities in which they are shot. Most of these shows are shot in southern cities, which challenges the idea of queer life being possible only in northern queer metropoles like New York or Philadelphia. While cities do dominate the web show landscape, they are often southern, and the communities of friends are almost, if not all, Black.

Between Women, *Skye's the Limit*, and *195 Lewis* not only create representations that speak to the subjectivity of these marginalized communities but also redefine the imagined audience as those very communities themselves. Digital media makers are less concerned with creating content that reaches privileged out-group members than creating content for their own networks. This work is less about creating positive or respectable images that would appeal to normative audiences, but rather a means for creating networks and representations that speak to communities not acknowledged in mainstream media. These productions create opportunities for the viewing audience and the creators to see and make content that centers their experiences, a process that Black queer theorists Aymar Jean Christian and Faithe Day call "quare-shared recognition."[3]

For Black queer web show producers, their creative projects represent a realness redefined where Black queer life is central, not peripheral. Queerness and Blackness are not the source of the dramatic tension in these shows. These shows offer aspirational visions of Black queer women's lives and as such offer their own possibility models for Black queer existence. The otherwise generative digital alchemy these shows' worldbuilding efforts provide still leaves unexamined tropes of toxic masculinity, domestic violence, and capitalist success. The liberatory worlds these shows attempt to build are not utopias. A feminist future is not necessarily being called forth in these Black queer web shows, which exist somewhere between the real world and fantasy.

"Worldbuilding" is a term generally reserved for the creation of sci-fi and fantasy universes, but I find it useful for thinking through the settings that Black queer web shows construct. Viewers are invited into a Black queer space that reflects some contemporary realities of Black queer life but also imagines what might otherwise be possible.[4] Whether it's the city of Atlanta legalizing gay marriage or a James Baldwin writer's award for a Black queer American to go to Paris for a year, these web shows build worlds with the realities they want to exist, even as they depict the messier realities of their existence.

This chapter investigates the proliferation of Black queer women's YouTube series. Through close readings of scenes in the series' episodes, I argue that *Skye's the Limit* (2013), *Between Women* (2011–), and *195 Lewis* (2017) critique familial relationships, relationships between friends, and the relationships characters have with themselves through narratives that challenge the centrality of romantic relationships and stress the importance of healthy social networks beyond sexual partnerships. These web shows both trouble and perpetuate misogynoir, especially with the way that masculinity and femininity are portrayed by the characters. On the one hand, these shows offer a window into the world of Black queer women, but in so doing, they expose the messy reality that misogynoir can and does live there too. Though these web series often have short runs due to the unpredictable nature of crowd-sourced funding and a lack of professional talent, they still offer important insights into the worldbuilding of Black queer women. Further, these worlds address misogynoir through the generative digital alchemy of making Black women's health needs central to the plot of many of the storylines of the webisodes. Rather than defensively critique misogynoir directly, these shows offer a transformed view of Black queer life by creating the worlds they want through generative digital alchemy.

The web shows I explore in this chapter all center queer and trans characters assigned female at birth. Each show addresses their communities in different ways depending on their location and the socioeconomic realities of the characters they center. *Skye's the Limit*, *Between Women*, and *195 Lewis* are all set in queer communities in different parts of the country: DC, Atlanta, and Brooklyn, respectively. These three series exemplify the transformative power of generative digital alchemy while still showing that we have so much further to go in terms of what we imagine for our futures. Each show relied on community support to raise the funds to produce the show as well as spread the word to build its audience.

Skye's the Limit

Skye's the Limit (2013) is a web show created by Black queer writer and producer Blue Telusma that follows a group of Black queer friends living in the DC metro area. Launched on YouTube in 2013, the show had only one season of nine episodes. *Skye's the Limit* follows lead character Skye as she makes questionable choices that complicate both her professional and personal lives. Skye struggles to find stability after blowing through her life savings, being laid off from her job, and reconnecting with an old love. Though *Skye's the Limit* traffics in the classic plot points of uncommunicated desire and miscommunication between lovers, there are refreshing moments within this web series that trouble these tropes and even push back on in-group stereotypes.

Telusma used the show as a vehicle to discuss many aspects of Black queer life that are largely absent from mainstream media, including gender roles, kink, and queer sex, among other topics. Telusma invited viewers behind the scenes of the series by including outtakes in the credits of episodes, hosting Pride engagements around the country, and using social media platforms that allowed viewers to invest in the show and actors beyond the episodes themselves. Telusma built and generated innovative content, all while developing a digital network of fiercely loyal fans. For Telusma, transforming the process of production included ensuring that the sensory experience of the filming was central. She stated, "I'm a visual/tactile learner so if something doesn't appeal to all five senses . . . I'm out, but being that way means it takes more to make a project happen. . . . I made the cast shoot every scene a dozen times just so we could get different angles, like a real show."[5] This attention to detail, to make the web show "like a real show," speaks to the transformative potential of digital projects. Telusma was raising the bar for web series production while also helping the cast bond through the additional time they spent together because of the additional filming. At the level of content and production, Telusma was interested in creating a different experience for cast, crew, and audience alike.

In behind-the-scenes footage that rolled during the credits of some episodes, as well as a stand-alone blooper reel, the audience gets to see the cast taking tea breaks on set and being silly together. In the credits following episode 2, cast member Romy Simpson recounts the strange looks received by others in the building where they were shooting as she dons the teddy and trench coat required for her scene. Simpson laughs as she says, "The lady in the elevator asked, 'Are y'all shooting a porno?!'" Her castmates laugh and express shock at how their production is being perceived by other people. These moments provided an opportunity for the cast to connect and build relationships that translated to their on-camera chemistry. To the degree that she could, Telusma tried to create an atmosphere that rivaled a mainstream TV production, ultimately making the show a YouTube fan favorite, with nearly a million views of the series before it moved to a paid platform.

Skye's the Limit's titular character is an extroverted and impulsive cis femme who—upon returning from a self-motivated *Eat Pray Love* vacation to India, Spain, and Italy—finds herself out of a job.[6] Skye's best friend, Taylor, and her cousin Cassie work together to lift Skye's wilted spirit by sending her to a life coach and orchestrating a rent party in her honor. Over the course of the season, viewers are treated to a bevy of Black women of different sizes, gender presentations, and sexualities, as they all try to navigate life in their late twenties.

Despite what the title implies, *Skye's the Limit* is not focused solely on its titular character. Rather, it is an ensemble-driven show centered on a group of people who are all friends with Skye. We meet her friends and her love interest, Jay, who all challenge mainstream representations of beauty in some way. Skye is a dark-skinned protagonist, a rarity in traditional television. She is the object of desire for both of her college friends, the masculine-of-center and light-skinned Jay as well as the also masculine-of-center and brown-skinned Ronnie. Dark-skinned feminine love interests as well as light-skinned masculine love interests subvert a subtle tendency in mainstream media to equate masculinity and melanin. Misogynoir is predicated on the idea that Black women are too masculine and too dark to be desirable, so when these web shows make room for more diversity on-screen, it challenges these fixed notions of who can be attractive. Masculine lesbians are rarely seen on mainstream screens whether big (movies) or small (television), particularly if they are Black.[7] Marisol is a fat Black femme, as is Jay's girlfriend, Maya. Both women are portrayed as desirable and sexy, and their size is never the butt of a joke or something they talk about changing. *Skye's the Limit*, like many of these shows, does not overtly tackle colorism, but it features a diverse range of bodies and skin tones. This unnamed diversity in the cast does the silent work of challenging mainstream representations that allow only thinness and light skin to be beautiful. Through casting, *Skye's the Limit* and other web shows provide a more heterogeneous picture of what relationships in queer communities of color can be. The show provides a real reflection of the diversity of the Black lesbian community because it is made by that community.

But even as I discuss this show as made for and by a Black lesbian community, the show goes further, complicating notions of what queerness looks like for Black women. Skye's best friend, Taylor, identifies as queer, and when the series begins, she is dating Tyler, a cis straight man, while nursing an unarticulated crush on Skye. Taylor's queerness is never questioned despite her current relationship. Here, as in the other Black queer web shows I discuss, there is no valorizing of gold star status (the supposedly coveted position of a lesbian who has never had sex with a man) among the characters, reflecting the reality that many of these characters, like the members of the communities they represent, have sexual practices and pasts that are not neatly encapsulated under the label "lesbian." Taylor plays the role of educator in some of these episodes, introducing the ostensibly straight cousin Cassie to queer terminology and ideas.

In episode 2, "Trapped in the Closet," Skye witnesses Jay, her unrequited college love, "getting strapped"—or being penetrated—by Jay's current and more feminine girlfriend, Maya. Shocked, she tells Taylor and Cassie. Taylor chastises Skye and Cassie for limiting Jay's sexuality because of their homonormative beliefs about how Jay should behave in bed.

> CASSIE: Wait, but isn't Jay supposed to be the boy? Is she supposed to do that?
> TAYLOR: Neither of them are the boy, Cassie, they are both women. Just because Jay is more masculine-of-center doesn't mean she can't enjoy her full womanhood just like everybody else. No. I say more power to her.
> CASSIE: Masculine of what? Isn't that a fancy way of saying she's the boy?
> TAYLOR (*ignoring Cassie, and speaking directly to Skye*): So let me get this straight. You ignore your guests for half the night and then you leave your own party early so that you could . . . what? Watch some woman who broke your heart get fucked by somebody else? Does that pretty much sum up this long ass story you've been telling?

SKYE: It sounds silly when you put it that way. I mean it's easy to criti-
cize in hindsight, but at the time I just totally shut down.

Taylor's comments serve to broaden and expand both her scene partners' and her audiences' worldview by defending the sexual agency of
Jay and Maya. Telusma offers viewers the narrative that they might be
familiar with, one in which the more masculine person is assumed to be
the one who wears the strap, but then challenges that narrative through
what Skye witnesses and then recounts. By having Taylor serve as a foil
to this homonormative assumption of sexual gender roles, *Skye's the
Limit* introduces the possibility of another option, where sexual roles
and gender roles do not have to be aligned. Taylor is not concerned
about Jay's masculinity or her sexual proclivities; she focuses on the hurt
Jay caused Skye. Her recap of the previous night's events is designed
to make Skye question her interest in Jay, given the disrespect Jay has
shown by forcing her to hide in a closet and sneak out of the apartment
when Maya arrives unexpectedly. Cassie's naivete as the "straight girl" in
the scene provides an opportunity to reflect homonormative messages
that queer viewers might have internalized through the cover of an out-
group member. Telusma cleverly uses Taylor's responses to open a conversation about gender and sexuality in a community that may generally
regard itself as progressive when it comes to sex. This scene exposes the
socially acceptable but ultimately limiting frames within queer spaces,
inviting the audience to question their own assumptions about sex and
gender.

Cassie struggles to make sense of what she has just learned about Jay's
sexual predilections given Jay's masculine appearance. As Cassie tries to
talk through her perception of Jay as a tomboy and how she imagines
that must line up with her sexual practices, Taylor provides another narrative by using herself as an example. Taylor gives Cassie an education
in queer identity and expression by explaining why the term "bisexual"
does not quite work for her:

TAYLOR: Sexuality is a very personal thing. You can't stigmatize someone for liking what they like.
CASSIE: Well, since you're bi, I bet you have a lot more experience with
that stuff than I do.

TAYLOR: I am not bi.

CASSIE: Well, Skye said you dated women in college, and now you have a boyfriend. Doesn't that make you bi?

TAYLOR: I identify as queer.

CASSIE: But you date both men and women. What is the difference?

TAYLOR: Okay. The difference is that I am not only open to men and women in the traditional sense, I am also attracted to trans men, gay men, bisexual women, androgynous, the whole spectrum. I don't get caught up in all of those boxes people like to check off. What is most important is if you are sexy.

Taylor's explanation of her sexuality again pushes the show beyond a simple Black lesbian representation of sexuality into one that addresses queerness as its own identity. For Taylor, the term "bisexual" does not fully capture her sexual identity. As discussed in chapter 2, in relation to CeCe McDonald's own sexual identity journey, "bisexual" does not have the dimorphic connotation that "bi" implies or that Taylor assumes. However, despite efforts to reeducate community around the word, biphobia persists in an aversion to the word and its perceived binarism. Taylor wants to be understood as queer because for her, queer includes her attraction to genders beyond the gender binary.[8] Her explanation of her queer identity provides a more fluid representation of sexuality, one that explicitly names gender as a spectrum. Taylor's words highlight the connection between our ideas about gender and sexuality. Queerness becomes Taylor's way to name her multifaceted desire. Both Cassie and the viewing audience are invited into a perspective on sexuality that they may not have considered before.

Taylor provides a window into the diversity of sexual play in episode 6, "Rockin Robin." Taylor introduces the shy "straight" Cassie to bondage and other forms of light BDSM. At Cassie's behest, Taylor blindfolds her, drips hot wax on her body, and ties her up as they have sex. The scripting of this encounter introduces more challenges to mainstream depictions of sex on television, with explicit verbal consent and visual consent centered on-screen. When Cassie asks Taylor to teach her, she not only gives consent but establishes the dynamic she wants for their sexual encounter. Though Taylor is positioned as the teacher, Cassie is the one who initiates their play and seeks to be taught.

That Taylor and Cassie are both feminine Black women having a sexual encounter makes the scene disappointingly unique for two reasons: it is rare in Black queer media for feminine women to be partnered together, and it is equally rare for Black characters in traditional media to have Black romantic partners.[9] Lena Waithe's *Master of None* (2015–2017) character Denise and Bre-Z's Coop on *All American* (2010–present) have Black love interests, but these love interests are more feminine than their counterparts, maintaining a subtle homonormative relationship dynamic. For most of the Black lesbians on mainstream television now, white lovers are the norm. *Pretty Little Liars* (2010–2017) featured the only other Black lesbian/Black lesbian pairing; also bucking the generally homonormative system, both characters are feminine.[10] There have been no mainstream representations of masculine-of-center women with masculine-of-center women, though Waithe does her own form of queer baiting—the practice of teasing a queer relationship between characters but never allowing them to get together, to attract a queer audience without distancing straight viewers—in her new BET vehicle, *Twenties* (2020), in which two masculine-of-center characters flirt for a few episodes, only for the flirtation to be decidedly ended after an awkward conversation.[11] Web shows offer slightly more versatility with series like *Choiices*, offering some masculine for masculine representation on-screen.

Web shows both reinforce and challenge dominant ideas about sexuality. They can become a space where sexual pleasure, gender expression, and desire can be pushed beyond the limits of mainstream television. When a range of gender expressions and sexual possibilities is presented, sexual health expands to include discussions of kink, consent, and fluidity. In the last scene of episode 8, "Feasting on Scraps," Cassie admits to a friend that she is questioning her sexuality and her understanding of herself as straight given the sexual experiences she has had with Taylor. *Skye's the Limit* allows for characters' sexual fluidity and shifting identity. Unlike mainstream television, which might present this ambiguity as a source of angst, Cassie expresses excitement in exploring this new side of her sexuality. The fluidity of sexuality and sexual practice is made visible in the varied relationships and encounters we see take place on the show. Whether it's Taylor's description of all the different kinds of people and sex she enjoys, or Jay's busting open the taboo of masculine lesbian penetration, *Skye's the Limit* presents a variety of queer sex and sexualities. The drama of the show does not come from the queer sex on-screen but rather the very human issues of dealing with the love and heartache that accompany these sexual relations.

In the main plotline of the series, Skye struggles to handle the fallout of being laid off from her job. Taylor suggests she see a therapist as she starts to put the pieces of her life back together. Skye's therapist is Mutha Indigo, a Black trans elder who sternly counsels Skye about the reemergence of her college love interest, Jay. In their second scene together, Mutha Indigo does not allow their client to retreat into fantasy regarding her "friendship" with Jay.

> MUTHA INDIGO: Look, no offense, love, but from what you just told me, this woman seems to be under the impression that she can come and go whenever she very well pleases without any regard to your feelings.
>
> SKYE: No, it wasn't like that. She didn't know that I liked her.
>
> MUTHA INDIGO: Trust me, she knew. One look in those big brown eyes of yours and even Ray Charles could see what you were feeling. She knew. And she used your silence against you. So again, this time around, is she single? Or has she at least grown up enough to make herself emotionally available to you?
>
> SKYE: It is not that simple. She was in a previous relationship way before we reconnected.
>
> MUTHA INDIGO: So the answer is no, she is not single.
>
> SKYE: Not yet.
>
> MUTHA INDIGO: And you're still waiting?
>
> SKYE: No, we're rebuilding our friendship while she transitions out of her last relationship. That's it. It's totally legit.[12]

Skye rationalizes her connection to Jay as Mutha Indigo asks pointed questions that reveal the one-sided nature of their friendship. Jay is not single and, once again, is using Skye's feelings for her to get the attention she needs as Skye is left wanting.

Nowhere in Skye's conversation with Mutha Indigo does it seem that Skye is concerned about her identity as a queer Black woman. It is not Skye's queerness that is the "problem" here or the reason she sought therapy. In an important pivot away from mainstream media representation, a queer Black woman is in therapy where her queerness is not the reason she is in therapy. Mutha Indigo does not care about Skye's potential love interest's gender, but they do care about how this potential suitor treats Skye. The focus of their conversation is Skye's lopsided connection to Jay and what that means for the friendship going forward. When anxiety about queer identity is off the table, characters can go further into big human questions that concern all of us: love, self-worth, and connection.

As Skye and Mutha Indigo continue to talk, the conversation shifts from Jay's questionable treatment of Skye to Skye's questionable treatment of herself. Through an extended metaphor, Mutha Indigo helps Skye process the ways Skye is actually hurting herself by trying to maintain her relationship with Jay.

> MUTHA INDIGO: When was the last time you ate?
> SKYE: What? I thought we were talking about me and Jay.
> MUTHA INDIGO: Just humor me. When was the last time you ate?
> SKYE: It's been a pretty busy day, so I haven't eaten anything since this morning.
> MUTHA INDIGO: So are you hungry?
> SKYE: Now that you've mentioned it, yes. I am starving.
> MUTHA INDIGO: And from what you've told me in the past, you're a bit of a health nut, yes?
> SKYE: I do my best to stay in shape, so?
> MUTHA INDIGO: So, if you were starving even more than you are now, and I offered you a bag of chips, would you take it?
> SKYE: As hungry as I am right now, yes, I probably would.
> MUTHA INDIGO: And that's the problem. Our spirit body isn't that different from our physical one. You, my dear, are so spiritually starved for affection that you're willing to consume any bit of emotional junk food that comes your way.
> SKYE: Wait, I don't think that is a fair comparison.
> MUTHA INDIGO: It most certainly is. This woman isn't offering you anything of substance. She is in a relationship with another woman and is giving you whatever is left over. When, and how, she feels like it. You are feasting on scraps, Skye. Little bits and pieces of ambigu-

ous romance. It is leaving you full, but never truly satisfied. And for some strange reason, you have actually convinced yourself that that's okay. Why is that?

SKYE: What the hell am I supposed to do, Indigo? She has a girlfriend. We're friends. I am doing the best I can with the cards I've been dealt. My hands are tied.

MUTHA INDIGO: You don't get it, do you?

SKYE: Get what?!

MUTHA INDIGO: Darling, you only get the love that you think you deserve. If you can't see fit to make yourself a priority, how can you expect anyone else to? Jay is only getting away with this because you are letting her.

SKYE: But I don't know any other way to be.

MUTHA INDIGO: And that's why you have me.

Mutha Indigo provides Skye with the reality check she needs to come to grips with the ways she is being used in her friendship with Jay. Jay is not attentive to Skye because she does not have to be; Skye admits to accepting what little attention Jay offers her. Mutha Indigo's "feasting on scraps" metaphor invites Skye to see how she is limiting her own desires through her willingness to be there for Jay even as Jay does not reciprocate Skye's care. Mutha Indigo's retort is for both Skye and the viewing audience, asking her and those watching to consider how we allow ourselves to be treated in relationships. Mutha Indigo ends their comments by reminding Skye that the reason she is in therapy is to learn to respond differently to the world, and she need not have all the answers yet. Therapy is a journey and Mutha Indigo is a resource to help Skye imagine a different way of relating to Jay and other potential love interests.

Part of undoing the damage of misogynoir is making room for Black women to heal and transform their relationships to themselves and others. Skye is being guided to address the harm she allows Jay to cause in her life through the metaphor of gorging on unhealthy food. By comparing the spiritual body to the physical body, Mutha Indigo is expanding notions of health. This dialogue transforms misogynoir by offering a moment of process to viewers, where the audience can reflect on their own patterns and perhaps establish new ones. Unlike traditional television that might linger on this unhealthy dynamic without naming it, *Skye's the Limit* allows for character growth by identifying the issue and suggesting that a therapist's job is to help the client address it.

Scenes like these offer a surprising fact-from-fiction experience that transcends any one group to proffer insights on universal human questions of self-worth and self-sacrifice. In being specific and accountable to queer Black women's community, *Skye's the Limit* offers insights that go beyond their niche, countering an oft-lobbed charge that marginalized communities' creative productions are too specific to appeal to a mainstream (read: white) audience. Part of the human condition is learning to regulate our interaction with others so that we are not being taken advantage of or we are not taking advantage of others, and the exchange between a Black queer woman and her Black trans therapist can do just that.

Mutha Indigo's presence in the series challenges narratives about Black people's beliefs about therapy and what a therapy session can look like. By creating on-camera scenes of Skye in two separate counseling sessions, particularly a session that pushes back on a dominant media representation of therapists and clients as white, wealthy, and straight, *Skye's the Limit* presents a redefined representation of therapy for Black people. This intergenerational healing dyad is not readily accessible in popular media. To have an older Black trans person unfazed by her client's sexuality presents an alternate reality that is often missing from mainstream television. Therapy is presented as a regular health practice, accessible to Black queer and trans people, and the therapeutic relationship is a transformative element in the show. Contemporary organizations like the Black Emotional and Mental Health Collective are creating opportunities for Black women's mental health to be adequately cared for through the creation of a national Black therapist provider list and creating "heart space" or healing circles specifically for Black queer and lesbian women.[13]

That this scene comes in the penultimate episode of the short-lived series is promising, as it hints at the possibility of Skye changing her behavior. For Skye to continue to remain in right relationship with the values she claims to have, she will have to evaluate what she has allowed to happen between her and Jay. The web show provides a vehicle for character transformation that is missing on mainstream television. The significance of a queer Black woman in therapy working on changing her harmful habits cannot be understated as a possibility model for audiences engaging the show. *Skye's the Limit*'s intentional use of therapy as a healing modality is a powerful example of generative digital alchemy in the service of Black women's health.

The androgynous character Bryn Daniels serves as another possibility model in the series. Bryn is a writer interested in pursuing a James Baldwin Fellowship that would allow her to write in Paris for a year. Baldwin famously emigrated to France in his mid-twenties in hopes of escaping the racism of the United States. His time in France allowed his writing to flourish and nurtured his activism, a defining feature of the fellowship to which Bryn plans to apply. While the season (and series) ends before the realization of Bryn's dream, its conjuring provides another way to imagine Black queer life as a life of the mind, a vision that some Black queer women may not have thought possible. Given the dearth of mainstream Black queer media I have described, the aspirational yet attainable dream of this fictional fellowship imagines a path forward for the regeneration of new Black queer creators working in another creative discipline. *Skye's the Limit* expands what is possible for Black queer life by imagining a new opportunity for one of its characters.

In the final episode of *Skye's the Limit*, titled "Bienvenidos a Miami," the masculine-of-center Carter gets into a near-physical altercation with her more feminine girlfriend. The episode opens with the more feminine (and uncredited) of the partners going through Carter's phone and finding suggestive text messages sent to other women. Carter erupts, grabbing the phone out of her girlfriend's hand, grabbing the keys out of the girlfriend's hand when she tries to leave the apartment, and ultimately throwing the keys to the ground so that her girlfriend has to pick them up before she can leave the apartment. This violent and loud altercation stands in stark contrast with the generally measured reactions of the characters in earlier episodes. This scene fully paints Carter as someone whose masculinity is toxic. Like the protective masculinity exhibited by Lena Waithe and Syd discussed in chapter 1, toxic masculinity hinges on the ill treatment of femmes and feminine women and is defined by aggression.

According to a 2018 study by the National Coalition Against Domestic Violence, Black LGBTQ victims were "more likely to experience

physical intimate partner violence, compared to those who do not identify as Black/African American."[14] It is also difficult for Black lesbians
to seek help for intimate partner violence (IPV) because of community
stigma, most notably in Christian churches.[15] By showing this reality,
Skye's the Limit and the other web shows I examine accurately depict a
problem within the community. Unfortunately, this storyline and others
like it are not always resolved in ways that exemplify best practices for
survivors and those who cause harm.

Carter's violent behavior toward her girlfriend is depicted, but it is
not cast in a critical light within the show. Given that this is the last
episode of the season, it is reasonable to imagine that Telusma would
have picked the storyline up if crowdfunding for season 2 had been successful. However, as it stands, Carter and other masculine-of-center
characters in Black queer web shows display a toxic masculinity steeped
in patriarchal violence that rivals the violence of cishet men but generally remains unchallenged. Whether it is through depictions of IPV or
cheating, masculinity portrayed in these shows does not always seek to
upend heteronormative conceptions of what a masculine person should
be or how they should behave. Like the aforementioned Syd of Odd
Future and The Internet, masculine-of-center characters use their masculinity to protect themselves from misogynoir as they actively participate in and direct misogynoir against the more feminine people around
them.

By not presenting this violent behavior as problematic, *Skye's the
Limit* perpetuates the stereotype and sometimes reality of the masculine
abuser. Carter's character does not exemplify a feminist revisioning of
queer masculinity, nor are the other masculinities of the characters on
the show presented in a nuanced or critical light. As Black queer anthropologist Savannah Shange notes, there is a culturally relevant way
of understanding this archetype. Shange writes, "As an archetype, 'fucknigga' is related to, but distinct from the carcerally-derived pejorative
'fuckboy.' In this context, a fucknigga is a Black masculine person with
all of the patriarchal trappings that spark desire in the beloved, and none
of the ethics that make loving such a person sustainable."[16] Whether it's
Jay's manipulation of Skye and Maya, or even Gina's cheating on Marisol, Black masculine-of-center characters in *Skye's the Limit* treat their
more feminine counterparts dismissively. Ironically, Tyler, the one cishet

man character, is the only masculine person who treats his partner with respect.

In an attempt to defang the bite of Carter's problematic behavior, the extended behind-the-scenes footage following the final episode presents the actors from the scene in a loving embrace. Telusma prompts, "Hug her so that we know you're not really a violent crazy person. Hug her."[17] This moment encourages viewers to remember that the show is just a show, but still leaves the violence of the scene unaddressed within the world the series built. The ableist language of calling the character "crazy" pathologizes the violence portrayed and makes it exceptional as opposed to the sadly ordinary occurrence it is.

Perhaps because shows like *Skye's the Limit* are passion projects, and there is often the understanding that there may not be additional seasons or episodes, writers and producers are compelled to allow for more character growth more quickly than in other mediums. We see Jay's girlfriend Maya leave their relationship because Jay's roommate Ronnie exposes the ambiguous nature of Jay's relationship to Skye; we also see Cassie grow into a queer or at least questioning Black woman over the course of the season; Skye herself, with the help of Mutha Indigo, questions the reciprocity of her friendship with Jay. Traditional television series have the benefit of renewal timelines that allow the cast and crew to know whether the show will return for another season. The ephemerality of the web show can become an asset and not a liability in that it can allow for more expedient story arcs and character development.

The initial viewing success of *Skye's the Limit* prompted an upgrade in the show's website and the development of a new series by Telusma, but the unsuccessful crowdfunding of the second season meant the suspension of these advancements. Ultimately, Telusma put away her director's chair and has become a writer for outlets like the *Grio* and the *Root*. Telusma has her own YouTube channel, which features some self-generated video content, but *Skye's the Limit* remains on a subscription viewing platform.

Both the content of the show and the actors' experiences on set address relationships, health, and well-being. Queer sex and relationships get more attention through this web show than is possible in mainstream television media. Additionally, by normalizing the health-seeking behavior of seeing a therapist, *Skye's the Limit* is effectively destigmatizing self-care practices within the Black community. Telusma gives viewers a peak behind the fourth wall, reminding her audience that the show is constructed by Black queer women and for Black queer women. I mark these intentional choices as possibility models that signal the importance of process over product.

Misogynoir is mostly out of frame on *Skye's the Limit*, with the notable exception of the way Jay and Carter treat the Black women love interests in their lives. The toxic masculinity that informs the IPV and cheating of these queer characters is an outgrowth of misogynoir that disproportionately impacts their femme paramours. While easily able to pass the Bechdel Test, unlike *Shit Black Girls Say*, the dialogue from this series does prompt a potential revision of the questions, where rather than asking whether the women characters speak to each other about something other than a man, one might ask whether they speak to each other about something other than a masculine-of-center person. *Skye's the Limit* would pass the revised test, but the way toxic masculinity predominates in the plot should be explored as its own form of misogynoir.

Between Women

Where *Skye's the Limit* offers an aspirational yet somewhat attainable queer possibility model through characters that are largely portrayed as the college-educated middle class, Atlanta's *Between Women* (2011–2015) attempts to create a world of unrealistic wealth and respectability even as it struggles to make it believable to its audience. *Between Women* is the most watched of all the Black queer web shows I discuss and is in the top five of all time. The first episode of the series amassed over one million views during its time on YouTube.[18] The success of the show is unparalleled: showrunners were able to successfully produce three seasons of content before moving on to other creative projects.

The cast and crew of *Skye's the Limit* made many references to Howard University, a historically Black university. The characters' educational background was highlighted through dialogue and Bryn's potential James Baldwin Fellowship. The college experience of the characters suffused the show, providing a texture to the way class was made visible in their interactions and values. As Telusma said during our interview, "My Howard University intern once said some scenes, like the dinner party one, made her think of the sort of 'grown folks' elegance she wants when she gets older and has a home of her own. And that was the point. I think some film makers, especially in minority or marginalized groups, get so caught up in keeping it real they forget to be aspirational."[19] This "elegance" exists in stark contrast with the differing class statuses of the characters on *Between Women*.

Despite the air of sophistication it attempts to inspire, *Between Women* features a cast with widely varying occupations and resultant class status, making some of their friendships a bit hard to believe. Miller, the central masculine-of-center character, is an upper-level administrator in a multimillion-dollar corporation, while her girlfriend Rhonda's job is not discussed. Their good friends Beautiful and Ray struggle to make ends meet with a kid in tow. Miller's cousin Winnie has a job, but the audience is not privy to what it is. Sunny still lives at home with her homophobic mom at the beginning of the series. The friends come from these different class backgrounds, which is made visible through the differences in aesthetic and ethical choices of the characters.

For example, when gathering to celebrate the end of the work week, the friends in *Between Women* drink cheap liquor and even cheaper chasers out of Styrofoam cups. The friends on *Skye's the Limit* do brunch with mimosas and host dinner parties with wine. While Bryn dreams of Paris, Beautiful dreams of marriage and financial stability. Both shows provide an aspirational take on Black queer women's lives, but the aspirations presented are quite different. Black lesbians are more likely to live in poverty than their cishet counterparts, so the range of Black lesbian employment options portrayed on these web shows is a deliberate act of generative digital alchemy.[20] *Skye's the Limit* is able to build a world in which the arts are central, whereas *Between Women* seems to focus on a more capitalistic and homonormative set of ideal relationships.

Cheating is a central element of the dramatic tension on the show, with none of the characters expressing interest in consensual nonmonogamy. Gay marriage is presented as a desirable relationship outcome, as the show's world builds a fictional Atlanta where the institution is legalized before the federal judgment in favor. The series opens with Rhonda calling her live-in masculine-of-center girlfriend, Miller, excitedly explaining that the radio has announced Atlanta's new legislation supporting same-sex marriage. But Rhonda's excitement is tempered by the realities of her rocky relationship with Miller. As Black queer media studies theorist Faithe Day explains, "Even with this venture into a world where the seeming fullness of gay citizenship has been realized, the realm of *Between Women* does not fall into the trap of neoliberalism by glossing over difference and the realities of the queer of color experience in the world."[21] Day highlights the tension between the fantasy of gay marriage and the messy realities of the characters we meet in the series.

Miller, like Carter and Jay, uses her masculinity to seduce the more feminine women around her. She lies to and cheats on Rhonda, all the while expecting an unreciprocated loyalty. Miller's infidelity is introduced in the opening scene of the series. As Rhonda shares the news about gay marriage becoming legal in Atlanta, the camera cuts to Miller holding her secretary in her lap in her large office. Misogynoir is masked through the veneer of the masculine-of-center characters in these shows. Miller's infidelity is a thread that runs through the series and, like Jay and Carter's, largely goes uncritiqued by the series itself. In fact, Miller becomes a mentor to her newly out friend Sunny, cultivating her into a toxic masculinity in her own image.

In episode 4 of the first season of *Between Women*, titled "I Can't Believe You!," Miller schools Sunny on the various ways a more masculine woman can properly seduce a more feminine partner. Sunny's gender expression is portrayed as formless; she tries on a more feminine persona, but is undone by the heels she feels required to wear. Sunny is not allowed to exist in this state of ambiguity, and she actively seeks to find where she fits in the femme/stud binary. The maintenance of gender roles is enacted through Sunny's exploration of how she wants to portray herself, ultimately leading her to Miller for tutelage.

MILLER: I got an idea; I got an idea.
    (*Miller puts on Marvin Gaye's "Sexual Healing."*)
SUNNY: Oooh, I like this.
MILLER: You gotta get in the groove. You know what I am saying? Right?
SUNNY: All right, okay.
MILLER: You know, when Rhonda comes home, this is what you gotta do. Put on the smooth sounds and she be loving it. Okay? Marvin

Gaye will get them every time. That's when the clothes start falling off. You don't even have to peel them off! They just fall off! All right? Turn Marvin on, and it's on. (*Miller dances.*) You gotta get your little groove together. You know what I am saying? We gone work on that.

Miller's instruction to use Marvin Gaye's music for seduction, that it "will get them every time," implies both her successful use of the technique and women's powerlessness in the face of it. While not overtly predatory, the image of "clothes falling off" suggests an ease with this approach that neglects to see feminine women as individuals with agency. Miller's use of passive voice to describe the clothes falling off dislocates the agency of the woman losing her clothes as well as the agency of Miller and Sunny as the implied more assertive partners. The casual expressing of the inevitability of sex furthers the myth of the masculine Lothario or "fuck nigga."[22] Miller continues,

MILLER: So you come in slow, bring her in. Now you have to touch her. You can't grab her aggressively. You gotta touch her. Touch her waist, right? And caress her. And bring the hands down. Right? And then bring her in. All right . . . now we groovin' (*Miller hums a few notes of the song*). Softly. Now bring her in, bring her in. Remember what I was saying? You gotta kiss the shoulder. Kiss her on the shoulder. Then like, slowly come up her neck. Right? Cool. Then at that point—

SUNNY: (*Dives in for a kiss.*)

MILLER: (*The kiss lands lightly. Miller pushes Sunny away immediately and so hard, she falls to the ground.*) What is wrong with you?!

SUNNY: I am sorry! I am sorry!

MILLER: I didn't say kiss me! I am talking about the girl, man!

SUNNY: I'm sorry (*laughing*). I am sorry. I'm sorry! I'm sorry. You okay?

MILLER: Are you okay? I am starting to wonder about you now.

SUNNY: My body is hurtin.' My arms ache.

MILLER: C'mon. Let's finish this. I don't have all day. Don't kiss me again.

SUNNY: So sorry. I misunderstood. I thought we was practicing. (*Jokingly*) No homo!

From intimately grabbing Sunny's hips, moving her hands to her hips, and even humming the song for a few bars, Miller sets up the scenario with meticulous and extensive detail. When Sunny tries to kiss Miller, the audience literally hears a record scratch. Sunny violated the implied gender limits of the role play by trying to kiss her more masculine friend. Since they are two non-femme lesbians, their kiss is made comical through its projected inappropriateness. Sunny's "no homo" comment is supposed to be funny to the audience because they are both lesbians but also because a kiss between two masculine-presenting lesbians is considered inappropriate.

Ironically, Black masculine-of-center lesbians who express romantic interest in each other can be ostracized for violating an unspoken rule of queer community that has an implicit preference for butch/femme partnering. Miller's visible and articulated disgust when Sunny goes in for a kiss and Sunny's deflecting "no homo" comment are both evidence of the deeply embedded norm of masculine/feminine partnering. The 2015 documentary *The Same Difference*, directed by Nneka Onuorah, addresses this taboo with an hour-long exploration of queer people's discomfort with stud for stud relationships and masculine-of-center people being pregnant.[23] With the notable exception of *Choiices*, masculine women dating masculine women is not an acceptable plot point in Black queer web shows.[24]

Despite the clear omission and critique of the stud for stud part of queer community, *Between Women, Skye's the Limit*, and *195 Lewis* all make space for femme/femme relationships. Winnie, Miller's cousin, is depicted as primarily dating feminine women. When Winnie finds out she is pregnant, she and her fellow feminine lover decide to keep and raise the baby together. Miller even compliments Winnie, saying she admires her cousin's ability to approach women "aggressively" despite being "super feminine."[25] This backhanded compliment solidifies the assumptions made about feminine characters and the differential reading of femme/femme connections within these Black queer web worlds. Taylor's crush on Skye and dalliance with Cassie are visually represented in *Skye's the Limit*. *195 Lewis* hints at a future femme fellowship between Camille and "Fishnets" in the first episode, though the latter character is absent from the rest of the season. Unsurprisingly, masculine on masculine romantic connection is never in the picture in any of these three web show worlds. Even within the generative digital alchemy these web shows provide, some norms remain that enact their own misogynoir by foreclosing the libidinal possibilities of studs with studs.

With toxic masculinity a prominent feature throughout the series, *Between Women* addresses IPV directly through the relationship between the characters Allison and Brooke. In addition to being extremely jealous and controlling, Brooke, the more masculine partner, engages in increasingly dehumanizing acts of abuse, including forcing Allison to eat and drink out of a dog bowl and chaining her to the toilet. The friend group calls out Brooke's abusive behavior and encourages Allison to leave the relationship. Unlike the abuse in a Tyler Perry production, this violent behavior is named as such and the friends rally to help their friend.

In a scene directly following the aftermath of the abuse, Allison tells her friends that she is staying in her relationship with Brooke. Her friends struggle to understand her decision, especially since Brooke hovers nearby as they talk.

> MILLER: Allison, how you doing? You feeling okay? Your sister let us in. You look better.
> WINNIE: Brooke?
> BROOKE: I'll give you some time alone.
> MILLER: Yeah, do that.
> BROOKE: Look. I fucked up, okay. I fucked up big time. I know sorry don't fix it. But Allison has forgiven me. I am just asking that you, Winnie, and everyone else does too.
> ALLISON: Please don't look at me like that. I just need you guys to be here for me. Don't judge me.
> MILLER: I am not judging you. I don't know . . . what is she even still doing here?
> ALLISON: I dropped the charges.
> MILLER: You what?!?!
> WINNIE: Wait, so you mean to tell me after all that, you two are back together?

MILLER: I just don't get it. I don't understand.

ALLISON: I don't expect you to understand. It was part my fault too. I mean with the phone. And me not respecting her. Look, she apologized and she vowed never to do it again.

WINNIE: Allison! They always say that.

MILLER: You know, I can't see you like this anymore. As much as Rhonda nags me, there is no way I'd ever put my hands on her. Ever. You don't deserve that. She doesn't have the right to put her hands on you.

Again, Miller illustrates the "correct" protocol of a masculine-of-center person in a situation of disagreement with a femme partner. Miller offers that she would never "put my hands" on Rhonda, evoking an uninterrogated chivalry that concretizes gender roles. Even as Miller is telling Allison to want and expect more from Brooke, she is reinforcing a benevolent patriarch ideal in which the masculine person does not use their perceived superior strength to assault the feminine person. Rhonda is dismissed just as she is invoked. Miller suggests that Rhonda's nagging might incite someone else to violence, but Miller is able to exercise restraint. Proper masculinity is framed as control over one's emotions, and Brooke is castigated for not living up to the implicit standard of comportment.

Allison continues providing the classic narrative of survivors still embroiled with the person who harmed them, an important on-screen decision that humanizes IPV and the partners who stay.

ALLISON: And Brooke said she won't do it again. Can't you guys see this hurts her?

WINNIE: Did you forget that she was feeding you out of a dog bowl? You almost died, Allison. Let me show you something. (*Winnie pulls out a mirror to show Allison her own bruised face.*) This! Look at this! This is not love! Love is not supposed to look like this!

ALLISON: I didn't die. I am still here. And all I am asking is for my friends to support me.

MILLER: Support you?

ALLISON: Yes!

MILLER: Really? It's not gonna happen. You keep dealing with Brooke, we won't be visiting you in this bed, we will be visiting you at your funeral.

WINNIE: Allison, Brooke needs help. Not the kind of help you can give her. You two need some space.

ALLISON: We are taking it one day at a time. She agreed to go to therapy. We all mess up. We all get carried away sometimes. But who would we be if someone we love didn't forgive us? Or give us a second chance?

WINNIE: I get what you're saying. But what I am saying is don't give her a "get out of jail free" card. You can love her from a distance.

ALLISON: Okay.

WINNIE: She needs help!

ALLISON: I can't, Winnie, I love her.

MILLER: You know what? Let's just go. Let's go, Winnie. Allison, I love you, okay? Be good.

WINNIE: I love you too . . . Allison, it's not too late.

ALLISON: I love you guys. Thanks for coming.

WINNIE (*to Brooke, who has reentered the room*): You know I could slap the shit out of you right now, but you're not even worth it because then I'd be just like you.

MILLER: Winnie, let's just go.

WINNIE: I can't even look at you the same way.

MILLER: Come on. Let's just go.

The scene provides an empathetic and realistic portrayal of what happens when women go back to their abusers. Friends do not understand and do not know how to support their survivor friend when she chooses to return to her abuser. Allison accurately reflects the reality that many women do not leave their abusers. In most cases, battered partners just want the abuse to stop, not to end the relationship. In fact, leaving creates its own dangers; up to 75 percent of women killed by their abusers are killed after they leave the relationship.[26] By depicting lesbian IPV, *Between Women* offers its audience a glimpse into a problem within the community, with both unhelpful and helpful solutions, chivalry and therapy, respectively.

An earlier scene in the previous episode showed the friend group struggling to decide whether they were going to call the police on

Brooke at all. The friend group tries its own form of harm reduction by assessing the need for police intervention following their discovery of Allison's deteriorated condition. For Black and queer people who are already targets of police attention, inviting them in, even in a situation where violence has occurred, creates additional risk for their collective survival. This small moment of indecision is what prison abolition looks like in practice in our communities. Choosing not to engage the police is one way to work toward reducing the harm that the criminal (in)justice system causes. That this group of Black queer women friends struggle with the choice before them illustrates the concerns that multiply marginalized communities face while trying to mitigate the excessive surveillance and targeting of their communities.

Ultimately, the group does call the police but remains silent or slow to answer the officer when she asks about the situation leading up to the call for help. The group wrestles with their loyalty to their friend and the harm she caused her partner, a reality faced by so many communities trying to figure out ways to enact transformative justice that moves us toward the world we want. Allison's decision to stay in her relationship offers an opportunity for a more granular look into Brooke's abusive behavior, as viewers are invited into a session between Brooke and a therapist.

Not only is the abuse depicted, but episode 5 of the first season provides a rare rendering of an abuser's state of mind. In a therapy session, Brooke discusses her feelings that make her feel like she needs to control Allison. She describes feeling more in control and calmer when she can exert power over her girlfriend.

> DR. GOLDSTEIN: I just want you to relax. We're just gonna talk today. Okay? Looking over your profile, and it seems like this wasn't necessarily a voluntary visit for you. Can you tell me more about what brings you here today?
>
> BROOKE: They said I have to be here.
>
> DR. GOLDSTEIN: Okay. Who said you have to come here?
>
> BROOKE: Allison.
>
> DR. GOLDSTEIN: Okay, Allison is making you come.
>
> BROOKE: Well, Allison said that in order for us to be together I have to come here. So I'm here.

Brooke's participation in therapy, unlike Skye's on *Skye's the Limit*, is court-ordered and a condition Allison set for their relationship to continue. Brooke's nervousness and involuntary presence in therapy mirror the reality for many abusers who initially feel compelled to comply with their partners' wishes as a form of making amends. Despite her initial reluctance to be in therapy, Brooke opens up and describes her anger.

> DR. GOLDSTEIN: Okay. I am just kind of looking at the things that we talked about over the phone. It seems that you've got a lot of issues with anger. And that is where I want to start with you. Let's talk a little bit about your anger issues. What is making you so angry?
>
> BROOKE: Okay. I get mad.
>
> DR. GOLDSTEIN: Okay.
>
> BROOKE: And when I get mad, I want to hit the wall or . . . slam a door. Or break something. You know?
>
> DR. GOLDSTEIN: Okay. Okay. And, when you're angry, do you ever hit your girlfriend?
>
> BROOKE (*quietly*): Yeah.
>
> DR. GOLDSTEIN: Okay. And how many times since y'all have been together would you say that this has happened?
>
> BROOKE: About . . . not too many times . . . no more than twenty, no less than fifteen.
>
> DR. GOLDSTEIN: Okay. (*Takes notes.*) Um, do you feel like this behavior is normal?
>
> BROOKE: I get confused. And like . . . I just don't know. People just don't understand me. And I just don't know what to do. I forget, and then it is happening.
>
> DR. GOLDSTEIN: Okay. That is honest. How do you feel when you hit Allison?
>
> BROOKE: Honestly?
>
> DR. GOLDSTEIN: Yes, I always want you to be honest in my office. Okay? This is a safe space for us to talk. So I want you to be honest.
>
> BROOKE (*pausing for a moment*): I feel like I am back in control. I feel like, now she's gon listen. Now I have power.
>
> DR. GOLDSTEIN: Okay. Power. Okay. And then tell me how do you feel after?

BROOKE (*pausing again*): I get upset with myself, 'cause she's crying.
I don't like to see her cry. And I feel disappointed because I know
I told her I wouldn't hit her anymore, the last time. I just . . . we go
from . . . talking to yelling to screaming . . . and then everything goes
black. And the next thing I know my hands is around her neck. That's
when she listens.

Brooke's commentary takes viewers into the mindset of someone who
has caused harm. Brooke remains a multidimensional character, one
with work to do, but she is not cast as a monster. This humanizing of
Brooke and the presentation of the possibility of her rehabilitation is a
welcome shift from movies and television that depict those who cause
harm as always already abusive, with no seeming motivation for their
violence toward others. In her 1999 piece "Representations of Black
Lesbians" in the *Harvard Gay and Lesbian Review*, Black lesbian poet
and author Jewelle Gomez describes the dearth of Black lesbian images
and the disproportionate impact that a character like Cleo, the Black
masculine lesbian violently murdered in the film *Set It Off* (1996), has on
the way other Black people imagine Black lesbians.[27] Gomez described
overhearing Black people express disapproval for gay rights, in large part
because their images of Black lesbians were colored by portrayals like
Cleo, who is presented as sexually aggressive, one-dimensional, and violent. Misogynoir is mitigated because Brooke's transformation does not
lock her into a singular reality.

The show does an excellent job of providing a deep dive into Brooke's
state of mind, but falls short of connecting her behavior to toxic masculinity. She and her therapist discuss her violence using the language
of anger and control. While accurate at the level of the interpersonal
violence Brooke inflicts on Allison, the connection between power and
control to antiquated notions of traditional (read: toxic) masculinity is
not explored. *Between Women* offers some important social commentary by bringing IPV within Black queer communities forward, but it
does not go the extra mile to challenge the way toxic masculinity exacerbates this reality in our communities.

When Allison finally does leave Brooke, it is due to an elaborate daydream sequence in which she predicts her own death at Brooke's hand.

Showrunner and creator Michelle A. Daniel highlighted the real-world implications of this fictional storyline by inviting the actors who play these characters to do a PSA about IPV at the end of the third episode of the first season. In an important message of contextualization following the scenes of domestic violence, the show ends the third episode with the two actors who play Allison and Brooke addressing the camera directly.

> ONYX KEESHA: Abuse is never okay.
>
> NOBLE JULZ: Abuse is physical, sexual, emotional, economic, and psychological threats and threats of actions that influence another person. That is any behavior that frightens, intimidates, manipulates, terrorizes, hurts, humiliates, blames, injures, or wounds someone.
>
> ONYX KEESHA: Domestic violence can happen to anyone. Of any race, age, sexual orientation, religion, or gender. It can happen to friends. People who are living together, dating, or married. Domestic violence affects people of all socioeconomical levels and educational backgrounds.
>
> NOBLE JULZ: There is never an excuse for abuse.
>
> ONYX KEESHA: If you or anyone you know is in need of help, please log on to www.thehotline.org.

Daniel recognized the serious nature of her subject matter and offered a way for her audience to get the help and resources they might need should they see their own lives reflected on-screen. By breaking the fourth wall, as was done on *Skye's the Limit*, Daniel reminds the audience that the violence is staged and that these are actors portraying characters. She also asks the audience to think seriously about the impact of IPV in their own communities and whether they or someone they know needs the resources the hotline provides. Breaking the fourth wall makes for a more "cognitively involved" experience for the audience, forcing them to consider what they are watching at the level of content and production.[28] Where other aspects of the show are portrayed as over-the-top and even rely on the use of slapstick comedic schemes, the attention to the realities of survivors of assault provides a welcome tonal shift. In an interview with Leyla Farah of the lesbian culture website AfterEllen.com, Daniel explains why addressing domestic violence was important to her:

Domestic violence is the one topic that is particularly close to me because I grew up in a violent home. As an adult, I was also in a relationship that included both emotional abuse and physical aggression. I want people to know that they aren't alone when it comes to serious topics. When we are going through difficult times, we tend to question life, faith, and fairness. The truth is that those things happens to people all the time, they just don't talk about it! When people see what they're going through on screen—whether it's a web series or TV show—they have a chance to engage with their own issues in a different way.[29]

Daniel also considers the power of media to transform how people engage with their own trauma. Media provides a little distance from the difficult topics people struggle to address in their own lives. Representing IPV on-screen gives viewers a new way of thinking about similar experiences they may have had and recognizing patterns of abuse that they might otherwise miss. Web shows have the unique ability to reflect both the reality of Black queer life and a vision for its future. The decisions made around how violence is depicted and contextualized are important.

Like *Skye's the Limit* and *195 Lewis*, *Between Women* addresses misogynoir by imagining otherwise. IPV becomes a transformative justice moment where the person who caused harm is allowed the possibility of being accountable to the person they harmed. Brooke is presented as a person with flawed logic but not as a one-dimensional evil shell who cannot change their behavior. Daniel gives the cast room to grow, though she limits the types of romantic connections that are possible between masculine characters. Web shows create options for liberatory representations even as they foreclose others.

195 Lewis

195 Lewis (2017) has the best production value of all the shows I examine in this chapter, and it also appears about five years after the initial deluge of Black queer web shows on YouTube. It is arguably the most sophisticated, no doubt in part because it reflects the oldest cast and production team in terms of their ages, with most in their early thirties as opposed to early or mid-twenties. The show was eventually released online through the show's own webpage; writers and creators Rae Leone Allen and Yaani Supreme initially shopped the series to mainstream television outlets by doing the festival circuit. The show was directed and produced by Chanelle Aponte Pearson, who also produced and starred in the critically acclaimed film *An Oversimplification of Her Beauty* (2012). Cinematographer Jomo Fray lights the all-Black cast incredibly, drawing on color palettes that are reminiscent of *Pariah* (2011) and *Moonlight* (2016).

The spared-no-expense production style was a deliberate choice to set the series apart from its peers. Not only does *195 Lewis* differ from other web shows because of its production quality, it also addresses a controversial form of consensual non-monogamy. The show introduces polyamory and sets the parameters to explore how polyamory functions in Black queer women's community. The audience enters the world of college-educated Brooklyn Black queers through the Paper Over Pussy Party, a fundraiser for the character Uri's art show of the same name. Portrayed by show creator Rae Allen, Uri and fellow partygoers engage in witty repartee that recalls the loquaciously (in)elegant dialogue of *Dawson's Creek* (1998–2003) and *Clueless* (1995). Where *Skye's the Limit* visually and contextually gives off an air of collegiate sophistication, *195 Lewis* makes it apparent with every syllable the cast utters. Uri's conversation with Simone in the first scene with dialogue in the series' first episode evokes not only their college educations but also their left politics.

SIMONE: So the "Paper Over Pussy" thing though . . . really?
URI: Yes.
SIMONE: Really? You're serious?
URI: I am.
SIMONE (*smiling*): You can't say things like that, though! It's not a joke.
URI: I am attracted to very basic language. Turns of phrases that have a sort of surprise.
SIMONE: Surprise! I thought I read on the bio thing that you were a teacher.
URI: Chill. It's not what you think. When you see the paintings, and the image-making traditions they're critiquing, the satire will be obvious to you. Then any anger you are feeling because of hyper-capitalism, misogyny, or the sheer eloquence of the phrase "Paper. Over. Pussy"

(POP) will evaporate. It is a double-entendre with a time-based trigger.

SIMONE: Double-entendre? I could see that. For instance, when you were just talking, I had two distinct reactions.

URI: What were those?

SIMONE: Well, the first was, I really wanna do something to you right now. And the second was that it is a really fresh revisioning of the linguistic parameters of double-consciousness.

URI: I think I like the first one better.

SIMONE: Yeah?

URI: It's more of a conversation starter.

SIMONE: What kind of conversation are you trying to have?

URI: I ain't catch your name?

SIMONE: I ain't throw it at you yet.

URI: We should get all of that out of the way. I need your name, your phone number, your email, favorite position, dietary restrictions . . .

SIMONE: I am not sharing my favorite position with you yet.

URI: On a piece of paper?

SIMONE: Ha! Old school with it. Simone.

URI: Simone. Word. Imma put you on the contact list so you can get the information about the opening. That way you'll know this fundraising isn't for nothing. But more importantly, the title will make sense to you.

SIMONE: I'll hear from you before then, though, right?

This exchange introduces both the class and political positionality of the show. By using the character Simone to comment on the blatant misogyny of Uri's art show title, *195 Lewis* engages feminism as an explicit task of the show. Uri's verbose rebuttal to Simone's distaste for the art show's name allows the audience to reevaluate the misogyny they may have taken for granted. Uri's word choices signal an intelligence that belies the "very basic language" she used to describe her show. Uri's knowledge of the incendiary nature of her art show's title is presented as a clever conceit to be fully interrogated by the show itself.

Uri's discussion of "hyper-capitalism" is the first and only overt acknowledgment of capitalism in the three series I examine. By using the language of "hyper-capitalism," Uri invokes a series of leftist political associations that hail a particular Black queer audience that is far and away from that of *Between Women*. Misogyny is a literal topic of discussion among characters who are meeting for the first time and with the quick and flirtatious mention of "dietary restrictions," a socially conscious class ethos deployed. These are Black queer women with political commitments that extend beyond a homonormative agenda of gay marriage. Not only are these characters queer in terms of their sexual and gender identities, they express a queer feminist politics in their conversations.[30]

In episode 5, the last of the short inaugural and final season, Uri's best friend and business manager, Ciara, talks at a party with Chris, who is new in town. Ciara explains the different types of lesbians in the Brooklyn scene. While giving the detailed rundown, Ciara's voice is accompanied by the camera panning over people who match her auditory descriptions.

> CIARA: Listen, if you live in Brooklyn, you need to know. And Imma tell you. There are five kinds of lesbians. Okay? Five. Police Officers. You know, they like chinos. Butches. But not trans. Gentlemen-like. Opens doors, pays for things on principle. They hang out with men, work with their hands, with young people, but not necessarily an artist. Aggressive. Pretty much only dates femmes. Now, if they stud for stud, that is a whole 'nother conversation.

While there is no visual stud for stud couple for the camera to pan to, the acknowledgment of this sexual/gender pairing is unique in the Black queer web shows I examined. *195 Lewis* acknowledges the possibility of masculine for masculine relationships where *Between Women* visually rebuffs it. *195 Lewis* acknowledges the tendency for "police officers" to mostly date femmes but provides a nuance that broadens the possibilities beyond these expectations. In giving these archetypes, Ciara both reinforces the norms for the community and complicates them by extending beyond the usual bifurcation of queer women's identities.

Ciara's certainty that there are five types pulls the viewer in, implicitly calling on them to assess where they fit in the hierarchy. Ciara continues with her taxonomy, moving on to AGs.

> CIARA: Now, an AG/Dom Stud. She is a masculine-of-center woman that is in touch with her womanness. Real feminine in her face and

body but with the swag and style of a dude. Now, she gon' wear a dress to a wedding for her mom. But reluctantly. She's like a tomboy but all grow up. They never smile in pictures for some strange reason.

CIARA: Now I know you know about the Beyoncés.

CHRIS: Of course.

CIARA: Beyoncés are the highest femmes. Makeup, that's her warrior paint. Never leaves the house without her warpaint or earrings. Only dates Doms/AGs. A pillow princess. They shave, they get manicures, they want kids . . . like from their womb. They want to bear their children. And none of them ever wanna pay for groceries! And . . . little known fact, most of these broads can't even cook! And you know, you never know they're gay unless you ask . . . or want them to be.

CIARA: And then you got your in-betweens. Not quite femme, not butch either. Okay . . . somewhere in between.

CHRIS: (*Laughs.*)

CIARA: (*Laughs.*) Androgynous even. And nobody really knows where to place them even. But that works to their advantage because they can sneak up on whoever they want. And you know what? I'd say that you're an in-between.

CHRIS: What's that make you, then?

CIARA: I am nameless and formless. I can't be contained by these human conceptions of sexuality and gender. I am at the top of the food chain. I am badder than Bette.

CHRIS: Who's that?

CIARA: Are you serious? You don't know who Bette is?! (*Literal record scratches as a frame of Jennifer Beals as character Bette Porter of* The L Word *(2004–2009) in GIF form dominates the screen.*) Imma need you to get up on your lesbian lore.

Chris, like Cassie in *Skye's the Limit,* becomes a device through which the writers can address subtleties of the queer scenes they navigate. Chris's education by Ciara mirrors Cassie's by Taylor, with both women being schooled on social dynamics to which they are new. In both cases, their instructors refuse the very dichotomies they set up, again treating readers to the fluidity of life and the slippery nature of these labels.

Additionally, the use of the record scratch in both *Between Women* and *195 Lewis* helps to make clear the in-group knowledge that characters are expected to possess. Sunny should know that they should not kiss their masculine-of-center friend, even if they have been role playing with greater and greater physical intimacy up until that point. Chris should know who Bette Porter is, as one of the few Black lesbian characters on television. Suffice it to say, Bette fits the socially acceptable version of Black women we see on mainstream television, with her feminine appearance, loose curls, and light skin. Even as she is venerated in this circle of Black queer women, she does not match the physical description of any of the women who are presented in the montages. Like *Skye's the Limit* and *Between Women* before it, *195 Lewis* does an excellent job portraying members of the community of various skin tones and sizes. By visually going through these five types, *195 Lewis* provides representation that is unparalleled in mainstream outlets.

Without actively attempting to do so, these web shows provide redefined representations of beauty through their casting. By casting friends, these shows accurately reflect their community because they *are* the community. As Michelle Daniel said of the scenes she writes for *Between Women*, media become vehicles through which people can change the way they think about their own realities. To see yourself reflected onscreen is such an important draw for audiences and the creators of these web shows alike. Creators can work through some of the tensions of society by reframing these issues for episodic web shows. *195 Lewis* offers opportunities to redefine desire by opening possibilities that might have seemed foreclosed. Polyamory is one of the ways this show attempts to do this, moving away from the explosive (and entertaining) dynamics of cheating to the interior complex emotions that make having many loves possible.

Polyamory is introduced in the first episode through Uri and her partner Camille "checking in" at the POP Party, deciding whether they are interested in pursuing any of their fellow revelers. Their exchange is loving, but when Chris pushes to become an uninvited houseguest for the month and Uri relents, Camille starts to feel jealous. In a daydream, Camille imagines looking at Uri's phone and finding suggestive text messages from party guest Simone and from Harlem, Uri's other paramour. Though identified through dialogue as the instigator of their non-monogamy experiment, Camille starts to doubt the benefits of their arrangement. She calls Uri on the phone, "forgetting" that Uri is spending time with Harlem. The show teases these mounting tensions, but the first five episodes are mostly a slow simmer foreshadowing Camille's future resentment.

Over the course of her time in Uri and Camille's home, Chris begins to put the pieces together regarding Uri's other lover, Harlem. It is not until the last episode, however, that she finally has what she believes is the full picture. As they smoke outside the latest party, Chris and Uri discuss Uri's romantic situation.

CHRIS: No, because I am conservative (*laughing*).

URI: Well, me too! I am just warning you.

CHRIS: No. No you are not.

URI: Stop playing! I am all about my work, that's it. Wake up, do art, come home.

CHRIS: Oh . . . and you come home every night?

URI: What you mean? Oh, you talking about Harlem?

CHRIS: Yes, what are you doing, anyway? I thought Camille was your wife.

URI: Camille is my life.

CHRIS: Well, it doesn't seem like it.

URI: You see? Did you hear that in your voice?

CHRIS: What?

URI: You just took that hushed, high-pitched maternal tone people take when they think Camille doesn't know about Harlem. They take that tone when they think that this is some traditional monogamous, infidelity-type situation.

CHRIS: And it's not?

URI: Stop judging me! Harlem's not some other woman. Camille and I are polyamorous. Non-monogamous, many loves.

CHRIS: That sounds like some complicated shit. How is that working out for you?

URI: You know what? Imma have to get back to you on that.

CHRIS: Do she live in Harlem too?

URI: Nah, she don't live in Harlem.

CHRIS: Oh, 'cause I was gonna say, that is too much.

URI: I am lying, she do. It's an hour on the train.
CHRIS: That's ridiculous.
URI: It's a long ride.
CHRIS: It must be good.

Chris remains skeptical of Uri's romantic arrangement and Uri admits that it is more complicated than she would like. But Uri's callout of Chris's admonishing tone marks the social consequences of polyamory. Chris struggles to view Uri's relationship with Harlem as more than infidelity, illustrating the still relatively novel nature of polyamorous relationships even in progressive Black queer circles. The judgment that can accompany an admission of engaging in polyamorous relationships is signaled here through a raised eyebrow and the direct talk of two old friends. The show endeavors to bring polyamory out of the proverbial closet, but does so by honestly acknowledging the challenges of unconventional arrangements even in progressive spaces.

While Uri does not display a manipulative toxic masculinity like Jay, Carter, or Miller before her, her masculinity is still prized in her community. Simone, Camille, Harlem, and even Chris all have some romantic/sexual energy with Uri, while none of these more feminine women seem to have other romantic interests beyond Uri. When Chris arrives in New York unannounced and hoping to crash with a long-lost friend, Uri worried about how Chris's presence might disrupt the "delicate balance" of the non-monogamous connections she has cultivated with her wife and girlfriend. Camille, on the other hand, had a brief flirtation with a woman at the party in the first episode of the series, but seems to have no other prospects in later episodes. The gravitational center of the non-monogamy of the series is Uri, one of the more masculine characters in the series. The potential for femme for femme consensual non-monogamy remains out of frame. Once again, masculinity becomes a tool for misogynoir by delimiting the possibilities for Black women's romantic connections. While Uri is not cheating, the way Uri's masculinity coheres sexual possibility while Camille's femininity does not elicit similar attention, speaks to unarticulated gender norms just below the show's progressive surface.

The dynamic of Uri and Camille's poly relationship foreshadows some potential plotlines that the first season was not able to see through. The fact that the partners had been in a monogamous relationship and then chose to open it up, a new paramour for one partner and not the other, sets the stage for some emotional fallout that just did not quite make it on-screen in five episodes. Though Uri makes the expressed point that Harlem is not "some other woman," her appearance in the show suggested otherwise. As viewers, we meet Harlem through Uri's computer as they FaceTime, and we see cuts of Harlem's mouth as she and Uri talk on the phone. She does not attend any of the social gatherings that pepper the first five episodes of the series. Harlem's physical distance from the other characters on the show reinforces the otherness of her character. When Uri visits Harlem, Uri is inaccessible to Camille and is also no longer part of the visual storytelling of the show once arriving on Harlem's doorstep. The centrifugal force of Uri and Camille's relationship keeps Harlem spinning far from the center of the show, making her character seem ancillary and convenient for plot's sake all at once. Polyamory is presented through a lens that centers a previously established relationship that inadvertently makes Harlem, and to some degree Chris, the rising tension that propels the plot forward.

In addition to addressing the idea of many loves, *195 Lewis* offers an important subplot on physical health through the sexually transmitted infection (STI) of one of its characters. The fourth episode is titled "Pussy Burning," echoing the crass way that Anne tells the doctor's receptionist that she might have an STI. Anne, Camille's little sister, has trouble urinating and complains of a burning sensation when she does. Anne's experience negotiating her sexual health presents an opportunity for admonition from her sister that Anne should use protection, even when sleeping with multiple assigned-female-at-birth partners. Lurking in Anne's surprise and even Camille's initial downplaying of Anne's symptoms is the erroneous assumption that women who have sex with women will not contract STIs.[31]

> ANNE: Bacterial-vaga-what? It's normal to have it? Okay . . . a fishy-smelling odor? What the f——. (*Camille enters the apartment.*) Camille! Camille! Now, something terrible has happened. Now, don't be tripping. But I think . . . how do you know if you got an STD?
> CAMILLE: You do not have an STD, Anne. Anne . . . has my damn apartment been like this all day?

ANNE: SIS! I have a sexually transmitted disease! I was on the
computer . . .

CAMILLE: On the computer . . . ?

ANNE: Gonorrhea! chlamydia, Hepatitis H through Z! Fucking . . .
you know what? The government did this shit. Yeah, they are always
doing shit like this. I knew I shouldn't have gone to the doctor that
one time. See, he probably infected me on purpose. You know they
always doing this shit. They're always infecting us, and quarantining
us and shit.

CAMILLE: You went to the doctor for an HPV vaccination. I got the
same one. Remember?

ANNE: Okay, okay. How's it feel when you pee?

CAMILLE: It feels good, it's a relief.

ANNE: Argh! Help me, Camille. I'm feeling like Pompeii right now. It
feels like hot molten magma is, like, coming out every time I pee.

CAMILLE: Well, you should've thought about that before you just dove
off into any wet vag that was in your field of vision.

ANNIE: I am mad discreet about my assignations. And you know that.

CAMILLE (*laughing*): I can't with you right now. You're discreet? I can't
take you right now.

Anne moves to her sister's bedroom and begins pacing in front of the
altar before deciding to kneel and pray. The altar contains crystals, rose
water, mini statues, vases, alcohol, incense, prayer beads, and a succu-
lent, among other things.

ANNE: Dear God, I don't really know how this works. There is like fifty
of you over here. But I guess that is a good thing because I need all
the help I can get right now. I guess I should start by confessing, or
coming clean, or whatever, before I start asking for things. So . . . first
my bad for all of the promiscuity. In the future, I promise to practice
ab—moderation.

CAMILLE: (*entering the room*): Just make an appointment with the
doctor. It is probably nothing. Actually, I shouldn't, but I'll dial
the number for you. It is probably stress-related, because you
habitually be doing the most. What is going on with your music,

anyway? I thought you were making a beat a day. You know, musicians, you know, real musicians, they get up with one thing on their mind—music. They get up and they go about the business of making their work. You get up with other priorities in mind. I am not saying that to be harsh. I am just telling you what it looks like to me, okay? So, don't start catching feelings. An—it's gonna be okay.

ANNE (*picking up the phone to call*): Hi, I'd like to make an appointment. My pussy burning!

Anne's comical refrain lessens the mounting tension of her concern about her potential STI. It is also a literal call for her to consider her health. Like Skye's conversation with her therapist, Anne's interaction with her sister shows the power of Black women and Black nonbinary, agender, and gender-variant folks working together for better health. The mutual support of the interaction is an essential tool in the arsenal of Black women's health praxis. Sometimes it is easier to do it together rather than do it alone.

However, Camille's own admonishment to herself that she should not place the call for Anne speaks volumes about their relationship. Camille is the older, responsible sibling to Anne's dependent freeloading. Anne lives with Camille and Uri while in school and "working on her music," but in the few episodes of the season, we do not see or hear her work. Again, gender works to assign the greater share of caretaking to Camille, and in turn, Anne lives into lowered expectations. Anne seemed perfectly content to travel through life on the good-natured support of her sister, but the STI serves as a wake-up call for her to take better care of herself and might be a turning point for her character's development in the show.

That Anne also moves to consider the spiritual realm as a source for potential help further illustrates the degree of pain she is feeling. Admittedly new to prayer, she imagines that there are gods on the altar. She begins by suggesting that she will "abstain" from sex, but before the word has left her mouth, she changes it to "moderation." This linguistic choice furthers the comic relief of the moment but also provides a window into Camille's spiritual practice. There is a growing movement among millennials and their next-generation counterparts to reclaim religious and spiritual traditions beyond Christianity.[32] Camille's altar reflects this reality and offers a possibility model for Black queer women looking beyond the Christian church for spiritual support.

Anne dealing with her STI by talking to her sister and making a doctor's appointment on-camera is important. It challenges the nefarious notion that is perpetuated within the medical community that women who have sex with women are less susceptible to STIs. Healthcare providers falsely assume that women who have sex with women are not able to pass STIs to one another because of antiquated notions about the kinds of sex these women have with each other.[33] By allowing Anne to deal with her issue on camera, *195 Lewis* opens up another area of conversation that is still considered taboo for traditional television. Additionally, in the context of a Black queer web series, Anne's STI is not a feature of misogynoiristic caricature. Her experience becomes another important representation that can lead to STIs becoming less stigmatized in Black queer women's communities.

In all these series, issues of Black women's mental and physical health are brought to the fore by the central characters. The Black women behind these web shows consciously endeavored to tackle issues that never make it into mainstream media outlets. Therapy, IPV, and sexual health were featured in these web series because of the creative freedom possible when stories are made for us and by us. We see characters negotiating their romantic relationships as well as their relationships to themselves, and even with short series runs, transformation is possible.

But still, even in the things we make for ourselves, misogynoir persists—most notably in the masculine/feminine romantic relationships between characters. Being oppressed does not prevent one from being an oppressor. The romantic relationship dynamics these web series explore harken back to the Pat Parker poem from the introduction, proving that the fists that hit do not have to be attached to cis men. Toxic masculinity and its connection to IPV need to be much more thoroughly addressed in the web show worldbuilding we produce, especially since each series included IPV in its run.[34]

Skye's the Limit, like many of these web shows, finally acknowledges female masculinity in Black communities, but the types of masculinity portrayed end up replicating harmful tropes about masculinity itself. To be legible as masculine, many of the women, even in these fictional portrayals, adopt a masculinity that is antagonistic to more feminine people. Even in *195 Lewis*, where polyamory is presented as a real possibility for the characters, the more masculine partner seems to benefit most from the arrangement on camera. Black queer cultural critic Kara Keeling also sees the relationship dynamics between Black masculine and feminine queer woman doing work for the heteropatriarchy. In particular, Keeling argues that Black female masculinity is not "enough" on its own and must often be shored up by a femme to prevent queerness from being seen as completely abhorrent.[35] Black queer web shows display the toxic masculinity that exists in their communities but have not yet endeavored to offer a possibility model for a reimagined feminist masculinity. Again, as discussed in the introduction, not all the digital alchemy I observed in these productions is feminist.

In my imagining of our liberatory futures, I cannot help but wonder whether the toxic masculinity that Black queer masculine-of-center people can enact will mean that misogynoir will still exist. In each of the web shows I describe, the specter of toxic masculinity looms, but in varying degrees. Will polyamory be the solution that enables the possibility for a nontoxic masculinity that is not predicated on its relationship to the feminine? Will we create a social media platform built on transformative and design justice principles that transforms misogynoir before it's even noticeable? My hope is that this text provides an opening, a possibility model for a new way of relating to each other and the potential for the complete transformation of misogynoir.

Despite limited runs, uneven production values, and amateur actors, these web series have and had dedicated followings. These shows do not only deal with the positive and aspirational side of life for Black queer women, they also deal with the challenges and places of contention. Whether it is the therapy they seek or the friends who offer counsel, these characters provide a different way of doing family outside a normative frame. Siblings, cousins, chosen family, and friends are essential relationships for these characters. Yes, romantic partners are important, but characters spend more time engaging their non-romantic relationships than their romantic ones, even with the reliance on cheating and polyamory for narrative tension. Mainstream television does not tell these stories. The web show is a place for Black queer women to build worlds where misogynoir is muted and even transformed into a liberatory art show or a fellowship in France. Black queer women are making the world that they want and crafting the world that they want to see. They are not waiting on traditional television to make space for them; they are making space for themselves and their communities online.

4

Alchemists in Action against Misogynoir

I initially said (to no one) that I would not write about the social media platform Tumblr. As my favorite digital dimension, Tumblr was sacred protected space where I thought my research should not go. I would leave it be, to just enjoy it as a user, and let other scholars do the critical work of analyzing its political significance. But two things have happened that changed my opinion: one, Tumblr lost prominence among the social justice activists who popularized it, in part because of Tumblr's misunderstanding of the significance of its own platform, which led the company to make decisions that alienated longtime users; and two, my friends and beloved Tumblr users moved on to other platforms like Twitter and Instagram.

Tumblr launched in 2007 as a microblogging website that allowed users to create sites that were content-driven as opposed to personality-driven. What set Tumblr apart in the world of social media platforms was that the short blog posts users produced could be reblogged and/or liked by other users. Whatever you put on your blog could "tumble" through the site, picking up reblogs and likes from other users much like a snowball rolling downhill. The site was designed for viewing, as users could scroll an endless stream of GIFs, images, videos, and blurbs of text from the users they followed. Rather than spending time looking at one person's profile or blog, user dashboards highlighted the most recent content produced by the blogs you followed. The format was notoriously difficult to access for new users, who were sometimes confused about the way the platform worked. It was not an easy site to navigate for users with visual impairments, as it relied so heavily on users' ability to follow the internal and atypical interface. In the early days of Tumblr, from 2007 to 2012, a typical Tumblr post would include the reblogs of an original post with nested commentary that had narrower and narrower column widths of texts, appearing like a set of matryoshka dolls cut on a vertical axis. This visual display gave Tumblr the feeling of an echo chamber in which posts were amplified by the number of times they were reblogged, or how deeply nestled the original post was in relation to greater and greater commentary. Unlike Facebook or MySpace, Tumblr centered the content that was uploaded to the blog, not the user. More so than any other social media platform, the images and texts users posted were central to the interface.

A widely circulating meme from 2012 lists the kinds of posts on different social media platforms using a donut for comparison. The image describes Twitter first with imagined text from a post on the site that reads, "I'm eating a #donut," while the text next to Facebook reads, "I like donuts." Twitter as a platform is portrayed as what you do, while Facebook is portrayed as what you like. Tumblr was not listed among the social media sites, but Tumblr user Emergency Salsa reblogged the original meme, adding their own explanation of Tumblr via donut that read, "#this fucking donut #can we talk about this fucking donut for a minute #can we #because on this donut #the sprinkles just comfortably melt into the icing #you can tell that they are so perfectly in tune with each other #and they've come so far from when the sprinkles just sort of sat on top #barely touching for fear of rejection #just ugh I can't #otp: comfortably melting."[1]

Tumblr differs from Twitter and Facebook in a couple of ways. For a microblogging site, Tumblr posts are surprisingly lengthy when compared to their competition. Tumblr user Emergency Salsa's post also alludes to Tumblr fan culture in which users gush over their favorite shows and "ship"—hope for relationships between certain characters—sprinkles and icing. Fandoms often ship relationships that are not likely in the worldbuilding of the show, sometimes creating their own alternate universes where characters are queer or even different genders. The hashtag "#otp" means "one true pairing," a reference that these two characters are meant to be together. By describing Tumblr with this detailed and romanticized description of the sprinkles and icing on the donut, Emergency Salsa signals the longing and loving energy of Tumblr community. Tumblr is what you fangirl, or what you simply cannot stop yourself from ardently gushing over. A certain earnestness and care are evoked in this Tumblr post exemplar, in stark contrast to the performativity that can be prominent on other social media sites. The sincerity of Tumblr users was a part of the appeal of the platform when compared to others.

Tumblr's heyday (2009–2015) has come and gone, making me feel less protective of the platform and the friends I made on the site. I speak about Tumblr in the past tense because after being bought by Yahoo! in 2013, creating stricter rules regarding content in 2018, and being bought again by WordPress's parent company in 2019, Tumblr lost many of its early and long-term bloggers.[2] That this zenith was relatively brief, just under six years, means that I and others who were on the platform during its peak carry the stories of these blogs that will be lost if not recorded. Think of this chapter as an oral history, a glimpse behind the veil into the world of Black nonbinary femmes who ran Tumblr—or at least the corner of it that mattered to me—and provided so much of the popular education on social justice issues that has permeated the culture. Before woke was woke, these users provided an eye-opening popular education through the ways they curated their blogs.

Because Tumblr has (had) such a small portion of the social media market, research about the platform is limited. At the time of publication, only one book has endeavored to take a scholarly approach to the once vibrant community.[3] Researchers have done ethnographies of queer Tumblr users, but they tend to center cis white men. Queer and trans people of color (QTPOC) were a thriving component of Tumblr community and are responsible in large part for bringing "trigger" and "content" warnings into the mainstream consciousness, along with the more notorious practice of the "callout," alongside its more gregarious sibling, "calling in."[4] Black women and Black nonbinary, agender, and gender-variant folks were instrumental in making Tumblr a space where misogynoir could be theorized and introduced as an important concept.

This is also perhaps the most personal section of the book, the acknowledgments notwithstanding. For me, this section is a bit of a fangirl moment, an opportunity for me to geek out about the "early" days of Tumblr when we were young and didn't know any better and would confide and confess to anyone on the interwebs. In what follows, I interview two Tumblr activists-turned-friends and invite them to remember the significance of the site for them and how it helped them understand their work and place in the world. Danielle "Struggling to Be Heard" Cole and Antoinette Luna "Ancestry in Progress" Myers both defined Tumblr as a transformative space for me. They transformed misogynoir by uplifting critical content created by Black women and Black people. I asked them about their first forays into social media and how they make sense of the acclaim their posts generated for a time on the (formerly) popular platform.

One of the reasons Cole and Myers are so dear to me is that I got to meet them in person through my work with the Allied Media Conference (AMC) in Detroit. The AMC is an opportunity for social justice activists to share and learn media skills to improve their organizing. The conference began in 1999 as an anarchist zine conference in Bowling Green, Ohio. A critical mass of Detroit attendees convinced the conference to relocate to Detroit in 2007, a moment that also marked an influx of women of color leadership. Jenny Lee, the director of the Allied Media Conference, was the conference coordinator and hired women of color while also making connections with important WOC organizations like INCITE! Women of Color Against Violence.[5] These calculated moves by Lee made the AMC transform into a conference that welcomed women, queer, and trans people of color, making space for those who previously may not have seen themselves connected to an audience consisting mostly of white boys.

As a longtime attendee, I saw the AMC as a space that brought together powerful women, nonbinary, agender, and gender-variant folks of color who were also bloggers and activists. I organized, sometimes by myself but often with others, a multi-year event at the conference called Shawty Got Skillz Skillshare, in which members of these communities came together to share media strategies with each other. I titled this section Alchemists in Action Against Misogynoir because I imagine it speaking directly to young Black digital organizers who are using digital platforms in transformative ways. Danielle and Luna's stories are powerful and exemplify some of the best the Internet—Tumblr specifically— has to offer as an organizing tool because it gave them access to a whole world they had not previously thought possible.

Struggling to Be Heard

And if [Black women and Black femmes] are so [hated], if
somebody is always trying to put a foot on our neck, what
would it look like without any of those on ours?
—Danielle Cole

Danielle "Strugg" Cole is a Black nonbinary femme who was thirty-two years old when I conducted our interview, but we began to connect on Tumblr when they were twenty-two and I was twenty-seven. They grew up in New England with a white working-class mom and a younger brother and sister. Cole described being an early user of social media platforms, saying she was on message boards "hardcore" when she was thirteen and fourteen years old. Like those of us who grew up in this era, they remember when users had to have an official college email address to join Facebook. Because of the hierarchy of collegiate institutions during these early Facebook days, Cole's community college was lumped into the category "Massachusetts Colleges," making it difficult to find her classmates among such an amorphous and large group. As a result, Facebook held less appeal than other platforms that did not create hierarchies among users. Tumblr presented a new possibility for creating connections with other Black people, something that was missing from Cole's daily life in New England.[6] It was through the Crunk Feminist Collective (CFC) WordPress blog, which announced its foray into Tumblr with a new profile on the site, that Cole was first introduced to the platform.[7] Cole saw this post from the CFC, which then led her to Black queer feminist Alexis Pauline Gumbs's Tumblr site, which in turn pushed Cole to get her own. Cole said, "[Alexis] was doing this thing where you could send her anonymous questions and she would, like, dedicate a song. . . . I think I just got an account so that I could anonymously message [her to get a dedication]."[8] As innocuous as this act of requesting a song seems, it was a pivotal point for Cole. They wanted to message Gumbs anonymously to ask for a song about accepting their queer identity. Cole cites this initial foray into Tumblr as part of her coming-out process.

Being Black and having a white mom in New England presented challenges for Cole as a young child. As Cole described,

> I always wanted friends like the ones I made online, but they were never close to me. So, being in very white Massachusetts, being in very . . . you know, like, Worcester, where I grew up, is the second-biggest town in Massachusetts, but it is very spread out. And so, where I grew was very still kind of middle-class and it is still very segregated. . . . So for me, [Tumblr] was like I actually got a chance to connect with a lot of different

people. Um, a lot of Black people, a lot of queer people and then a lot of just people of color.[9]

Cole's words illuminate the power of Tumblr as a platform, to bring people together who are otherwise isolated from the communities they feel connected to in their everyday lives. Much like the hashtag #GirlsLikeUs, Tumblr provided a virtual space for queer people of color to find connections that were difficult to forge in real life. Cole goes on to describe the feeling of recognition when talking with other people of color on the site, the affirmation of people having similar experiences around racism and sexism. This feeling of isolation prior to connecting with Tumblr community was the impetus for her handle, StrugglingToBeHeard, a sentiment that had been brewing in her white and straight environment in Massachusetts.

Struggling to Be Heard represented a pent-up longing to be seen and heard in a community that actively tried to silence her. For those of us read as Black women, our silence is expected and sometimes coerced by the people around us. Cole tried to make connections within her immediate community, but the cold affect of New England white people made it difficult for her, even as a child with a white mother, to break through. Her frustration as illustrated in her handle is also reflected in some of the popular titles of Black feminist theory, including *All the Women Are White, All the Blacks Are Men, But Some of Us Are Brave* and the aptly titled *Longing to Tell: Black Women's Stories of Sexuality and Intimacy*.[10] Both texts voice the frustration of isolation and a long-silenced narrative of Black feminists' experiences of marginalization as well as their resistance. These texts, like Cole's blog, provide a new venue and opportunity to tell our stories without the self-imposed or socially imposed suspension of our own stories due to respectability concerns.

For Cole, one of the important features of Tumblr was the ability to connect with fellow users around shared interests. Whereas Facebook and earlier social media platforms like MySpace relied on users' offline relationships to build their cadre of connections on the platform, Tumblr made it possible to connect along lines of affinity. With Tumblr, users could follow different blogs, many of which had a specific theme or topic that shaped the types of posts users posted, reblogged, and liked.

Cole describes Tumblr as a gateway to more connection. Once Cole created their Tumblr account, they started building community with mostly Black and queer Tumblr users. Of the community of people Tumblr helped them to connect to, Cole said, "so all of those, almost all of those people . . . are Black. But they are all from different places, they are all different genders, sexualities, sexual orientation, so it was like super diverse still."[11] Tumblr was a digital platform that exposed the diversity within Blackness to other Black users like Cole. Like the Black queer web shows discussed in chapter 3, Tumblr as a platform was transformed through the generative digital alchemy of Black users who sought to build and fortify offline connections with their Black Tumblr friends that defied limiting ideas about who Black people could be. Cole continues, "Tumblr was a good space that a lot of people who needed each other migrated to, and then took the effort to make it offline, like a bigger network, offline, . . . of support." Not all these Black queer users were isolated from Black or queer community, but the type of support they developed for each other through the site bled out into their real worlds. Black queer users shaped the platform in ways that facilitated the growth of networks both online and off.

Cole echoes the sentiments of Janet Mock and other users of the #GirlsLikeUs hashtag who found the web an important tool for building community both on- and offline. In fact, digital networks often create the connections required for people to build meaningful relationships offline. As I explore in my coauthored text *#HashtagActivism: Networks of Race and Gender Justice*, there is a feedback loop between digital and in-person organizing that belies the dismissal of online organizing as "slacktivism."[12] The digital networks that Cole helped cultivate through the creation of her own Tumblr posts, reblogging and liking others, as well as general engagements with other users, opened up the possibility of the web being a place to be vulnerable and make friends.

But not all of Cole's experiences on Tumblr were positive. One of the many reasons I felt it was important to interview Cole was the incident that launched her into Internet notoriety. Tumblr allowed Cole to feel comfortable to explore their sexuality as a Black nonbinary femme in a relatively safe digital space—or so they thought. As Mother's Day 2014 approached, Cole wanted to do something fun for moms. She said,

[I had] this idea, especially for Black mothers to be able to celebrate, you know, celebrate their bodies, celebrate twerking, and celebrate the idea that not all Black mothers are straight. So they might like twerking too, in a different way, not just for themselves. And like, it's a gift. You know what I mean? Like, I am not a mother, but Black mothers do a lot of sacrifice, Black parents in general do a lot of sacrifice, and this was something specifically for Mother's Day to celebrate that and to celebrate femmes, and celebrate just in general.[13]

Cole created a video of themselves twerking for Mother's Day and posted it to Tumblr. Twerking, an African diasporic dance form that involves shaking your butt to the beat of the music, has been derided as lascivious and celebrated as art depending on context. Cole's celebratory twerking was understood by their Tumblr community of Black, queer, and allied users, but in the broader Black community, her twerking became an opportunity for misogynoir to emerge.

As the video made the Tumblr rounds, the community of users offered support and praise for Cole's dancing skills and her reason for creating the video. Tumblr users got it. However, as with most online media and especially Tumblr content, the video did not stay put with an appreciative audience. It was when the video was posted to World Star Hip Hop, a Black celebrity gossip blog and chat site, that the comments started to take a turn for the worse. Cole recounts, "For a while I was arguing with the people in the comments because they were trying to talk all this stuff and say really just derogatory comments, like not understanding comments, anti-Black comments, transphobic comments, I got a lot of comments on my body and my looks."[14] Misogynoir is precisely what motivated the caustic comments Cole received. Comments attacking her body, her gender, her Blackness are at the heart of how misogynoir operates online. A video expressly made for Black women and femmes, made by a Black nonbinary femme became a vehicle for misogynoir on World Star. In the context of this platform, Cole's video could only be viewed through the lenses of respectability and desirability and on both counts, Cole was judged to be lacking. Like Shakara before her, who was physically dragged out of her classroom by her school resource officer, Cole was being disciplined in the video's comments by commenters who felt authorized to critique her performance. Users participated in a digital public shaming with the aim of making Cole regret creating the video.

Like the Black men who participated in #RuinABlackGirlsMonday, mostly intracommunity members were the ones raging at Cole. Cole's experience of misogynoir was orchestrated by other Black people whose vicious comments also illustrated the ways misogynoir can be internalized by those who experience it. Black women (and Black men) used the comments to express anti-Black sentiments that implicitly challenged how they might view other Black women and Black agender, nonbinary, and gender-variant members of their own communities.

Cole's initial urge to fight and engage all of the negative comments they received began to wear on them: "You know, just after a long time of developing my own coping skills that I kind of just helped me navigate, and saying 'you know, I am not even going to interact with this person for my own health.'"[15] Cole made a connection between these misogynoiristic attacks on their video and their health, and decided that arguing with strangers over her humanity wasn't worth it, so she gave it up. Cole realized that energy was better spent on herself.

Digital feminist scholars like Kate Manne and Bailey Poland assert that the adages "don't feed the trolls" or "don't read the comments" have limited efficacy when one is trying to use the Internet to create connection.[16] "Just ignore it" is not a sustainable long-term strategy for those of us who are trying to make change through the digital platforms to which we have access. Cole's retreat from the comments was an act of self-preservation and harm reduction; it helped her health in the moment, but so did the initial video she created. Cole's celebration of Black women and femmes was a source of pleasure for her and for her community of Tumblr users, complicating the notion that "don't engage" is the best way to be safe online. Cole makes claim to Black women and femmes' pleasure while risking the possibility and then eventuality of misogynoiristic rebuttals from commenters who do not understand. Cole's experience is not unlike the misogynoiristic and transphobic violence against CeCe McDonald on the street. Both negotiated strategies to reduce the harm to their health, Cole by leaving the commentary fray and McDonald by literally fighting for her life.

These negative experiences transform the way that users like Cole think about these social media platforms. When I asked Cole how they understood their relationship to Tumblr and its ability to combat misogynoir like the kind they experienced on World Star, Cole explained,

> I think that Tumblr was a means to organize around misogynoir. I think it was a place to discuss it, to educate and to create networks around how to handle it. I don't think it necessarily combated misogynoir, I think it made more people willing to understand, more likely to listen and think of ways the replicated it in their life. I think it was a vehicle to help, to give us those tools offline or in different spaces online.[17]

Cole clarifies that Tumblr itself is not able to transform misogynoir, but the people who use it are able to have a conversation that creates the networks needed to address this anti-Black racist misogyny both on- and offline. Like the digital platforms discussed in previous chapters, Tumblr is a means to an end. In my work with Sarah J. Jackson and Brooke Foucault Welles, we found Twitter and Tumblr to operate similarly in that both tools are adapted by people multiply marginalized to do more than the corporations that created them ever imagined.[18] That Tumblr was a space to grow the kind of networks that do combat misogynoir is an important lesson. The platform provided a space for users to create the conversations and connections needed to deal with oppressive forces on the platform and off. As platforms go in and out of fashion quickly, it becomes important to take the lessons learned in these spaces and apply them to new ones.

This growing cadre of Tumblr users Cole was part of building wanted to connect to each other in other digital and in-person venues. They would gather in chat rooms to talk; through these conversations, users made plans to attend the Allied Media Conference. Coming off of her negative experience with World Star following her Twerk for Mother's Day video, Cole's "Twerkshop" at the 2014 AMC was an opportunity for women of color and agender, nonbinary, and gender-variant people of color to dance together outside the cishet male gaze. For those who participated, the space was incredibly liberatory because there was no shame in moving our bodies in ways that would otherwise make us hypersexual targets in the world outside the carefully curated space of the conference. Cole's skillshare was a reclamation of the dance that had incited misogynoir online. The Twerkshop served to transform the misogynoir Cole experienced into its own salvific salve for those who had been too afraid to "twerk" in public because of the ways their bodies moving to music are always already made hypersexual.

For those of us who are outside socially privileged categories of white, male, able-bodied, and straight identities, Tumblr became a place for affirmation and learning. Many users found the kind of connections and solidarity they were seeking online as opposed to IRL. For Cole, this meant an affirmation that her experiences and analysis of the world were valid and that she was not "crazy." Part of letting go of this feeling included having the language or, in their words, "the verbage just to push back, to recognize like, 'Yes, this is what is happening, there is a word for it, I am not going crazy, there are other people who have experienced this.' Which is important. That is a big piece for your mental health, because you're constantly being gaslighted into thinking that that's not what is going on."[19] When mainstream (read: white) society projects a narrative of post-raciality but you are feeling and witnessing the impact of misogynoir in your life, outlets like Tumblr where others share and validate your experience are incredibly important for mental well-being.

Another important component to mental health is feeling that you have the resources in your life to take care of yourself. Cole discusses the ways misogynoir impinges on that sense of security by showing that an education is not enough for surviving, let alone thriving, if you are read as a Black woman:

> I think just in general misogynoir has negatively impacted my life. I have my associate's degree, bachelor's degree, master's degree, and I am still making twenty dollars an hour. I have no health insurance; I don't have any guaranteed wage. The universities that I did go to, I had a lot of white women say they would help me and nothing ever pulled through. I noticed that I definitely got more callbacks [for jobs] once I took my thesis off my résumé about doing studies on Black women in predominantly white universities. That made a difference on who would call me back [about] my résumé. You know, I have a degree in qualitative sociological research, but the academy doesn't want what I am researching, because Black women aren't good research, that's not—knowing where Black women have come from historically, socially, academically, and financially, that's just not something that they're invested in.[20]

The message Cole received from these research companies was that research on the lives of Black women is not the type of research they want future hires to pursue. Black women are outearning Black men with degree attainment at both the collegiate and graduate level.[21] But despite being the most educated demographic, Black women still make less than every other demographic except Latinx women.[22] For Black women going to grad school and trying to invest in different fields, this sort of dismissal can be damaging not just to the ego but to success. Even when one is working twice as hard and achieving twice as much, the costs to one's health and wellness can be severe.

Misogynoir impacts Cole's ability to make money and have the necessary health benefits to live well. Whether it is the research institutions that might potentially hire Cole or the social media companies that provide our platforms for engagement, there is a reluctance to actually address the systemic nature of the social ills they perpetuate. When I asked Cole about what she thought these social media platforms should do to address misogynoir, she did not hold back:

> I think they can stop being cowards. I think they can take a stand and actually say [that] certain things are not allowed. Certain types of . . . all that right-wing propaganda, right-wing hate speech, . . . no, they shouldn't be allowed. Okay, if you want to make money off of that, okay, that's what you can do, but you aren't revolutionary in any way, and if you want to be better you need to take a clear-cut stand and ban or disallow some people from using it. And you know, when you live in a country where so many people talk about free speech, and it's like, no, there is . . . we get censored more than you get, so there really isn't freedom of speech. If I want to say "fuck white people," it is not the same as you saying "fuck Black people." It's just not.[23]

Cole makes clear that these platforms are actively shirking their responsibility to create a safer environment for marginalized users. Part of the challenge embedded in their words is a need for these companies to acknowledge the hierarchies at play between marginalized groups and those who are more privileged. When white people disparage Black people, it is connected to the long-storied history of slavery, Jim Crow, and other forms of racism in this country. When Black people disparage white people, it does not have the same impact because of these historical and contemporary power dynamics. When companies pretend to be appalled by or suggest that the type of derogatory language used by white people about Black people is equivalent to Black people's disparaging language about white people, it ignores these historic and contemporary fault lines.

Like Cole, I do not understand the equation that one prejudice is the same as the other without contextualizing the relative power of the parties involved. I would go further to say that I am not waiting on social media platforms to change their policies and suddenly start addressing these disparities on their platforms. Corporate America is both a reflection of the values that our society has shaped and a shaper of values. Until society is ready to address its systemic oppression, we should not be surprised when corporations do not. However, because of corporations' expressed capitalist interest, there is a way that people are able to show that racism is not good for their bottom line. The spate of extrajudicial killings of Black people in the summer of 2020 touched off by the murder of George Floyd by Minneapolis police officer Derek Chauvin led to national uprisings that pushed corporations like Aunt Jemima, Uncle Ben's, Cream of Wheat, and Mrs. Butterworth to pledge to change their branding and big retail stores like Walmart and Sephora to change their racist and misogynoirist corporate policies.[24] The longevity of these superficial changes and the prospect of more meaningful ones are beyond the scope of this book.

I asked Cole what their ideal social media platform might look like, and they were eager to share. Ideally, she would want a site that was for Black people only. When someone says something ableist, sexist, racist, homophobic, transphobic, and so forth, they'd be sent to a "time-out room" where they would have a chance to "cool down" and talk with others who are willing to educate them on why what they said was inappropriate.[25] If the person didn't want to change their behavior they'd be temporarily banned from the site, and they'd have to work at showing behavior change and a growth in outlook before being allowed to rejoin. Cole goes on to say that the real impetus behind these rules is her desire to see a site that is more "community wise" and where accountability is a shared value among the people using the site. Cole's vision is of a site that operates with transformative justice principles.

Transformative justice, as described by the activist organization Philly Stand Up, "is a way of practicing alternative justice which acknowledges individual experiences and identities and works to actively resist the state's criminal injustice system."[26] In the context of social media, this looks like rejecting punitive tactics for correcting behavior and repairing the harm caused to the satisfaction of the community of users on the site. As Cole states, someone who did not follow the group agreements would face consequences but would not be treated punitively. Incorporating transformative justice into a social media platform means getting the community of users to start thinking about its application in this digital space but also in their real lives. Cole is offering up a vision for an anti-misogynoir platform that allows for users' transformation.

Cole even described their own transformative experience around colorism that happened on Tumblr. Growing up in a very white town and being light-skinned, Cole had not fully considered how colorism operated in spaces with more Black people with a range of skin tones.

> I really was ignorant to what colorism was, and, you know, when people were talking about it [on Tumblr], I was just like, "I don't fully get it, I experienced this too . . . But, you are saying that it's different." I had a lot of people who I really respected like [Tumblr users] Blackraincloud, BadDominicana, SoTreu say, "Listen, we love you, but you're just out of touch, you just don't know, so we are going to put you together and tell you what's going on. We are not denying your own experiences, but think about it."[27]

Cole described this experience as a calling in. These fellow Tumblr users wrote to Cole and told her why what she was saying was simply wrong. She resisted at first but started to hear and see what they were saying in the lives of the dark-skinned people around her. Cole's best friend and younger brother became instrumental in her acknowledgment of colorism because of their experiences that she did not have, experiences she began to consider because of being called in on Tumblr.

Cole also discussed the need for this imagined new social media platform to be more attentive to issues of accessibility from the outset, such that different disability communities can access the site easily and be integrated into the platform with non-disabled users. They wondered about what kind of design features would be needed to make a site that is accessible to Deaf and blind users at once. Cole also calls for a site that allows the users to create the subcategories and sections of the site, where they are not guided by the site creators to use the site in a certain way because of its design. Giving some control back to the users opens possibilities that the creators of the site cannot envision. Letting users drive both content and design creates the opportunity for the kind of accountability Cole wants to see on the site.

Cole evoked some of the principles of design justice. In communications theorist Sasha Costanza-Chock's book *Design Justice: Community-Led Practices to Build the Worlds We Need*, they describe the practice as "an approach to design that is led by marginalized communities and that aims explicitly to challenge, rather than reproduce, structural inequalities."[28] In the context of redesigning a social media platform, Cole calls for those most impacted by the structural failures of previous platforms to be at the center of the planning. By instituting transformative justice policies in relation to the harm folks might cause on the platform, Cole challenges rather than reproduces the structural inequalities that make current platforms so troublesome.

I also asked Cole whether they thought that misogynoir—as the title of this book suggests—could be transformed. They said, "I think for me misogynoir being transformed would be, I guess in some ways would be seeing that there is so much power in Black women and Black femmes if we are so hated. And if we are so, if somebody is always trying to put a foot on our neck, what would it look like without any of those on ours?"[29] Cole makes a connection between the hatred spewed at Black women and femmes and the oppressive way that they are treated. For Cole, transforming misogynoir involves the removal of the barriers that keep Black women down, creating room for Black women and Black nonbinary, agender, and gender-variant folks to grow and thrive in new ways. This imagined reality, where Black women are not trampled by society, is a space not yet realized, and for Cole, that opens possibilities.

Cole adds that the stereotypical representations of Black women that feed misogynoir are not accurate. Cole states, "It's not like what they think about us is true, but they are living in an altered perception. How do you address that altered perception and use it to your advantage sometimes?"[30] For Cole, transforming misogynoir also involves using people's limited thinking, the way that you might be underestimated as a Black woman and Black femme, to actually gain some point of favor in the world. When you are judged unfairly and regarded as less than you are, when you are unseen, that can create opportunities to surprise those who doubted you.

The tactic of "playing small," or seeming innocent, is a clever deceit successfully employed by Black women against white people for generations. Black feminist historian Darlene Clark Hine writes of enslaved women who feigned pregnancy for extra rations and reduced workloads.[31] Historian Stephanie Camp discusses enslaved Black women's "relocation of goods" and need for night worship as cunning ruses that allowed them to throw illicit parties unbeknownst to their masters.[32] Edward P. Jones's novel *The Known World* chronicles the lives of Black people during slavery. His character Alice pretends to be "crazy," which grants her the freedom to roam the plantation and surrounding areas unrestricted, unlike her fellow enslaved compatriots.[33] Black women can cultivate personas that allows potential antagonists to underestimate their brilliance and emphasize their vulnerability.

But this strategy has its limitations. It is not a solution to be employed en masse when Black women and Black agender, nonbinary, and gender-variant folks are navigating so much abuse already. In Cole's own testimony we see the impact of this underestimation on their life. As Cole described, despite having multiple advanced degrees, earning a living wage and having health insurance are still difficult to manage. In so many ways, Cole has exceeded the limiting expectations society has of Black women and Black agender, nonbinary, and gender-variant folks, and yet the actual material benefit of that success remains elusive in Cole's life. Cole's call to remove the oppressive foot off the necks of Black women resonates so deeply given the depressing statistics surrounding Black women's existence in this country.[34] Black women are evicted from rental properties at rates "on par" with Black men's incarceration rates.[35] One in five Black women were evicted in Milwaukee between 2008 and 2009, making it impossible for them to save and get out of a cycle of poverty.[36] When it comes to health, Black women don't fare much better. A 2005 literature review of the major healthcare journals found that Black women had a maternal mortality rate that was three to six times higher than that of white women.[37] Black women had higher infant, fetal, and prenatal mortality rates than white women. They were also twice as likely to have pre-term delivery of their babies.[38] The pre-term birth rate was higher among Black women than any other racial/ethnic group in the United States. In the year 2000, mortality was higher for Black infants (14.0 deaths per 1,000 live births), who died at more than twice the rate of white infants (5.7 deaths per 1,000 live births).[39]

For Cole, social media platforms like Tumblr and the ideal social media platform they envisioned become tools that help build the networks and strategies that will address these negative health outcomes in the lives of Black women and Black agender, nonbinary, and gender-variant folks. Generative digital alchemy becomes a praxis that transforms misogynoir through what it facilitates. Giving users of digital spaces the tools to hold each other accountable outside corporate interests creates the possibility of a world where communities can self-regulate based on shared values. I for one am eager to see Cole's dream realized.

Ancestry in Progress

The Internet has a lot of memory, but somehow, for some
reason, it can't seem to remember that Black women were
the creators of things.
—Antoinette Luna Myers

Antoinette Luna Myers's Tumblr journey is similar to Cole's but differs slightly because of their respective ages. Luna was in high school when Facebook became the most popular social media platform, making her initial use of the site "very boring."[40] Facebook was built for a generation just before them and they didn't find the site compelling because they knew no one in college, the primary demographic of users at the time.[41] It was the now neglected social media site MySpace that allowed her to connect with other Black women and Black agender, nonbinary, and gender-variant folks. Their initial point of connection within this community was around hair.

Myers used to write haikus about Black hair that she called "nappykus" and initially saw her role on these social media sites as one of service. Myers would help their newfound Internet friends establish their

Black hair YouTube vlogs. Vlogs, or video blogs, were a popular way to use YouTube, with users creating videos as serial content that mirrored what they might write on a blog. Black hair vlogs included tutorials on perfecting certain hairstyles, chronicling the "big chop"—the moment someone cuts off the chemically relaxed part of their hair—as well as discussing the joys and challenges of wearing one's hair naturally. Myers developed titles for these blogs, helped script some of these videos, and offered behind-the-scenes editing help. It was one of these friends who suggested Myers investigate Tumblr as another platform to highlight her popular nappykus in one central place.

It was their love for Black singer and musician Zap Mama that inspired Myers to use the title *Ancestry in Progress* in homage to Mama's sixth studio album of the same name. *Ancestry in Progress* quickly became a go-to Tumblr blog for all content related to Black women and Black agender, nonbinary, and gender-variant folks. The blog took off once Myers returned from a trip to Brazil that left her at once energized by the connections among people across the African diaspora and disappointed by online collaborations with white allies.

Myers worked with two white queers on another blog, *Gurl Goes to Africa*, that was designed to call out white women's voluntourism on the continent. Working with these two required more energy than initially anticipated, as Myers had to do some political education with her collaborators. What started out as a savvy critique of white womanhood and postcolonial imperialism devolved into snarky and sometimes misogynist comments under pictures. The relationships soured and Myers decided that they did not want to co-curate the site any longer, which allowed them to turn their attention to their own blog.

On starting *Ancestry in Progress*, Myers said, "I started curating what I thought would be an online gallery that was reflective of what I, and how I, perceived Blackness and politics, and other people's perspectives. When I started thinking about my Tumblr as a gallery, a digital gallery, that I was the curator of, that is when it took off most."[42] Myers centered their own curatorial vision. They were not interested in responding to misogynoir but collecting content that reflected the Black experience and their political beliefs. Her framing of the site as a gallery is reflected in the predominance of images that populated *Ancestry in Progress*.

Tumblr was designed for the type of curation Myers had in mind, and with little effort, the site grew quickly.

I think it is important for me to attempt to describe the power of Myers's curatorial work. While the blog does not exist on the web, it exists in my memory and the memory of those who had the pleasure to experience it.[43] Because *Ancestry in Progress* was oriented around the idea of a digital gallery, Myers's posts featured images of Black women of all shapes, sizes, colors, and abilities from throughout the African diaspora, expanding viewers' notions of who and what is beautiful. Of her praxis Myers said,

> I wanted to make sure that on *Ancestry in Progress* especially, that, like, all Black women were seen as beautiful, but especially all the Black women that I grew up seeing . . . who were darker than a paper bag, whose hair was—quote un-quote—"nappy." That's why my [personal Blogger] blog was called *Nappy Like Yo' Pappy*. Like, nappy hair was it to me. I wanted the 4C, 4Z curls to be seen as beautiful and stylish. I wanted size 12, 14, 16, 18, 20, 22 and up to exist along with size 2, 0, 00, because we stan all of those sizes too.[44]

Part of their curatorial mission was to document those Black women who are never in the spotlight or on the national stage. These images were of the Black women who were denied representation in traditional media outlets. Black women who were deemed acceptable for traditional media were usually light-skinned and thin with loose curl patterns. Myers's insistence on representing Black women in their full range offers multiple possibility models of beauty on which users can draw. *Ancestry in Progress* was a repository of the extraordinary beauty of everyday Black women and Black nonbinary, agender, and gender-variant people.

As is evident in the remnants that remain visible in the Internet Archive of the site, *Ancestry in Progress* was filled with quotes, images, and essays that all spoke to the Black experience, especially for those of us directly impacted by misogynoir. In a snapshot captured by the Internet Archive Wayback Machine on August 13, 2012, Myers's Tumblr featured a black screen with white text, and posts laid out horizontally across the screen. One post praised gymnast Gabby Douglas for her 2012 Olympic history-making performance, where she became the first African American winner of the women's all-around individual gymnastics final. Just a bit further down and to the right was a quote from Nobel laureate Toni Morrison that read, "I tell my students, when you get these jobs that you have been so brilliantly trained for, just remember that your real job is that if you are free, you need to free somebody else. If you have some power, then your job is to empower somebody else. This is not just a grab bag candy game."[45] In addition to these celebratory and instructive posts, the site also included stories of violence. In the bottom left of the Tumblr page was the story of a yet unidentified Black lesbian who was murdered in Dallas, Texas, on July 23, 2012. Myers also discussed her own challenges, asking how people go to work with severe menstrual cramps, bleeding, and nausea when navigating their monthly cycle.

This disparate content is united by the fact that it is all in service to the lives of Black women and Black nonbinary, agender, and gender-variant folks. Whether it's celebrating Gabby Douglas or heeding the words of Toni Morrison, this blog is giving different windows into the lives of Black women while also addressing the parts of that life that are hard. The personal struggles of Black women and Black nonbinary, agender, and gender-variant folks with menstrual pain may seem insignificant, but given the continued social taboos around discussing menstruation and the realities of Black people's historic experiences with uterine health, the issue is critically important.[46] An astounding 80 percent of Black women will develop fibroids in their lifetime.[47] Like the Black queer web shows discussed in the previous chapter, Tumblr provides a platform for discussing reproductive health directly when mainstream media outlets are reluctant to include these conversations in their content.

Additionally, the murder of the yet unidentified lesbian in Texas is striking because it further illustrates the disproportionate amounts of violence that Black women experience in the world and the lack of concern for our suffering. In trying to find an update or an identification for the woman murdered, I came across the murders of two other women of color, both of whom were trans women, in the same county in the last decade.[48] The violence our communities face is disproportionate and often overkill, reflecting the special hatred and disdain that this book has named.

The growth of *Ancestry in Progress* from two hundred to over eight thousand followers occurred over the course of a few months, making the blog one of the top blogs on Tumblr. In fact, when Tumblr introduced a spotlight feature where it would highlight a popular post from one of the millions of blogs on the site, *Ancestry in Progress* was featured. Myers discussed the awkwardness of having her digital life intersect with her professional life once the site amassed thousands of followers after this special recognition. She said, "I went from like two hundred followers to nearly eight thousand, or maybe eight thousand and some change? I remember deleting it once I took my first job in higher ed because the students of the college knew my blog and followed me [on the blog]. So I was like, 'Uh oh! This is going to make my job awkward,' and that is why I ultimately deleted it. I couldn't have my professional life and personal life cross those lines. So I deleted it."[49]

Myers's decision to delete their blog rather than have their public and private lives merge is representative of how the web can be a digital respite from the societal expectations of a white cis heteropatriarchal world. The type of vulnerability that Myers fostered through her blog was ultimately something that she was unwilling to have bleed into her professional life. Like Cole, Myers found Tumblr to be a space where a certain level of collective intimacy could be cultivated. This intimacy is threatened when uninvited coworkers, students, and superiors encroach on what has in some ways become sacred space for lifting up and celebrating Black women who are often overlooked. Myers's self-described digital gallery highlighted people who were not generally part of the predominantly white institution where they worked. Tumblr provided a maroon resting site for Myers, and similarly, had to be destroyed once discovered.

Tumblr has been instrumental in educating a generation of users in social justice activism. The type of content people post is remarkable, as is the amount. For Myers, "Tumblr would help me have language that I was actually learning on the ground with my students."[50] As student affairs staff at an elite private university, Myers saw the way that students were using Tumblr to learn about their world in ways that their college professors were not. Tumblr was a space where language and sexual and gender identities knew no bounds. For those on Tumblr at this pivotal time between 2011 and 2015, there was an opportunity to learn from people who were experimenting and creating as they went, building the plane as they flew. The flexibility of the site made room for exploration in ways other social media sites did not. Myers was able to connect with their students in ways that those students' own professors could not because of the shared language that circulated on Tumblr.

Despite my reading of Myers as a central force in the Black queer feminist Tumblr spaces in which I traveled, Myers saw themselves as existing somewhat apart from this community. Where she saw them actively addressing white racism and misogynoir, she saw her own work as staying in her own corner of the Internet, curating things of beauty:

> I had noticed that there were a group of Black folks, of nonbinary Black folks and femmes, and Black folks who were nonbinary, . . . who spent a lot of time educating folks on issues, spent a lot of time battling with trolls, spent a lot of time responding or choosing not to respond to hate that was either direct towards them and their accounts anonymously and not so anonymously in a way that I did not face at all. And I found that to be very curious. I was not front and center like a number of others on the Internet. I like to think of myself as having been quite peripheral.[51]

Myers described her experience of Tumblr as though she was on the margins. They saw the misogynoir that other users experienced, and though they did experience some themselves, it was not to the degree that other users endured. These users were resultantly more vocal in directly responding to misogynoir on the platform. This feeling of being on the periphery of misogynoir was helpful in that it allowed Myers to focus on the content she wished to create and to ignore the content that would have dissuaded her from her curatorial efforts. Having a clear perspective for *Ancestry in Progress* as a gallery meant that Myers was not embroiled in the same types of arguments with commenters that their peers faced. This conscious choice by Myers was their own form of health praxis as it helped them stay out of anxiety-inducing interactions with other Tumblr users.

Myers's mercurial relationship to these social media platforms meant that she used the sites as long as they were useful, and when they no longer served their purpose, she could let them go. From Facebook to

YouTube, Blogger to Tumblr, Myers moved as needed to share the ideas and images that were important to them. They said,

> I feel like the Internet was—is and was—a tool for communication, and the more that I realized that I, that the Internet and its platforms can lead to miscommunication or misunderstandings or misinterpretations of the things that I am trying to communicate, the less I have engaged with it. I hunger for opportunities to express myself in new ways now, but I have to admit that since I have not been on the Internet or used Tumblr or social media in those ways that I feel like I am carrying around all of this energy, this kinetic energy that needs to be let out.[52]

For Myers, as for Cole, Mock, and McDonald, Tumblr is a tool, a platform that is helpful until it is not. It provides a space for Black women and Black nonbinary, agender, and gender-variant folks to share their thoughts, but it can also lead to miscommunication and misunderstandings that make continued use of the platform unsustainable. For Black women and Black nonbinary, agender, and gender-variant folks to keep using these platforms requires a redesign or a new platform altogether. However, as Cole's own handle attests, when people are invested in not hearing you and making up narratives, it does not matter what platform you use. Myers's experiences caused them to question the utility of the Internet altogether.

Myers described conflicting feelings about Tumblr. It's the space that allowed her to put some of her energy out into the world, but it also allows for people to perform the digital blackface and digital minstrelsy discussed in chapter 1. Myers asked, "Is anything authentic anymore? So I am just going to stay offline and read."[53] In the wake of longtime Tumblr and Twitter user EmoBlackThot's reveal that they were a cis gay man and not a cis woman, Myers was searching for the redefined realness of the everyday and not the performative digital drag of those pretending to be Black women.[54] Tumblr can be a hostile place to navigate, given the presence of those who use GIFs of Black women to react to digital content, actively pretend to be Black women to generate laughs and likes, or type, wear, and say things they never would with their real avatars.[55]

Like Cole, Myers also cites the 2014 Allied Media Conference as a turning point, an opportunity to meet many of the people behind the Tumblrs they followed and with whom they chatted. This AMC included a call from Black queer femme Tumblr user GlitterLion, to all QTPOC Tumblr users to come to the conference and meet in person. It was at this conference that lifelong friendships were forged. Tumblr users had the opportunity to meet the people behind the handles. Unfortunately, this was the unexpected zenith of Tumblr gatherings, as 2014 marked the height of Tumblr's blog posts per day, with a steady and then steep decline in subsequent years.[56]

Myers described her experience as a nonbinary Black femme who gets read as a Black woman. She said, "I, unfortunately, after leaving the very comfortable higher ed space that I was in, have kind of been pushed, in the past two to three years more specifically, away from the gender fluid identity that had become really comfortable for me. I had become comfortable in sitting in the space of not really having a gender that I fully identified with, or not really, you know. I felt comfortable being nonbinary, nonconforming, but femme-presenting."[57] Myers's gender identity and presentation had room to breathe in an elite liberal arts school setting and in the corner of the web they carved out for themselves. Students, no doubt emboldened by their own Tumblr journeys of self-discovery, pushed for more inclusive policies on their campuses, including gender-neutral bathrooms, easy name changes to official school documents, and even the practice of asking people's pronouns before an event begins. But outside the space of these institutions, innovations around gender are much less common. Myers is much more likely to be read as a Black woman in her day-to-day life now that they are no longer working in a university.

But Myers does not dislike being read as a Black woman. She said, "It does not feel like violence or misgendering when I am read as a Black woman. Particularly because of being a Black woman, being raised as a Black woman and then being read as one allots me a certain power."[58] For Myers, "Black woman" is not incorrect but rather one facet of a prism through which they still experience love and recognition. "Black woman" does not encapsulate all of her, but it is still a part of her that she understands that other people may recognize. "Black nonbinary femme" is yet another facet of the prism through which she can be seen and recognized. She connects her fluidity with labels and pronouns to her generation, as she has a wife who is of an older generation who still struggles with "they" pronouns and her nonbinary identity. For Myers, this is not disrespect but simply a matter of generational shifts, one they handle with grace and patience.

I asked Myers, as I had asked Cole, what she was looking for in a social media platform, and she said she missed "that we used to talk to each other more."[59] In the early days of the World Wide Web, when list-servs, message boards, and regular blogs reigned supreme, people would write lengthy posts that followers would read and respond to in equally lengthy posts. The Allied Media Conference figures into this early history as well, with the 2008 AMC hosting the first in-person gatherings of the SPEAK! collective of radical women of color, an organization that helped build the capacity of feminists of color online through poetry and song.[60] Building on their successes and others, a younger generation of QTPOC users felt compelled to make sure their voices were heard, participating in their own generative digital alchemy that helped them grow. There was a different sense of online community that has eroded away with the speed at which information and communication move on the Internet now. Myers said, "But there were collective threads. Right?! Where Twitter or even Facebook just allows for an individual's thread, and the people's commentary on that thread. But forums, they were collectively . . . co-created! I would like to see that happen again, co-creation. A genuine co-creation that doesn't silence or steal from origi-nators and creators."[61]

Myers also raised the point of continual friction between online con-tent creators and those who wish to profit from their work. In a guide for educators hoping to engage in social media research with students, femi-nist digital humanist T. L. Cowan and I noted the potential harm that can come from analyzing or aggregating social media posts without per-mission. We wrote, "Frequently, heightened attention by journalists, re-searchers, and others opens up a social media user to harassment, threats of violence, and actual violence."[62] Collaborative conversations without an agenda are difficult to produce in the current iteration of social media. Tumblr was one of the few platforms that allowed for the possibility, but with platform changes and ownership shifts, it is difficult to generate the kind of collectivity that was once commonplace on the site.

Myers wants an Internet that remembers the work of Black women creators who made the Internet what it is today. It was in this point in the conversation that she shared what became the epigraph that begins this section. She wants an archive, a digital repository, that shows how Black women have moved and shaped the Internet. Part of the reason I wrote this book was to begin to do some of that introductory archival work, but the history remains intangible and needs more people to tell it. Myers saw such an archive as "an interactive, digital gallery curated by Black women about the kind of things we've created online, the discussions, the threads, something that is an endless loop of hyperlinks to discussions."[63] Her vision conjures her own deleted site, *Ancestry in Progress*, with its discussions and galleries of images.

Myers continues her line of thought about how Black women's accomplishments in digital space can be made visible to a wider audience. Black women are copied and made into caricatures, which prevents us from being taken seriously, particularly around our contributions to the digital. She adds,

> And if misogynoir is transformed, can it be transformed in such a way that Black women are celebrated and appreciated authentically? Because there are ways where Black women are "appreciated" but it still feels . . . I wouldn't say appreciated. "Recognized," "celebrated," I guess, in the sense of visibility, but it so quickly can turn on its head. It can so quickly become we are parodied. It can so quickly become we are copied. We are made fun of, we are seen as a vehicle through which humor can be delivered to other audiences, like, you know . . . I am thinking of a white gay man who got a lot of power on the Internet acting and pretending to be a Black woman.

Myers returns to concerns of digital Blackface and drag, means by which Black women are ridiculed and not taken seriously. They remain cautious about visibility just as the trans advocates in chapter 3 do. Visibility makes you a target even as it helps you find your people. Visibility can be reactionary or generative digital alchemy, depending on how it is leveraged.

There is a way to imagine something otherwise, and I think that the work of *Ancestry in Progress*, *Struggling to Be Heard*, #GirlsLikeUs, and the work of people who create Black web shows are examples of the transformational power of generative digital alchemy.[64] I have been thinking about the digital media we put out there in cyberspace as medicine for us, by us. This medicine is not always made in reaction to misogynoir; sometimes it transforms. *Ancestry in Progress* was not created in reaction to misogynoir, but it existed as a beautiful antidote to and maroon site from the misogynoir floating through the web. *Ancestry in Progress*, like *Struggling to Be Heard*, is a possibility model for generative digital alchemy. As Myers says,

> When it feels precious to us, then we hold it close and near and dear because it came from us, because it was for us, and it never really had any intentions of being anything but what it was. When it reaches external communities, when it reaches other eyes, when it begins to catch on, when it grows larger than itself, doesn't that medicine begin to weaken?[65]

Myers calls for us to be guarded with our medicine and ensure that it does not get into the wrong hands. Like the hashtag #GirlsLikeUs, the medicine that a digital space like the one Myers described must ride the delicate balance between being public-facing while also being somewhat protected from those who would dilute its magic.

Both Cole and Myers, Black nonbinary femmes, center Black women in their digital space making. By creating the digital networks and spaces that support them, they graciously made space for others of us looking for a soft place to land in the misogynoiristic toxicity of the Internet. While neither of them can stop misogynoir, they were both able to transform their relationship to it by actively not engaging comments and turning away from it completely. Both Cole and Myers exemplify the power of digital resistance while also reminding us of the limits of the tools we do not create ourselves. Like "lesbian, mother, warrior, poet" Audre Lorde, I am not under the impression that the social media tools we have will bring down the structures of oppression that provide their scaffolding.[66] Like Cole and Myers, I imagine new tools and new tactics for transforming misogynoir and our relationship to it.

Conclusion

Misogynoir Transformed: #BlackWomenDragBack

> Drag me, Professor Sanders-Johnson. Drag me!
> —student

My dear friend and colleague Grace Sanders-Johnson told me of the moment one of her favorite students made the statement quoted in the epigraph above. Her student had said something about an issue and as Dr. Sanders-Johnson offered a counter-perspective based on other facts the student did not know, this was the student's prompt reply. "It kind of caught me off-guard because I didn't think of my additional points as particularly antagonistic to what [my student] said, but she felt that I was really telling her something she needed to know and in an authoritative way she needed to hear it."[1]

While I have heretofore discussed dragging as a tool used against Black women and girls, there are ways that Black women and girls reclaim the practice to suit their own needs. When Sanders-Johnson's Afro-Latinx student expresses exuberance at being dragged by her favorite professor, it becomes clear that there is more to drag than what meets the eyelash. For this student, to be dragged in this instance is an expression of care, one in which Sanders-Johnson is educating the student by alerting them to information they had not previously considered or known. To drag in this instance is to, as we say, "get you together," or tell you what you need to know so that you are not out in public looking raggedy. When Danielle Cole described the way that Black women "got them together" around their incorrect ideas on color, that was an instance of dragging back through "calling in."[2]

Black women social media users employ digital alchemy by digitally dragging those who need to be told about themselves, even when the interaction is not received as positively as it had in the scenario above.

As user @jiinandtonic demonstrated with her comments on the hashtag #RuinABlackGirlsMonday, dragging back can be a satisfying and even humorous way to upend misogynoir. Dragging back can be used to both call in and call out the problematic behavior of other social media users who are engaging in misogynoir. Maybe dragging can also be transformed and redefined.

The case of #YourSlipIsShowing is particularly stellar. In a poorly planned Trojan horse campaign called Operation Lollipop, men's rights and pickup artists on the social media platform 4chan attempted to mask their incendiary and falsely feminist posts to social media by adopting avatars and speech that mimicked Black women and social justice activists. These men tried and succeeded in getting the hashtag #EndFathersDay to trend on Twitter as an authentic feminist campaign that asserted that Father's Day was anti-feminist.[3] The hashtag predictably drew the ire of conservative news hosts like Tucker Carlson, who equated the hashtag with feminist hatred of men. These users tried to pass off tweets like "#EndFathersDay because I'm tired of all these white women stealing our good black mens" as tweets by actual Black women. By adopting both digital blackface and drag, they attempted to create a narrative that for Black women, social justice activism was again rooted in their concern about their desirability to Black men.[4] Actual Black feminist Twitter user @sassycrass immediately knew that something was up and created the hashtag #YourSlipIsShowing to call out the fake accounts spouting misogynoirist hatred. Her hashtag took off after being adopted and supported by research by another actual Black woman twitter user, @so_treu. Together, @sassycrass and @so_treu helped marshal a network of Black women Twitter users using the hashtag to out fake accounts.[5]

#YourSlipIsShowing is a powerful hashtag because it hails humor as it corrects. "Your slip is showing" is a southern Black aphorism born of the mother wit of Black sociality. To say your slip is showing is to slyly call you out for being careless with your appearance. But in calling out the indiscretion, one is calling for the offender to correct it. Whether they do or not is less important than the public pronouncement of the behavior as inappropriate. Black women who participated in #YourSlipIsShowing were not simply outing these imposter accounts with stolen avatars and poorly executed Black vernacular for sport; they were demanding that these users stop. After being outed as using fake avatars, these white users abandoned the strategy. The hashtag was accompanied by a link to the Twitter account in question and sometimes with the use of the official @Twitter handle to encourage Twitter management to get involved and delete the suspected accounts. Unsurprisingly, Twitter did little to address these concerns.

Since its initial birth in 2014, #YourSlipIsShowing had a resurgence as the 2016 US presidential election Russian bot debacle unfolded. Fake accounts created by Russian interests successfully influenced voters by spreading propaganda on Facebook, Twitter, and even Instagram. These accounts had hundreds of thousands of followers who liked posts that cast presidential hopeful Hillary Clinton in a bad light and portrayed Trump favorably.[6] For @sassycrass and @so_treu, this revived interest in the hashtag has not meant any financial compensation for their initiative or detective work. Rachelle Hampton, a Black woman journalist with *Slate* magazine, revived the story in April 2019, giving credit where credit was due by properly acknowledging the work the hashtag did. It continues to be a hopeful example of what digital alchemy can accomplish in terms of stopping a harmful practice.[7] I too see Black women's activism through #YourSlipIsShowing as semi-prescient, producing a strategy for addressing harmful fake Twitter accounts before Russian bots were part of the election narrative. But as @so_treu put it, there is no glory in being "a canary in the coal mine." Black women effectively said "She doesn't even go here" to hundreds of trolls, but that has not stopped their mistreatment online.[8] In some cases, it has been the very Black women who sound the alarm on racist misogynist content who get banned from social media.

Jane Oranika, a then nineteen-year-old writer and musician, took to Twitter after the Trump 2016 election to get a few laughs from coworkers. Borrowing from digital drag star Joanne the Scammer's tagline that she is "Caucasian," Oranika started to paint her face white with makeup as a form of self-protection now that Trump was elected. The video went viral, amassing over 100,000 views, but twelve hours after it was posted, Oranika's Twitter account was suspended. Twitter declined to answer journalists' inquiries as to why the account was suspended, but the backlash to her joke was severe. White Twitter users tried to compare her use of beige makeup to minstrel blackface, calling it a double standard that Oranika's video received positive attention before her Twitter suspension when blackface, in their mind, is routinely condemned. User @ Ann_Tagonist commented, "This is racist, she is doing 'white-face'—if black-face is bad, so is white-face. Report and Block."⁹ To suggest that there is a double standard seems to be supported, though not in the ways that these white users imagine. Misogynoirist content routinely goes unchallenged on social media, but when it is, it is Black women who are suspended, blocked, or removed from the platform. More interesting than Oranika's suspension is the fact that her inspiration, Joanne the Scammer, did not and has not received similar admonition. When a Black woman attempts to joke in a similar manner as a Black man by using drag, she somehow still ends up the punch line. Oranika is but one of the many Black women who have been suspended on social media platforms for calling out the misogynoirist abuse that they uniquely negotiate.

Simplistic solidarity strategies built on race or gender are not sufficient for the social transformation necessary to stop misogynoir. The digital resistance strategies deployed by the content creators I highlight utilize a queer Black feminist framework that eschews respectability or a quest for "positive" counternarratives. The Black digital alchemists discussed here refashion social media to their own ends and create new possibilities for engaging in digital space, even as they are being suspended and blocked for it.

Misogynoir Transformed

In chapter 1, I discussed the viral videos of assaults on Black women and girls. The dragging of Black women via drag as well as the literal dragging of Black women and girls are captured on video and live online in perpetuity, only for the comments on these videos to drag Black women and girls further through the muck of misogynoir. Capturing the violence that Black women and girls endure on video may help some of these survivors gain financial compensation in court, but it does not facilitate redress for the trauma and harm that remain. In our current (in)justice system, the onus is on the individual to advocate for themselves, with no acknowledgment of the structural forces that created the conditions that contributed to the violence they experienced. Black women and girls use defensive and generative digital alchemy by speaking back to and advocating for new practices that better serve their collective needs. Niya Kenny worked with the ACLU to get a law changed in South Carolina that benefitted all K-12 students in the state. Similarly, the Black women who responded to #RuinABlackGirlsMonday used defensive digital alchemy to engage some of the trolls who attempted to mess with their mental health through a poorly planned hashtag. Black women used the tools available to them to mitigate misogynoir. Removing police from schools and jettisoning prejudicial policies are essential for creating new realities for Black girls and their Black nonbinary, agender, and gender-variant peers. Scholars like Bettina Love, Asha French, and Ruth Nicole Brown are leading the way with new possibility models for Black youth in educational settings.[10]

In chapter 2 I highlighted the advocacy and network building of Black women through the hashtag #GirlsLikeUs and the organizing to support CeCe McDonald. That #GirlsLikeUs was created by a Black woman to support a white woman or that many of the organizers of the #FreeCeCe movement were not Black illustrates the veracity of the Combahee River Collective's claim that if "Black women were free, it would mean that everyone else would have to be free since our freedom would necessitate the destruction of all the systems of oppression."[11] By centering the most vulnerable of Black women, fighting for their lives, and paying attention to their generative digital projects, we increase the possibilities for justice for all. CeCe McDonald used generative digital alchemy to write herself into a new world, transforming her inhumane conditions into a portal of possibility through reading and writing. Transforming misogynoir also meant the transformation of the Black women at the center of #GirlsLikeUs and #FreeCeCe. Supporting Black trans women, the Black women most vulnerable to deadly harm and devastating health outcomes, means changing the realities of all Black women's lives. Creating a world that makes it possible for McDonald and other Black trans women to walk down the street unmolested means rooting out misogynoir and transphobia wherever they live in society.

Chapter 3 provided a glimpse into the worlds built by Black queer women in digital spaces. Whether it's therapy, intimate partner violence, or sexual health, these web shows provide a critical lens into the health concerns of Black queer women, conspicuously absent from mainstream media. The creators of these shows combat misogynoir by centering the lives of Black queer women as Black queer women. The "for us, by us" approach to the digital projects they create ensures that the issues of the Black queer women's community are front and center, offering small transformative possibility models through the choices characters make. Seeking therapy, leaving an abusive relationship, and destigmatizing STIs are just a few of the liberatory actions taken by characters on these shows. Misogynoir is both transformed and present in the gendered dynamics of the characters, with masculine-of-center characters benefitting from their relative privilege and simultaneously enacting subtle forms of misogynoir on their more feminine counterparts. Even as we create the world we want to see, our radical imaginations can still be limited by the world as we know it.[12] We need to continue to stretch our imaginations, because another world is not only possible, it is required for more than mere survival.

Chapter 4 was an intimate and personal look at the way the social media platform Tumblr transformed the misogynoir experienced by two Black nonbinary femmes. For Danielle Cole and Antoinette Luna Myers, Tumblr was a means for making community, community that started online but led to real-world connections at events like the Allied Media Conference. Their digital lives helped them navigate a larger social reality that was hostile to their existence. Whether in their immediate communities or on the job, both Cole and Myers negotiated racist, sexist, and even transphobic antagonism. The networks of connection that Tumblr facilitated help to sustain them and provide new ways of thinking about the world as a result. For Cole, this new thinking included a calling in about their initial denial of colorism. A large part of my conversation with Myers was explaining what *Ancestry in Progress* meant to me as a conscious inattention to misogynoir on the platform. Tumblr became a place of respite and network building that fueled their engagements with others offline. Digital alchemy was alive and well during their engagements with the Tumblr platform, and we will undoubtedly continue to find our points of refuge in other social media sites, but we can also begin to build our own.

The Viral Video Lives On

In her book *Bearing Witness While Black: African Americans, Smartphones, and the New Protest #Journalism*, author Allissa Richardson tracks the growing number of smartphone videos used to capture police brutality against Black people, particularly Black women.[13] Videos that depict white people calling the police on Black people for violating perceived "rules" or social standards also show the disproportionate victimization of Black women and girls. In May 2018, Yale graduate student Lolade Siyonbola used Facebook Live to capture a video of her interaction with campus police when they were called on her by a fellow student, a white woman, while Siyonbola napped in a common room on campus.[14] The video went viral and received more than ten thousand comments. A month later, in June, a white woman dubbed "Permit Patty" called the police on an eight-year-old Black girl selling water outside her building without a permit.[15] These are but two examples in a laundry list of mounting cases that exemplify the ways that Black women and girls are deemed dangerous for simply existing. These videos, like those of the assaults on Dajerria Becton and Shakara, attempt to solicit a sympathetic audience where viewers can see the disparate way Black women and girls are treated.

Sandra Bland's story is a particularly frightening testimony to the deadly nature of misogynoir and the ambivalent results of these types of viral videos. In July 2015, Sandra Bland was stopped by state trooper Brian Encinia for purportedly failing to signal a lane change. Bland is seen on both the officer dashcam video and her own phone-recorded video expressing frustration with the stop and annoyance with Encinia. The video captured by Bland was only made publicly available in May 2019; it shows an unprovoked Encinia yelling at Bland to get out of the car or he will "light her ass up!," referencing the taser in his hand.[16] Encinia arrested a stunned Bland, who allegedly died by suicide in her jail cell three days later. Her arrest and mysterious death sparked protests and demonstrations around the country as Black women demanded that we #SayHerName.[17] Her death touched off its own viral movement of Black women and Black agender, nonbinary, and gender-variant Black folks talking about their own dangerous and deadly interactions with the police. #SayHerName has grown to be a vociferous movement, making connections between the extrajudicial killing of cis and trans Black women alike while also highlighting the unique vulnerabilities of non-binary Black folks to this type of violence.[18]

That Bland's story finds its way into this book that centers the digital alchemy of Black queer and trans women is a bit counterintuitive given that Bland used her YouTube channel to express some homophobic views.[19] But Bland need not have perfect politics to be deserving of Black queer feminist attention, especially when misogynoir played such a huge role in how she was treated by the police before, and likely during, her untimely death. As queer theorist Cathy Cohen has illustrated, the deaths of ostensibly healthy cis straight subjects still necessitate queer theoretical attention. In her keynote address at the 2010 Critical Ethnic Studies Association conference, Cohen began her talk with a horrific tale of young Black life lost too soon. Sixteen-year-old Derrion Albert was beaten to death by other teens on the street in the late summer of 2009. Of his passing and its connection to queer theoretical interventions Cohen offered the following: "Derrion and other young folks of color operate as queer subjects, the targets of racial normalizing projects intent on pathologizing across the dimensions of race, class, gender, and sexuality. By normalizing their degradation, marginalization, and invisibility, it becomes something to which we no longer pay attention."[20] Like Cohen, I see the ubiquity of Black extrajudicial killings queering those they touch. The visible markers of difference written into the bodies, clothes, and mannerisms of these queered subjects make them targets for violence and injury, despite being otherwise healthy individuals. For Black women, misogynoir exacerbates their vulnerability, making them frequent targets in the crosshairs of injustice and harm.

The hashtags and activism that come out of these events are also illustrating the role white women play in maintaining white supremacy and in enacting misogynoir. "Karens," as this litigious and vociferous group of white women that includes Permit Patty have been dubbed, further underscore the need to discuss misogynoir as an experience unique to Black women and Black agender, nonbinary, and gender-variant folks, as Karens can simultaneously experience misogyny while perpetuating misogynoir.[21]

There Is No Over There

Thrown away where? The world is round.
—Marge Piercy

The hashtag #GirlsLikeUs makes me smile just as Black queer web shows make me laugh. My Tumblr friends' words have been a balm when I have felt isolated and unsure that others were interpreting the world in a similar way. I love these imperfect and messy means for making something out of the scraps you have been given. But this practice of making a way out of no way is not sustainable. I envision a Black queer feminist future where we have what we need and misogynoir is truly transformed, so much so that it is unrecognizable. In the words of the character Luciente in Marge Piercy's *Woman on the Edge of Time*, there is no getting rid of the things we don't want because the world is round.[22] In womanist writer Alice Walker's classic text *We Are the Ones We Have Been Waiting for: Inner Light in a Time of Darkness*, she writes, "This is a time when consciousness really requires that we connect, that we don't just say 'oh, that's them over there,' because the other part of consciousness now is to understand there are no other people anywhere. They are all here on the planet, we are us, and that's it."[23] These are different ways of saying that even as I work toward the end of misogynoir, I know that it requires the transmutation of people. We cannot incarcerate or censor misogynoir away. We must work to liberate our visions of what is possible in the world, and this includes calling in those who have caused harm by promulgating misogynoir.

I see the work of Black trans feminist Dora Silva Santana on the Brazilian concept of *mais viva*—"more alive, alert, savvy"—as a brilliant way forward for building the worlds we want.[24] The activist and scholar Angela Davis; Mary Hooks, leader of the Black Mamas Bailout movement; Mariame Kaba, theorist on transformative justice; and Ruth Wilson Gilmore, co-founder of Critical Resistance, are just a few of the leaders who are asking us to rethink our relationship to those who cause harm and the way we deal with them in society.[25] Critical race and digital studies scholars Ruha Benjamin, Kishonna L. Gray and Alondra Nelson research at the intersections of Black lives, health, the carceral state, and technology, asking us to reimagine what our world might look like if the people were collaboratively working with the scientists and technologists that structure our institutions and world.[26]

In addition to these scholarly and activist forms of resistance, Black women and Black nonbinary, agender, and gender-variant folks are still carving out their digital and physical sites of respite in a misogynoiristic world. The restorative project the Nap Ministry was created by Tricia Hersey in 2016 with the founding belief that "rest is a form of resistance," naming "sleep deprivation as a racial and social justice issue."[27] Through installations and guided events, along with quotes and images on its Instagram and Facebook accounts, the Nap Ministry creates opportunities online and off for Black women to take time to prioritize rest in their lives, a generative digital alchemy that transforms the misogynoir that might cause us to lose sleep.

TikTok is another social media platform that is expanding the way misogynoir can be addressed. User UrDoinGreat became a viral sensation with clever short videos that center the experiences of Black nonbinary feminists trying to move through this world. In one of their most popular videos, with more than a million views, UrDoinGreat humorously exposes the well-intentioned misogynoir that often adheres to and harms those who are Black and assigned female at birth. With word bubbles, UrDoinGreat shows a Black nonbinary person being asked what their pronouns are. They respond with "They." Then another person, trying to be helpful says, "She uses they," to the consternation of the nonbinary person. Despite clearly articulating the pronouns they use, the nonbinary person is misgendered. The video reflects how deeply embedded ideas of gender are even in communities that are working to trouble the binary. During the onset of COVID-19 in the United States, UrDoinGreat and their partner purchased an RV with a plan to literally take their viral TikTok video making on the road. The traveling project provides a helpful example of the fluidity that can propel misogynoir's transformation.

In June 2020, UrDoinGreat also came under fire by the same community that helped propel their social media success when their rape of a fellow Black femme activist was brought to public attention again. Under the banner of accountability, Black femme activist and organizer Jewel the Gem hosted an Instagram Live conversation with UrDoinGreat in which she asked for them to deplatform or give their site to a Black woman or femme.[28] In addition to this request, UrDoinGreat was questioned about their process for making amends and for changing their behavior going forward. In multiple social media platforms, Black queer and trans people debated the efficacy of UrDoinGreat's callout or calling in, wondering out loud and through conversation what transformative justice looks like and at what threshold do consequences become punishment.[29] The process of transforming ourselves and the misogynoir we experience and/or perpetuate is a messy one that requires relationships built on trust and shared values. Social media ensures that this process does not happen behind closed doors and allows our fumbling toward repair to be evaluated by others whether we succeed or fail.[30]

Whether digitally or IRL, Black women and Black nonbinary, agender, and gender-variant folks are creating the spaces they need. Misogynoir causes harm, but Black women and Black nonbinary, agender, and gender-variant folks are using digital alchemy to transform that harm and reduce its negative impact. Through the hashtags created and challenged, the web shows launched and the Tumblrs tended, a new world is not only possible but essential if misogynoir is to be truly transformed.

ACKNOWLEDGMENTS

The acknowledgments were perhaps the hardest part of this book to write. I did not want to forget or leave anyone out but shied away from the comprehensive "thank yous" of my colleague Ronak K. Kapadia in *Insurgent Aesthetics: Security and the Queer Life of the Forever War*. Similarly, this acknowledgments section lacks the poetics of Savanah Shange's in her incredible text, *Progressive Dystopia: Abolition, Antiblackness, and Schooling in San Francisco*. What I do offer is heartfelt appreciation for many who helped me along the journey of this book. No text is a single-author text, and I know I did not finish this book on my own.

This book was two decades in the making, and as such was touched by more people than I can adequately list here. I would like to express my great appreciation to the universe for facilitating the completion of this text; there was something bigger than myself that made completing this book possible. This text was mostly written on the stolen land traditionally stewarded by the Wampanaog, Nipmunk, Pawtuckett, and Massachusett. I am deeply grateful to Suzanna Walters for her guidance and inclusion of the text in the Intersections series at New York University Press along with my press editor, Ilene Kalish. To my various writing partners, Tope Fadiran, Summer McDonald, Grace Sanders-Johnson, Shalanda Baker, Anima Adjepong, Eunsong Kim (Pom Partner extraordinaire), Shameka Powell, Katie Seitz, Juli Grigsby, Northeastern's Feminist Faculty Writing Group, Northeastern's Women of Color Writing Group, my book accountability group of Chanda Prescod-Weinstein and Natali Valdez, I could not have done this without you. To Ruha Benjamin, Elizabeth Todd-Breland, and Ashon Crawley, I thank you for being academic possibility models who showed me, through both your written work and the way you move through the academy, that we can imagine otherwise. I also extend my sincere thanks to Summer McDonald for her impeccable editing and "mat-talk" when I needed it. The work and camaraderie of my Internet family, Izetta Autumn Mobley, Jessica Marie

Johnson, Danielle Cole, Sydette Harry, Antoinette Luna Myers, Dr. Bianca Laureano, Mai'a Williams, Tourmaline, Trudy, and the late Stacey Park Milbern, were essential for ensuring an ethical and accountable text. And to Demita Frazier, I am so grateful for our connection and your work in the world that made *Misogynoir Transformed* possible.

While this is my first "solo" authored book manuscript, I learned so much about the writing process from my collaboration with Sarah J. Jackson and Brooke Foucault Welles on our co-authored book, *#HashtagActivism: Networks of Race and Gender Justice*. The ethical considerations developed in *#HashtagActivism* were employed here as well. Other collaborators, including Ayana Jamieson, Izetta Autumn Mobley, Whitney Peoples, and T. L. Cowan, among others, have helped me develop the skills and confidence to produce a "single-author" text. The work of graduate students Alanna Prince, Gregory Palermo, Dr. Miguel Montalva, and Devin Gaffney was essential for culling the scholarship that supports the arguments I make in the text. Collaborations with the Black Feminist Health Science Studies Collective have helped keep me energized when the content of this text weighed on me. Similarly, the Critical Race and Digital Studies Collective, #TransformDH community, Dark Room, Octavia E. Butler Legacy Network, Center for Solutions to Online Violence, and the recently formed Black Queer Feminists at the End of the Academy are generous collectives that remind me that there are more people who believe another world is possible.

I offer many thanks to the Allied Media Conference for being an unofficial collaborator on this text in every possible way. I would also like to thank the city of Atlanta and Spelman College for connecting me with the Big Mamas Collective, Queer Fit crew, Charis Books & More, as well as DeLaine Valdez Ferguson, Takkara Brunson, Grace Sanders-Johnson, Sarah Thompson, Golden Dreamsong Collier, Yolo Akili, Whitney Peoples, Taryn Jordan, and Cecilia Becerra, for their sustained friendship through these years. I am equally grateful for the support and kinship of the House of Mati (special shout-out to Jamie Bergeron) in Boston for making life above the forty-second parallel a joy. In particular, I am so glad to count Shameka Powell and Corshai Williams in my life as family. I am grateful for Whitney Peoples, Jalylah Burrell, Golden Dreamsong Collier, Yolo Akili, Amy Herring, and Summer McDonald for being the best of the best. Your friendship and encouragement over the years have been a stable and necessary presence in my life. Finally, I want to express my deep thanks and love to my Mama and Daddy, for whom I completed this effort.

This text is dedicated to my parents but also the Black women and Black nonbinary, agender, and gender-variant folks impacted by misogynoir. It was completed with the generous support of the Northeastern University NULab, College of Social Sciences and Humanities, Lisa Kahaleole Hall, as well as Jackie and Nadine of Easton's Nook Writing Retreats.

NOTES

PREFACE

1 Gilman, "Black Bodies, White Bodies."
2 Carpenter and Bailey, "Interview with Moya Bailey."
3 Bailey, "Guest Post."
4 Reid-Brinkley, "Essence of Res(Ex)Pectability."
5 Woman is perhaps the simplest and easiest way I conceptualize my gender, but it is not at all the most salient or accurate. See the introduction for more.
6 Bailey, "Race, Region, and Gender."
7 Hip hop feminism has a long history that includes Joan Morgan's foundational text, *When Chickenheads Come Home to Roost*. See additionally the pivotal essay by Durham, Cooper, and Morris, "The Stage Hip-Hop Feminism Built."
8 Cooper, Morris, and Boylorn, *Crunk Feminist Collection*.
9 An earlier version of the Crunk Feminists existed on Emory campus and included Black feminist activist Yolande Tomlinson as an organizing member.
10 Bailey, "They Aren't Talking."
11 Bailey and Trudy, "On Misogynoir."

INTRODUCTION

1 Bailey, "They Aren't Talking."
2 Facebook is the digital descendant of the yearbook, initially designed for college students to connect to other students at their school. I address these connections in my dissertation, "Race, Region, and Gender in Early Emory School of Medicine Yearbooks."
3 hooks, *Talking Back*, 14.
4 hooks, *Black Looks*, 4.
5 Collins, *Black Feminist Thought*, 85.
6 Axelsen, "Women as Victims of Medical Experimentation."
7 Foreman et al., "Writing about Slavery."
8 McGuire, *At the Dark End of the Street*.
9 Wallace-Sanders, *Mammy*.
10 Wallace-Sanders, *Mammy*.
11 Huddleston, "'Aunt Jemima' Heirs Sue."
12 Kesslen, "Aunt Jemima to Change Name."
13 Gomez, Shafiei, and Johnson, "Black Women's Involvement"; Hayward, "Ecological Citizenship"; Kwate, "Fried Chicken and Fresh Apples."

14 Strings, *Fearing the Black Body*.

15 Jackson et al., "Effect of Sex, Age and Race"; Kolata, "Why Do Obese Patients Get Worse Care?"; Racette, Deusinger, and Deusinger, "Obesity"; Office of Minority Health, "Obesity and African Americans."

16 Gay, *Hunger*; Sidibe, *This Is Just My Face*.

17 Fontaine, "From Mammy to Madea."

18 Digital blackface is a practice of using avatars of Black people to hide behind to spew racist and otherwise incendiary content and hopefully escape censure. Digital minstrelsy also describes the use of Black characters in video games and GIFs, where non-Black users perform a caricature of Blackness to move through the game or to land a joke. I discuss this further in chapter 1.

19 Burke, "Black Women and the New Magical Negro."

20 Tuchman, "Symbolic Annihilation."

21 Sommers, "Missing White Woman Syndrome"; Demby, "What We Know"; Stillman, "'Missing White Girl Syndrome.'"

22 Craven, "There's a Bigger Story."

23 Baragona, "White House Isn't Recognizing LGBT Pride"; Braidwood, "Munroe Bergdorf Speaks Out."

24 Roberts, *Killing the Black Body*, 92.

25 Lee, *For Freedom's Sake*, 21.

26 Clarke, "Subtle Forms of Sterilization Abuse"; Davis, "Racism, Birth Control and Reproductive Rights"; Volscho, "Sterilization Racism"; Blitzer, "Private Georgia Immigration-Detention Facility."

27 Clampett, *Coal Black and de Sebben Dwarfs*.

28 I use the term "US American" to acknowledge that there are other Americans in North, South, and Central America.

29 Kohler-Hausmann, "'Crime of Survival.'"

30 Albert, "Brett Favre to Repay $1.1 Million"; Harris-Perry, *Sister Citizen*.

31 Gilliam, "'Welfare Queen' Experiment."

32 Harris-Perry, *Sister Citizen*, 114–15.

33 "Moynihan Report."

34 Hirschenbaum, "When CRACK Is the Only Choice."

35 Stroud, "Our Opioid Crisis"; Newkirk, "What the 'Crack Baby' Panic Reveals."

36 Pilkington, "Black Americans Dying of Covid-19."

37 Gabriel, "Ohio Lawmaker Asks Racist Question."

38 Wilkinson and Marmot, *Social Determinants of Health* (World Health Organization, 2003); Marmot and Wilkinson, *Social Determinants of Health* (Oxford University Press, 2005); World Health Organization and Commission on Social Determinants of Health, *Closing the Gap*.

39 Crockett, "'Raving Amazons'"; Laur Jackson, "Memes and Misogynoir."

40 Carlson et al., "Self-Reported Racial/Ethnic Discrimination"; Harris, *Deepest Well*; Cooper-Patrick et al., "Race, Gender, and Partnership"; Boulware et al., "Race and Trust"; Johnson et al., "Patient Race/Ethnicity."

41 Skloot, *Immortal Life of Henrietta Lacks*.

42 Harriet A. Washington, *Medical Apartheid*.

43 Alondra Nelson, *Body and Soul*; Evans, Bell, and Burton, *Black Women's Mental Health*; Roberts, *Killing the Black Body*; Smith, *Sick and Tired*.

44 Roberts, *Fatal Invention*; Alondra Nelson, *Body and Soul*; Harriet A. Washington, *Medical Apartheid*; Imani Perry, *Vexy Thing*; Griffin, *Harlem Nocturne*; Davis, *Women, Race, and Class*; Strings, *Fearing the Black Body*; Hogarth, *Medicalizing Blackness*.

45 Crockett, "'Raving Amazons'"; Laur Jackson, "Memes and Misogynoir."

46 World Health Organization, "Preamble to the Constitution."

47 Quoted in Burns, "Black Women Are Besieged."

48 Sharpe, *In the Wake*.

49 Olayiwola, *Porsha Olayiwola—"Rekia Boyd."*

50 Weathers, "Argument for Black Women's Liberation."

51 Doroshwalther, *Out in the Night*.

52 Doroshwalther, *Out in the Night*.

53 Amuchie, "'Forgotten Victims.'"

54 Weathers, "Argument for Black Women's Liberation."

55 Crenshaw, "Mapping the Margins."

56 Stowe, "Sojourner Truth."

57 Spillers, "Mama's Baby."

58 Higginbotham, *Righteous Discontent*.

59 Tyler Perry, *Why Did I Get Married?*; Tyler Perry, *Daddy's Little Girls*; Tyler Perry, *Temptation*.

60 Bailey, "Why I'm Over Tyler Perry."

61 Transformative justice calls for consequences, not punishment. There are other ways to handle Marcus's violence besides doing nothing (which is what happens in the scene) or allowing Marcus to be arrested by the officer. For more on transformative justice, see Kaba and Hassan, *Fumbling towards Repair*.

62 Simmons, *No!*

63 Parker, *Movement in Black*.

64 Bailey, "Homolatent Masculinity."

65 "Sistagyny" was one I thankfully discarded.

66 Smythe, "Can I Get a Witness?"

67 "Femme" has meant a queer woman who embraces femininity because she enjoys it, not because society says that is the way she is supposed to be. "Femme" has been broadened to be inclusive of people who do not identify as women and debatably, do not identify as queer. In some contexts, "femme" seems to be a substitute for "feminine" in ways that erase its origin in queer lesbian communities.

68 If, as author and anthropologist Zora Neale Hurston wrote, Black women are "de mules of the world," what then are Black nonbinary, agender, and gender-variant folks? Are we the less desirable and rarer-to-find hinny? A mule is the offspring of a male donkey, a jack, mating with a female horse, a mare; a hinny is produced

through the opposite cross, a jenny with a stallion. According to *The Official Horse Breed Standards Guide* (2009), jennies and stallions are highly selective when it comes to mating and their offspring are less likely to make it through gestation, making the particular cross of hinnies rare. Their rarity and their proximity to mules make for an interesting analogy intellectually but one I quickly abandoned because of the way Black women are already imagined as bestial and animalistic, though Zakiyyah Iman Jackson's *Becoming Human: Matter and Meaning in an Antiblack World* raises important inquiries about this simplistic equation. In attempting to make clear the differences and similarities between Black women and Black nonbinary and gender queer folks who are subject to misogynoir, I do not wish to replicate the very abuse I am trying to name. Hurston's declaration makes visible the amount and type of labor Black women do in and for the world that is impossible to translate in a modern era where a hinny is not known for its particular dexterity or tenacity in the face of endless and unjust work to do.

69 The word "variant" recalls the passionate testimony by Hilda Viloria during a San Francisco Human Rights hearing about intersex surgeries in 2004. Viloria refutes the medical community's claim that intersex is abnormal, countering, "It's a variance," one that need not be medicalized, as we do not medicalize the variances of children who are extremely intelligent or beautiful to fit the perceived norm. See the film by Ajae Clearway, *One in 2000*. "Gender expansive" is a new term, but it does not have the same queer valence that "variance" connotes.

70 Bailey and Trudy, "On Misogynoir."

71 Smythe, "Can I Get a Witness?"; Ellison, "Black Femme Praxis"; Ellison et al., "We Got Issues."

72 Noble, *Algorithms of Oppression*.

73 On November 7, 2017, Twitter expanded the limit of characters in a tweet from 140 to 280. The original 140 character limit was set because tweets were initially sent via texts, which had a character limit of 160.

74 Hartman, *Lose Your Mother*.

75 Sobande, *Digital Lives of Black Women in Britain*.

76 The People's Gogo (@GogoMagosha), "Sisters came from Johannesburg," Twitter, November 1, 2019, https://twitter.com/GogoMagosha/status/1190162319860518912; Mwasi-Collectif (@MwasiCollectif), "Merci au collectif," Twitter, November 24, 2019, https://twitter.com/MwasiCollectif/status/1198673311510794243.

77 adrienne maree brown, *Pleasure Activism*.

78 TransformHarm.org, "Transformative Justice."

79 World Health Organization, "Preamble to the Constitution."

80 Collins, *Black Feminist Thought*; hooks, *Black Looks*; Harris-Perry, *Sister Citizen*; Giddings, *When and Where I Enter*; Kuumba, *Gender and Social Movements*; Cooper, *Beyond Respectability*.

81 Cathy J. Cohen, "Punks, Bulldaggers, and Welfare Queens"; Keeling, *Witch's Flight*; Ferguson, *Aberrations in Black*; Holland, *Erotic Life of Racism*.

82 José Muñoz's *Disidentifications* (1999) has such a beautiful cover, but the black-and-white still images inside are not as evocative as Muñoz's own words.

83 Jackson et al., *#HashtagActivism*, 205–6.

84 Browne, *Dark Matters*.

CHAPTER 1. MISOGYNOIR IS A DRAG

1 Park and Yan, "Gorilla Killing."

2 Lee Brown, "Amazon Pulls 'Joe and the Hoe' Election Shirts after Backlash," *New York Post*, August 20, 2020, https://nypost.com.

3 Lexico Dictionaries, s.v. "drag," accessed July 16, 2019, www.lexico.com.

4 Livingston, *Paris Is Burning*.

5 Hall, *Representation*.

6 Ramsey, *Well, That Escalated Quickly*, 26–27.

7 Sorrells, *Shit Black Girls Say*.

8 The Bechdel Test is a measure created in artist Alison Bechdel's comic *Dykes to Watch Out For* that asks whether a film meets the following basic feminist criteria: there are more than two women, the women talk to each other, and they talk to each other about something other than a man.

9 Andrews and Juilliard, *Holy Mackerel*; McLeod, *Original Amos 'n' Andy*.

10 Cole and Guy-Sheftall, *Gender Talk*, xxxiv.

11 Ramsey, *Well, That Escalated Quickly*, 27.

12 Sorrells, *Shit Black Girls Say*.

13 Feder, *Disclosure*.

14 I do not use "male" in this text, as I am speaking to the racial gender identities that people use. "Male" and "female" are contested categories that are not useful in this text. Though we are used to seeing "male" and "female" as descriptors, I invite my readers to challenge this expected formulation for one that is more accurate.

15 Jenkins, "Queering Black Patriarchy," 971.

16 Jenkins, "Queering Black Patriarchy," 973.

17 Lyle, "'Check with Yo' Man,'" 948.

18 Peoples, "(Re)Mediating Black Womanhood," 151.

19 Blameitonkway, YouTube channel, accessed May 16, 2019, https://www.youtube.com/channel/UCt42rXiddaMx0QSVHNnEkFQ.

20 *TiTi Do You Love Me*.

21 Willis, "'And Still We Rise.'"

22 *Jay Versace—On & On (Triller)*; Church Stars, *NOT KARLTON BANKS*.

23 Joanne the Scammer is another of these characters/caricatures that has gone on to have a significant cultural imprint. Played by Branden Miller, Joanne the Scammer is a character who lies about her race (she is light-skinned and tries to pass as white) and class position (she breaks into palatial homes and pretends to live there), all the while trying to deceive and scam her way into the lifestyle she purports to have. The character even hosted red carpet interviews for the 2016 MTV Video Music Awards.

24 "Cishet" is shorthand for "cis heterosexual."

25 Nissen, "Lena Waithe on Jason Mitchell Allegations."

26 Lane-Steele, "Studs and Protest-Hypermasculinity."

27 Bailey, "Homolatent Masculinity."

28 *Syd of OFWGKTA.*

29 In 2019 Lena Waithe was embroiled in a controversy regarding when she knew that Jason Mitchell, an actor on her series *The Chi,* was inappropriate with two Black women co-stars. Waithe was accused of not acting swiftly and not firing Mitchell, even though firing him was not in her power to do. For more, see Jasmine Washington, "Lena Waithe Says She Talked to Jason Mitchell."

30 Riley, "Tyler Perry on Saying Goodbye."

31 Madeline Berg, "From 'Poor as Hell' to Billionaire: How Tyler Perry Changed Show Business Forever," *Forbes,* September 1, 2020, www.forbes.com; Katie Burkholder, "Tyler Perry's Atlanta Studio to House Homeless LGBTQ Youth," *Georgia Voice: Gay & LGBT Atlanta News,* October 9, 2019, https://thegavoice.com.

32 According to Twitter, "Trends are determined by an algorithm and, by default, are tailored for you based on who you follow, your interests, and your location." When a hashtag or topic "trends," it is visible to users in the Twitter interface, making it easier to find and alerting you to activity you might otherwise miss.

33 Evolve Media House (@EvolveAndGo), "'@RyanGucciThomas: I don't participate,'" Twitter, July 21, 2014, https://twitter.com/EvolveAndGo/status/491389345354358785.

34 suzzie (@gabrielleSTORM_), "#ruinablackgirlsmonday wtf is this?," Twitter, July 21, 2014, https://twitter.com/gabrielleSTORM_/status/491366916507045888.

35 liz (@emptysovl), "Looks at the #ruinablackgirlsmonday trending topic," Twitter, July 21, 2014, https://twitter.com/emptysovl/status/491381726963175426.

36 michiko (@trillosophy), "#ruinablackgirlsmonday ?? Why would you disrespect a black woman," Twitter, July 21, 2014, https://twitter.com/trillosophy/status/491402359151423488.

37 Bailey, "#RuinABlackGirlsMonday Twitter Data."

38 Bailey, "#RuinABlackGirlsMonday Twitter Data."

39 Bailey, "#RuinABlackGirlsMonday Twitter Data."

40 Bailey, "#RuinABlackGirlsMonday Twitter Data."

41 Bailey, "#RuinABlackGirlsMonday Twitter Data."

42 Bailey, "#RuinABlackGirlsMonday Twitter Data."

43 Nett, "For Trans Women"; Lucas, "Illegal Butt Injections."

44 Klostermann, Profile.

45 Brooks, *COPS CRASH POOL PARTY.*

46 Brooks, *COPS CRASH POOL PARTY.*

47 Kennedra, "Meet the Teen."

48 Moye, "Black Texas Teenager."

49 Wiltse, "Black–White Swimming Disparity."

50 Jarvie, "Girl Thrown from Desk."

51 Blad, "She Recorded Her Classmate's Arrest."
52 Blad, "She Recorded Her Classmate's Arrest."
53 *Police Officer Slams S.C. High School Student.*
54 *Police Officer Slams S.C. High School Student.*
55 Zaveri, "Florida Deputy Charged."
56 Eligon, "A Black Officer, a White Woman."
57 Blad, "She Recorded Her Classmate's Arrest."
58 Blad, "She Recorded Her Classmate's Arrest."
59 Weathers, "Argument for Black Women's Liberation."
60 Helm, "Ex-SC Cop."
61 Robinson, "Black Lives Matter Is Still Here."
62 Morris, *Pushout*, 12.
63 Epstein, Blake, and Gonzalez, "Girlhood Interrupted."
64 Blake and Epstein, "Listening to Black Women and Girls."
65 Blake and Epstein, "Listening to Black Women and Girls."
66 Viglione, Hannon, and DeFina, "Impact of Light Skin."
67 Blake and Epstein, "Listening to Black Women and Girls," 7.
68 Blake and Epstein, "Listening to Black Women and Girls," 9.
69 Blake and Epstein, "Listening to Black Women and Girls," 6.
70 Jacobs, "Texas Jury Awards $68,000."
71 Jacobs, "Texas Jury Awards $68,000."
72 Jacobs, "Texas Jury Awards $68,000."
73 Jacobs, "Texas Jury Awards $68,000."
74 Combahee River Collective, *Combahee River Collective Statement.*

CHAPTER 2. TRANSFORMING MISOGYNOIR THROUGH TRANS ADVOCACY

 1 The book was initially titled *Fish Food*, but Mock opted to change the name because she worried that mainstream audiences wouldn't understand "fish" and misinterpret it as only a misogynistic way of referencing cis women.
 2 *Conversation with Janet Mock.*
 3 Butler, *Gender Trouble.*
 4 Big Think, *Judith Butler.*
 5 Mock, *Redefining Realness*, 116.
 6 Budson, "CDC," 5.
 7 Talusan, "Unerased."
 8 Mock, *Redefining Realness*, 172.
 9 Bolles, "Janet Mock."
10 Dunye, *Watermelon Woman*; Simmons, *No!*; Lorde, *Zami*; Jordan, *Soldier.*
11 Mey, "Flawless Trans Women."
12 McIntyre, "How Janet Jackson's Super Bowl."
13 Larson, "Welcome to a World."
14 Trudy, "Explanation of Misogynoir."

15 Janet Mock (@janetmock), "Please sign & share," Twitter, March 27, 2012, https://twitter.com/janetmock/status/184606253136347136.

16 Benoit, "Image Repair"; Barbaro and Twohey, "Crossing the Line"; Claire Cohen, "Donald Trump Sexism Tracker"; Libby Nelson, "Donald Trump's History"; Stuart, "Timeline"; John Walsh, "11 Insults."

17 Fisher, "Pageant Politic."

18 Feder, *Disclosure*.

19 Mock, "My Journey (So Far)."

20 This research is indebted to this repository and would not be possible to conduct currently, as Twitter has limited researchers' ability to collect large quantities of tweets.

21 Estes, *I Am a Man!*

22 "Trans women of color" is not and should not be read as a synonym for "Black trans women." However, some of the Twitter users I highlight seem to have this practice.

23 "Help Support Egyptt!"

24 National LGBTQ Task Force, "Injustice at Every Turn."

25 Bailey, "#GirlsLikeUs Twitter Data."

26 *MAJOR!*

27 The user changed her name and is now @tourmaliiine.

28 Cecilia Chung (smallglimpses), "See you next time," Instagram, June 15, 2013, https://www.instagram.com/p/alM6KjmJpy/. The Philly Trans Health Conference changed its name to the Philly Trans Wellness Conference but continues to use the same hashtag.

29 Cisnormativity (@cisnormativity), "Criminalizing the body," Twitter, April 30, 2013, https://twitter.com/cisnormativity/status/329262733499461633.

30 Janet Mock (@janetmock), "@Lavernecox Love you, Laverne," Twitter, June 27, 2013, https://twitter.com/janetmock/status/350343716499763200.

31 Riggs, *Tongues Untied*; Laverne Cox (@LaverneCox), "@ddirty531 @Splash_T thanks for the love," Twitter, October 29, 2013, https://twitter.com/Lavernecox/status/395193341962248192.

32 Allen, "Transgender Woman's Murder."

33 National Coalition of Anti-Violence Programs, *Lesbian, Gay, Bisexual, Transgender, Queer, and HIV-Affected Intimate Partner Violence*.

34 Laverne Cox (@LaverneCox), "For those trans women," Twitter, December 23, 2012, https://twitter.com/Lavernecox/status/282924209443848192.

35 Human Rights Campaign, "Dismantling a Culture of Violence," 19.

36 ChannelRichard, *For CeCe*.

37 Gossett, Stanley, and Burton, *Trap Door*.

38 Feder, *Disclosure*.

39 Gamson, *Freaks Talk Back*.

40 Janet Mock (@janetmock), "MT @allan_macdonell guess who used 'Mrs. Doubtfire,'" Twitter, January 15, 2013, https://twitter.com/janetmock/status/291288896447336449.

41 Fleischer, "Guess Who Used 'Mrs. Doubtfire.'"

42 National LGBTQ Task Force, "New Analysis."

43 Michaelson, "Media Ignores Rash of Assaults."

44 Janet Mock (@janetmock), ".@thedailybeast challenges media," Twitter, June 6, 2012, https://twitter.com/janetmock/status/210332514038984707.

45 Michaelson, "Media Ignores Rash of Assaults."

46 Michaelson, "Media Ignores Rash of Assaults."

47 Bailey, "#GirlsLikeUs Twitter Data."

48 Out2Enroll, "Plan Information for 2019."

49 Cecilia Chung (@cecilia_c_chung), "We want trans-competent health care," Twitter, July 19, 2014, https://twitter.com/cecilia_c_chung/status/490648267005255680.

50 *TEDMED Great Challenges.*

51 Raun, "DIY Therapy."

52 Bailey, "#GirlsLikeUs Twitter Data."

53 Bailey, "#GirlsLikeUs Twitter Data."

54 Bailey, "#GirlsLikeUs Twitter Data."

55 Fenway Health, "New Policy Brief."

56 Newbury, "Open Letter."

57 Fenway Health, "New Policy Brief."

58 Laungani and Brassard, "Gender Confirmation Surgery."

59 Seelman et al., "Transgender Noninclusive Healthcare."

60 Janet Mock (@janetmock), "Stop obsessing over our bodies," Twitter, October 9, 2012, https://twitter.com/janetmock/status/255707729010757632.

61 Laura J. Nelson, "As Demand for Illegal Silicone Injections Grows."

62 Baker and Schweber, "Woman in Group of Transgender Performers Dies."

63 Monica Roberts (@TransGriot), "#Girlslikeus rock," Twitter, March 28, 2013, https://twitter.com/TransGriot/status/317319118141399042.

64 Abby Louise Jensen (@Arizona_Abby), "So many tears," Twitter, August 10, 2012, https://twitter.com/Arizona_Abby/status/233929818922680322.

65 Bailey, "#GirlsLikeUs Twitter Data."

66 Bailey, "#GirlsLikeUs Twitter Data."

67 Bailey, "#GirlsLikeUs Twitter Data."

68 Mannix, "CeCe McDonald Murder Trial."

69 UC San Diego Center on Gender Equity and Health, "Measuring #MeToo."

70 Bailey, "On Appropriate Victims."

71 Mannix, "CeCe McDonald Murder Trial."

72 ChannelRichard, *For CeCe.*

73 Goldman, "Transgender Activist."

74 McDonald, "Pursuit of Happiness."

75 McDonald, "Pursuit of Happiness."

76 McDonald, "Pursuit of Happiness."

77 McDonald, "January 8, 2013."

78 McDonald, "Help Find Sage Smith!"

79 McDonald, "Support Estrellita!"

80 McDonald, "Drama from the DOC."

81 McDonald, "Drama from the DOC."

82 adrienne maree brown, *Emergent Strategy*.

83 "What CeCe's Reading."

84 Despite its corporate-driven disappointing ending arc, *The Hunger Games* trilogy provides a window into the horrors of a not-so-distant dystopia where the poor are subject to the whims of the rich.

85 Stanley and Smith, *Captive Genders*.

86 Janet Mock (@janetmock), "We can't bring Paige back," Twitter, April 22, 2012, https://twitter.com/janetmock/status/194071841508306944.

87 Paul Walsh, "Graffiti Backing 'CeCe.'"

88 Solomon, "CeCe McDonald."

89 Hill, "Why Aren't We Fighting."

90 Brock, "MSNBC's Melissa Harris-Perry."

91 Fischer, "#Free_CeCe."

92 Open Society Foundations, Soros Justice Fellowships listing for CeCe McDonald, accessed October 12, 2019, www.opensocietyfoundations.org.

93 Donnelly, "Janet Mock Signs."

CHAPTER 3. WEB SHOW WORLDBUILDING MITIGATES MISOGYNOIR

1 Issa Rae, *Misadventures of Awkward Black Girl*.

2 Johnson, *Lovers and Friends*.

3 Day and Christian, "Locating Black Queer TV."

4 Crawley, "Otherwise Movements."

5 French and Bailey, "'Skye's the Limit' Web Series."

6 Gilbert, *Eat, Pray, Love*.

7 *The Watermelon Woman* (1996), *Set it Off* (1996), *Pariah* (2011), *Stud Life* (2012), and *Rafiki* (2018) are five films that feature a Black masculine lesbian as a central character. Similarly, Snoop on *The Wire* (2002–2008), Samira Wiley's characters on *Orange Is the New Black* (2013–2019) and *Handmaid's Tale* (2017–present), Lena Waithe's *Master of None* (2015–2018) character Denise, and newcomer Bre-Z on *Empire* (2015–present) and *All American* (2018–present) account for the handful of Black queer masculine representation on television.

8 As bisexual activists have articulated, "bi" does not mean being attracted to men and women; rather, it means being attracted to more than one gender.

9 Onyejiaka, "Why Is TV So Afraid."

10 And then, in the tradition of the "dead lesbian syndrome" that afflicts these characters in film and television, one of the characters was killed off. For more on this trope, see Millward, Dodd, and Fubara-Manuel, *Killing Off the Lesbians*.

11 *Twenties*.

12 Telusma, *Skye's the Limit*, ep. 8, "Feasting on Scraps."

13 Black Emotional and Mental Health Collective, "What We Believe."

14 National Coalition Against Domestic Violence, "Domestic Violence."
15 Messinger, *LGBTQ Intimate Partner Violence*, 138.
16 Shange, "Play Aunties and Dyke Bitches."
17 Telusma, *Skye's the Limit*, season 1 finale, "Bienvenidos a Miami!"
18 In order to monetize viewing, the creators moved the show to their own sponsored platform. Viewers may now subscribe to see the series' three seasons and other Black queer web shows. Unfortunately, as a result of the move, YouTube viewing and comment data are no longer available.
19 French and Bailey, "'Skye's the Limit' Web Series."
20 Chisolm, "LGBTQ+ People of Color."
21 Day, "Between Butch/Femme."
22 Shange, "Play Aunties and Dyke Bitches."
23 Onuorah, *Same Difference*.
24 Warith, *Choiices*.
25 Daniel, *Between Women*.
26 Kasperkevic, "Private Violence."
27 Gomez, "Representations of Black Lesbians."
28 Auter and Davis, "When Characters Speak."
29 Farah, "Checking In."
30 "Crazy" is uninterrogated in this series, which speaks to the ubiquity of ableism and disability justice's nascent penetration into some leftist enclaves. For more on Black people's relationship to the word "crazy," please see Bailey and Mobley, "Work in the Intersections."
31 Fethers et al., "Sexually Transmitted Infections"; Muzny et al., "Sexual Partnership Characteristics."
32 Roy, "Must Reads"; Wise and Wakeam, "Millennials Are Leaving"; Samuel, "Witches of Baltimore."
33 Gorgos and Marrazzo, "Sexually Transmitted Infections."
34 While never overtly stated, Chris's arrival in Brooklyn from Dallas seems to have been precipitated by a bad breakup that at least involved unwanted and insistent texts and calls, alluding to a more serious lack of respect for her boundaries that is consistent with those who cause abusive harm.
35 Keeling, "'Ghetto Heaven,'" 37.

CHAPTER 4. ALCHEMISTS IN ACTION AGAINST MISOGYNOIR
1 Emergency Salsa, "Know Your Meme."
2 Fox, "Yahoo to Buy Tumblr"; Liao, "After the Porn Ban"; Alexander, "Verizon Is Selling Tumblr."
3 McCracken et al., *Tumblr Book*.
4 Trân, "Calling IN."
5 Allied Media Conference, "About the AMC."
6 Danielle uses both "she" and "they" pronouns. I alternate between sentences as is their preference.

7   I curated the CFC Tumblr blog from 2011 to 2013.

8   Cole, "On Your Time on Tumblr."

9   Cole, "On Your Time on Tumblr."

10 Hull, Bell-Scott, and Smith, *All the Women Are White*; Rose, *Longing to Tell.*

11 Cole, "On Your Time on Tumblr."

12 Jackson et al., *#HashtagActivism.*

13 Cole, "On Your Time on Tumblr."

14 I elected not to put the comments in the text because they need not be repeated for you, dear reader, to know what they said. Please see my comments in the introduction regarding not including visual images in this text.

15 Cole, "On Your Time on Tumblr."

16 Manne, *Down Girl*; Poland, *Haters.*

17 Cole, "On Your Time on Tumblr."

18 Jackson et al., *#HashtagActivism.*

19 Cole, "On Your Time on Tumblr."

20 Cole, "On Your Time on Tumblr."

21 National Center for Education Statistics, "Degrees Conferred."

22 Sonia Thompson, "Despite Being the Most Educated."

23 Cole, "On Your Time on Tumblr."

24 Zhang, "After Aunt Jemima"; García-Hodges and Sottile, "Walmart Will Stop"; Hou, "Sephora Is Making a Big Move."

25 Cole, "On Your Time on Tumblr."

26 TransformHarm.org, "Transformative Justice."

27 Cole, "On Your Time on Tumblr."

28 Costanza-Chock, *Design Justice.*

29 Cole, "On Your Time on Tumblr."

30 Cole, "On Your Time on Tumblr."

31 Hine and Wittenstein, "Female Slave Resistance."

32 Camp, "Pleasures of Resistance."

33 Jones, *Known World.*

34 Cole's framing is astonishingly prescient given the murder of George Floyd on May 25, 2020, by Minneapolis police officer Derek Chauvin, who held his knee to Floyd's neck as Floyd cried, "I can't breathe!"

35 Robertson, "Study."

36 Abbey-Lambertz, "How the Eviction Epidemic Is Trapping Black Women."

37 Parham and Hicks, "Racial Disparities," 941.

38 Anachebe and Sutton, "Racial Disparities."

39 American College of Obstetricians and Gynecologists, "ACOG Committee Opinion."

40 Myers, "On Your Time on Tumblr."

41 Like Cole, Myers uses the pronouns "she" and "they" interchangeably, so I will alternate my use of them in the text.

42 Myers, "On Your Time on Tumblr."

43 There are a few screen grabs on the Internet Archive Wayback Machine.

44 Myers, "On Your Time on Tumblr."

45 Internet Archive Wayback Machine, June 1, 2012, https://web.archive.org/web/20120601000000*/twitter.com/gzlegalcase.

46 Axelsen, "Women as Victims of Medical Experimentation."

47 Dionne, "What No One Tells Black Women."

48 Martinez and Law, "Two Recent Murders."

49 Myers, "On Your Time on Tumblr."

50 Myers, "On Your Time on Tumblr."

51 Myers, "On Your Time on Tumblr."

52 Myers, "On Your Time on Tumblr."

53 Myers, "On Your Time on Tumblr."

54 Angus, "Why @EmoBlackThot's Identity Reveal"; Wheeler, "He Pretended."

55 Lauren Michele Jackson, "We Need to Talk"; Wanna Thompson, "How White Women on Instagram Are Profiting."

56 Statista, "Tumblr."

57 Myers, "On Your Time on Tumblr."

58 Myers, "On Your Time on Tumblr."

59 Myers, "On Your Time on Tumblr."

60 SPEAK! Women of Color Media Collective, contributors list, March 19, 2009, https://speakmedia.wordpress.com.

61 Myers, "On Your Time on Tumblr."

62 Bailey and Cowan, "Research Ethics."

63 Myers, "On Your Time on Tumblr."

64 Crawley, "Otherwise Movements."

65 Myers, "On Your Time on Tumblr."

66 Lorde, "Master's Tools."

CONCLUSION

1 Sanders-Johnson, "A Good Drag?"

2 Trân, "Calling IN."

3 Broderick, "Here's How a Fake Feminist Hashtag."

4 Laur Jackson, "Memes and Misogynoir."

5 Hampton, "Years Ago."

6 Roose, "Russian Trolls."

7 #EndFathersDay reemerges every year since it was created, but references to #YourSlipIsShowing have effectively prevented the hashtag from trending again.

8 Popularly memed dialogue from the 2004 teen comedy film Mean Girls.

9 Sanusi, "This Teen's Twitter Account."

10 Love, Hip Hop's Li'l Sistas Speak; Ruth Nicole Brown, Hear Our Truths.

11 Combahee River Collective, Combahee River Collective Statement.

12 Kelley, Freedom Dreams; Boggs and Kurashige, Next American Revolution.

13 Richardson, Bearing Witness While Black.

14 Wootson, "Black Yale Student."

15 Levin, "California Woman."

16 Weber and Silber, "Sandra Bland's Own Video."

17 Lewis, "Four Years Later."

18 See, for example, African American Policy Forum, "#SayHerName."

19 Wells, "Members of LGBT Community."

20 Cathy Cohen, "Death and Rebirth of a Movement."

21 Lang, "How the 'Karen Meme.'"

22 Piercy, *Woman on the Edge of Time.*

23 Walker, *We Are the Ones.*

24 Santana, "Mais Viva!"

25 Davis, *Abolition Democracy*; Lindsey, "Negro Women May Be Dangerous"; Kaba and Hassan, *Fumbling towards Repair*; Kaba, "Transformative Justice"; Gilmore, *Change Everything.*

26 Benjamin, *Race after Technology*; Gray and Sarkeesian, *Intersectional Tech*; Alondra Nelson, "Social Life of DNA."

27 Hersey, "About."

28 Jewel the Gem, video, Instagram, June 30, 2020, https://www.instagram.com/tv/CCFJuP4lOaf/?utm_source=ig_web_copy_link.

29 Jewel the Gem, video, Instagram, June 30, 2020.

30 Kaba and Hassan, *Fumbling towards Repair.*

BIBLIOGRAPHY

Abbey-Lambertz, Kate. "How the Eviction Epidemic Is Trapping Black Women in Poverty." *HuffPost*, March 17, 2016, www.huffpost.com.

African American Policy Forum. "#SayHerName: Toward a Gendered Analysis of Racialized State Violence" webinar, March 30, 2015. www.aapf.org.

Albert, Victoria. "Brett Favre to Repay $1.1 Million in Federal Welfare Funds after Mississippi Spending Scandal." *CBS News*, May 7, 2020. www.cbsnews.com.

Alexander, Julia. "Verizon Is Selling Tumblr to WordPress' Owner." *Verge*, August 12, 2019. www.theverge.com.

Allen, Karma. "Transgender Woman's Murder Underscores Problem of Partner Violence Plaguing Community, Advocates Say." *ABC News*, September 13, 2019. https://abcnews.go.com.

Allied Media Conference. "About the AMC." October 30, 2019. https://amc.alliedmedia.org.

American College of Obstetricians and Gynecologists. "ACOG Committee Opinion Number 317, October 2005. Racial and Ethnic Disparities in Women's Health." *Obstetrics and Gynecology* 106 (October 2005): 889–92.

Amuchie, Nnennaya. "'The Forgotten Victims' How Racialized Gender Stereotypes Lead to Police Violence against Black Women and Girls: Incorporating an Analysis of Police Violence into Feminist Jurisprudence and Community Activism." *Seattle Journal for Social Justice* 14 (Spring 2016): 617.

Anachebe, N. F., and M. Y. Sutton. "Racial Disparities in Reproductive Health Outcomes." *American Journal of Obstetrics and Gynecology* 188 (April 2003): S37–42.

Andrews, Bart, and Ahrgus Juilliard. *Holy Mackerel! The Amos 'n' Andy Story*. New York: Dutton, 1986.

Angus, Haaniyah. "Why @EmoBlackThot's Identity Reveal Hurt Black Women So Much." *Paper*, October 16, 2019. www.papermag.com.

Auter, Philip J., and Donald M. Davis. "When Characters Speak Directly to Viewers: Breaking the Fourth Wall in Television." *Journalism Quarterly* 68, nos. 1–2 (1991): 165–71. https://doi.org/10.1177/107769909106800117.

Axelsen, Diana E. "Women as Victims of Medical Experimentation: J. Marion Sims' Surgery on Slave Women, 1845–1850." *Sage* (Atlanta, GA) 2, no. 2 (1985): 10–13.

Bailey, Moya. "#GirlsLikeUs Twitter Data." Northeastern University, 2014.

———. "Guest Post: 'An Open Letter to Nelly.'" *Black Youth Project* (blog), November 14, 2013. http://blackyouthproject.com.

———. "Homolatent Masculinity and Hip Hop Culture." *Palimpsest: A Journal on Women, Gender, and the Black International* 2, no. 2 (2013): 187–99.

———. "On Appropriate Victims: More on Trayvon Martin and Other Names You Need to Know." *Crunk Feminist Collective* (blog), March 26, 2012. www.crunk feministcollective.com.

———. "Race, Region, and Gender in Early Emory School of Medicine Yearbooks." PhD dissertation, Emory University, 2013.

———. "#RuinABlackGirlsMonday Twitter Data." Northeastern University, 2014.

———. "They Aren't Talking about Me. . . ." *Crunk Feminist Collective* (blog), March 14, 2010. www.crunkfeministcollective.com.

———. "Why I'm Over Tyler Perry." *Emory Report*, June 23, 2008. www.emory.edu.

Bailey, Moya, and T. L. Cowan. "Research Ethics for Students and Teachers: Social Media in the Classroom." Center for Solutions to Online Violence, January 1, 2016. http://femtechnet.org.

Bailey, Moya, and Izetta Autumn Mobley. "Work in the Intersections: A Black Feminist Disability Framework." *Gender and Society* 33, no. 1 (February 2019): 19–40. https://doi.org/10.1177/0891243218801523.

Bailey, Moya, and Trudy. "On Misogynoir: Citation, Erasure, and Plagiarism." *Feminist Media Studies* 18, no. 4 (2018): 1–7. https://doi.org/10.1080/14680777.2018.1447 395.

Baker, Al, and Nate Schweber. "Woman in Group of Transgender Performers Dies in Brooklyn Fire." *New York Times*, May 12, 2012. www.nytimes.com.

Baragona, Louis. "The White House Isn't Recognizing LGBT Pride Month for the Second Year in a Row—And It Sets a Dangerous Precedent." *Insider*, June 8, 2018. www.thisisinsider.com.

Barbaro, Michael, and Megan Twohey. "Crossing the Line: How Donald Trump Behaved with Women in Private." *New York Times*, May 14, 2016. www.nytimes.com.

Benjamin, Ruha. *Race after Technology: Abolitionist Tools for the New Jim Code.* Medford, MA: Polity, 2019.

Benoit, William. "Image Repair on the Donald Trump 'Access Hollywood' Video: 'Grab Them by the P*ssy.'" *Communication Studies* 68, no. 3 (2017): 243–59. https://doi.org /10.1080/10510974.2017.1331250.

Big Think. *Judith Butler: Your Behavior Creates Your Gender.* YouTube, 2011. https:// www.youtube.com/watch?v=Bo702LYATDc&t=3s.

Black Emotional and Mental Health Collective. "What We Believe." 2017. www.beam. community.

Blad, Evie. "She Recorded Her Classmate's Arrest, Then Got Arrested, Too." *Education Week*, January 25, 2017. www.edweek.org.

Blake, Jamilia, and Rebecca Epstein. "Listening to Black Women and Girls: Lived Experiences of Adultification Bias." Georgetown Law Center on Poverty and Inequality, May 15, 2019. www.law.georgetown.edu.

Blitzer, Jonathan. "The Private Georgia Immigration-Detention Facility at the Center of a Whistle-Blower's Complaint." *New Yorker*, September 19, 2020.

Boggs, Grace Lee, and Scott Kurashige. *The Next American Revolution: Sustainable Activism for the Twenty-First Century*. Berkeley: University of California Press, 2012.

Bolles, Alexandra. "Janet Mock Becomes New York Times Best Selling Author with Redefining Realness." *GLAAD.org* (blog), February 13, 2014. www.glaad.org.

Boulware, L. Ebony, Lisa A. Cooper, Lloyd E. Ratner, Thomas A. LaVeist, and Neil R. Powe. "Race and Trust in the Health Care System." *Public Health Reports*, 2016.

Braidwood, Ella. "Munroe Bergdorf Speaks Out for Black Trans Women: 'Statistically I Only Have Four Years Left to Live.'" *PinkNews*, June 7, 2018. www.pinknews.co.uk.

Brock, Marcus. "MSNBC's Melissa Harris-Perry Covers Stop and Frisk & CeCe McDonald." *GLAAD.org* (blog), June 11, 2012. www.glaad.org.

Broderick, Ryan. "Here's How a Fake Feminist Hashtag Like #EndFathersDay Gets Started and Why It'll Keep Happening." *BuzzFeed News*, June 16, 2014. www.buzzfeednews.com.

Brooks, Brandon. *COPS CRASH POOL PARTY*. YouTube, June 6, 2015. https://www.youtube.com/watch?v=R46-XTqXkzE.

brown, adrienne maree. *Emergent Strategy: Shaping Change, Changing Worlds*. Reprint, Chico, CA: AK Press, 2017.

———. *Pleasure Activism: The Politics of Feeling Good*. Chico, CA: AK Press, 2019.

Brown, Ruth Nicole. *Hear Our Truths: The Creative Potential of Black Girlhood*. Urbana: University of Illinois Press, 2013.

Browne, Simone. *Dark Matters: On the Surveillance of Blackness*. Durham: Duke University Press, 2015.

Budson, Sarah. "CDC: Black Women Have Highest Homicide Rate." *News 5 Cleveland*, August 11, 2017. www.news5cleveland.com.

Burke, Chesya. "Black Women and the New Magical Negro." In *African American Cinema through Black Lives Consciousness*, edited by Mark A. Reid. Detroit: Wayne State University Press, 2019.

Burns, Janet. "Black Women Are Besieged on Social Media, and White Apathy Damns Us All." *Forbes*, December 27, 2017. www.forbes.com.

Butler, Judith. *Gender Trouble*. Tenth anniversary ed. New York: Routledge, 1999.

Camp, Stephanie M. H. "The Pleasures of Resistance: Enslaved Women and Body Politics in the Plantation South, 1830–1861." *Journal of Southern History* 68, no. 3 (2002): 533–72. https://doi.org/10.2307/3070158.

Carlson, Sonia, Luisa N. Borrell, Celeste Eng, Myngoc Nguyen, Shannon Thyne, Michael A. LeNoir, Nadine Burke-Harris, Esteban G. Burchard, and Neeta Thakur. "Self-Reported Racial/Ethnic Discrimination and Bronchodilator Response in African American Youth with Asthma." *PloS One* 12, no. 6 (2017).

Carpenter, Faedra Chatard, and Moya Bailey. "An Interview with Moya Bailey." *Callaloo* 29, no. 3 (2006): 753–60. https://doi.org/10.1353/cal.2006.0132.

ChannelRichard. *For CeCe*. YouTube, January 19, 2014. https://www.youtube.com/watch?v=oMoL17MVP9c&t=2s.

Chisolm, N. Jamiyla. "LGBTQ+ People of Color More Likely to Live in Poverty Than Whites." *Colorlines*, October 23, 2019. www.colorlines.com.

Church Stars. *NOT KARLTON BANKS* | *"WHEN THEY SERVE FOOD AFTER THE CHURCH ANNIVERSARY."* YouTube, December 5, 2016. https://www.youtube.com/watch?v=tnPi5y_Z3Zo.

Clampett, Bob, dir. *Coal Black and de Sebben Dwarfs*. Animation. Los Angeles: Warner Brothers, 1943.

Clarke, Adele. "Subtle Forms of Sterilization Abuse: A Reproductive Rights Analysis." In *Test-Tube Women: What Future for Motherhood?*, edited by Rita Arditti et al., 188–212. London: Pandora, 1984.

Clearway, Ajae. *One in 2000: A Documentary on the Lives of Intersex People*. University of Texas, 2006.

Cohen, Cathy J. "Death and Rebirth of a Movement: Queering Critical Ethnic Studies." *Social Justice* 37, no. 4 (2010–2011): 126–32.

———. "Punks, Bulldaggers, and Welfare Queens: The Radical Potential of Queer Politics?" *GLQ: A Journal of Lesbian and Gay Studies* 3, no. 4 (May 1997): 437–65. https://doi.org/10.1215/10642684-3-4-437.

Cohen, Claire. "Donald Trump Sexism Tracker: Every Offensive Comment in One Place." *Telegraph*, June 4, 2016. www.telegraph.co.uk.

Cole, Danielle. "On Your Time on Tumblr." Interview by Moya Bailey, July 30, 2019.

Cole, Johnnetta B., and Beverly Guy-Sheftall. *Gender Talk: The Struggle for Women's Equality in African American Communities*. New York: Ballantine, 2003.

Collins, Patricia Hill. *Black Feminist Thought: Knowledge, Consciousness, and the Politics of Empowerment*. London: Routledge, 2000.

Combahee River Collective. *The Combahee River Collective Statement: Black Feminist Organizing in the Seventies and Eighties*. New York: Kitchen Table: Women of Color Press, 1986.

Cooper, Brittney C. *Beyond Respectability: The Intellectual Thought of Race Women*. Urbana: University of Illinois Press, 2017.

Cooper, Brittney C., Susana M. Morris, and Robin M. Boylorn, eds. *The Crunk Feminist Collection*. New York: Feminist Press, 2017.

Cooper-Patrick, Lisa, Joseph J. Gallo, Junius J. Gonzales, Hong Thi Vu, Neil R. Powe, Christine Nelson, and Daniel E. Ford. "Race, Gender, and Partnership in the Patient-Physician Relationship." *JAMA* 282, no. 6 (1999): 583–89.

Costanza-Chock, Sasha. *Design Justice: Community-Led Practices to Build the Worlds We Need*. Cambridge: MIT Press, 2020.

Craven, Julia. "There's a Bigger Story behind the Viral Tweets about Missing Black and Latinx Teens in DC." *Huffington Post*, March 17, 2017. www.huffingtonpost.com.

Crawley, Ashon. "Otherwise Movements." *New Inquiry* 19 (2015).

Crenshaw, Kimberlé. "Mapping the Margins: Intersectionality, Identity Politics, and Violence against Women of Color." *Stanford Law Review* 43, no. 6 (1991): 1241–99.

Crockett, I'Nasah. "'Raving Amazons': Antiblackness and Misogynoir in Social Media." *Model View Culture*, June 30, 2014. http://modelviewculture.com.

Daniel, Michelle A. *Between Women*. 2011. www.betweenwomentv.com.

Davis, Angela Y. *Abolition Democracy: Beyond Empire, Prisons, and Torture.* New York: Seven Stories, 2005.

———. "Racism, Birth Control and Reproductive Rights." In *Feminist Postcolonial Theory: A Reader,* edited by Reina Lewis and Sara Mills, 353–67. New York: Routledge, 2003.

———. *Women, Race, and Class.* New York: Vintage, 1983.

Day, Faithe. "Between Butch/Femme: On the Performance of Race, Gender, and Sexuality in a YouTube Web Series." *Journal of Lesbian Studies* 22, no. 3 (2018): 1–15. https://doi.org/10.1080/10894160.2018.1383800.

Day, Faithe, and Aymar Jean Christian. "Locating Black Queer TV: Fans, Producers, and Networked Publics on YouTube." *Transformative Works and Cultures* 24 (2017). https://doi.org/10.3983/twc.2017.0867.

Demby, Gene. "What We Know (And Don't Know) about 'Missing White Women Syndrome.'" *NPR,* April 13, 2017. www.npr.org.

Dionne, Evette. "What No One Tells Black Women about Fibroids." *Zora,* January 31, 2020. https://zora.medium.com.

Donnelly, Matt. "Janet Mock Signs Landmark Overall Netflix Deal." *Variety,* June 19, 2019. https://variety.com.

Doroshwalther, Blair. *Out in the Night.* Documentary. 2014.

Dunye, Cheryl. *The Watermelon Woman.* 1996.

Durham, Aisha, Brittney C. Cooper, and Susana M. Morris. "The Stage Hip-Hop Feminism Built: A New Directions Essay." *Signs* 38, no. 3 (2013): 721–37.

Eligon, John. "A Black Officer, a White Woman, a Rare Murder Conviction: Is It 'Hypocrisy,' or Justice?" *New York Times,* May 3, 2019. www.nytimes.com.

Ellison, Treva Carrie. "Black Femme Praxis and the Promise of Black Gender." *Black Scholar* 49, no. 1 (2019): 6–16. https://doi.org/10.1080/00064246.2019.1548055.

Ellison, Treva, Kai M. Green, Matt Richardson, and C. Riley Snorton. "We Got Issues: Toward a Black Trans*/Studies." *TSQ: Transgender Studies Quarterly* 4, no. 2 (2017): 162–69. https://doi.org/10.1215/23289252-3814949.

Emergency Salsa. "Know Your Meme: Meme This Donut!" Know Your Meme, 2020. https://knowyourmeme.com/photos/951754-tumblr.

Epstein, Rebecca, Jamilia Blake, and Thalia Gonzalez. "Girlhood Interrupted: The Erasure of Black Girls' Childhood." Georgetown Law Center on Poverty and Inequality, 2017.

Estes, Steve. *I Am a Man! Race, Manhood, and the Civil Rights Movement.* Chapel Hill: University of North Carolina Press, 2005.

Evans, Stephanie Y., Kanika Bell, and Nsenga K. Burton. *Black Women's Mental Health: Balancing Strength and Vulnerability.* Albany: State University of New York Press, 2017.

Farah, Leyla. "Checking In with 'Between Women' Creator Michelle Daniel." *AfterEllen,* May 25, 2012. www.afterellen.com.

Feder, Sam. *Disclosure: Trans Lives on Screen.* Documentary. Disclosure Films, Bow and Arrow Entertainment, Field of Vision (II), 2020.

Fenway Health. "New Policy Brief Outlines Best Practices for Retaining Transgender Women in HIV Care." April 10, 2018. http://fenwayhealth.org.

Ferguson, Roderick A. *Aberrations in Black: Toward a Queer of Color Critique.* Minneapolis: University of Minnesota Press, 2003.

Fethers, Katherine, Caron Marks, Adrian Mindel, and Claudia S. Estcourt. "Sexually Transmitted Infections and Risk Behaviours in Women Who Have Sex with Women." *Sexually Transmitted Infections* 76, no. 5 (2000): 345–49. https://doi.org/10.1136/sti.76.5.345.

Fischer, Mia. "#Free_CeCe: The Material Convergence of Social Media Activism." *Feminist Media Studies* 16, no. 5 (2016): 755–71. https://doi.org/10.1080/14680777.2016.1140668.

Fisher, Danica Camille Tisdale. "The Pageant Politic: Race and Representation in American Beauty Contests and Culture." PhD dissertation, Emory University, 2012.

Fleischer, Matthew. "Guess Who Used 'Mrs. Doubtfire' to Illustrate a Story on Transgender Healthcare." *TakePart*, January 15, 2013. https://news.yahoo.com.

Fontaine, Nargis. "From Mammy to Madea, and Examination of the Behaviors of Tyler Perry's Madea Character in Relation to the Mammy, Jezebel, and Sapphire Stereotypes." MA thesis, Georgia State University, 2011. *African-American Studies Theses.* http://digitalarchive.gsu.edu/aas_theses/5.

Foreman, P. Gabrielle, et al. "Writing about Slavery/Teaching about Slavery: This Might Help." Google document, June 19, 2020. https://docs.google.com/document/d/1A4TEdDgYslX-hlKezLodMIM71My3KTNozxRvoIQTOQs/edit.

Fox, Emily Jane. "Yahoo to Buy Tumblr for $1.1 Billion: Report." *CNNMoney*, May 19, 2013. https://money.cnn.com.

French, Asha, and Moya Bailey. "'Skye's the Limit' Web Series Shows SGL Sisters Living and Loving." *Ebony*, July 22, 2016. www.ebony.com.

Gabriel, Trip. "Ohio Lawmaker Asks Racist Question about Black People and Hand-Washing." *New York Times*, June 11, 2020. www.nytimes.com.

Gamson, Joshua. *Freaks Talk Back: Tabloid Talk Shows and Sexual Nonconformity.* Chicago: University of Chicago Press, 1999.

García-Hodges, Ahiza, and Chiara Sottile. "Walmart Will Stop Putting 'Multicultural' Products in Locked Cases." *NBC News*, June 10, 2020. www.nbcnews.com.

Gay, Roxane. *Hunger: A Memoir of (My) Body.* New York: Harper Perennial, 2018.

Giddings, Paula J. *When and Where I Enter: The Impact of Black Women on Race and Sex in America.* 2nd ed. New York: William Morrow, 2007.

Gilbert, Elizabeth. *Eat, Pray, Love: One Woman's Search for Everything across Italy, India and Indonesia.* New York: Riverhead, 2007.

Gilliam, Franklin D., Jr. "The 'Welfare Queen' Experiment: How Viewers React to Images of African-American Mothers on Welfare." Center for Communications and Community, July 1, 1999. http://escholarship.org.

Gilman, Sander L. "Black Bodies, White Bodies: Toward an Iconography of Female Sexuality in Late Nineteenth-Century Art, Medicine, and Literature." *Critical Inquiry* 12, no. 1 (1985): 204–42. https://doi.org/10.2307/1343468.

Gilmore, Ruth Wilson. *Change Everything: Racial Capitalism and the Case for Abolition*. Chicago: Haymarket Books, 2021.

Goldman, Russell. "Transgender Activist CeCe McDonald Released Early from Prison." *ABC News*, January 13, 2014. http://abcnews.go.com.

Gomez, Antoinette M., Fatemeh Shafiei, and Glenn S. Johnson. "Black Women's Involvement in the Environmental Justice Movement: An Analysis of Three Communities in Atlanta, Georgia." *Race, Gender & Class* 18, nos. 1–2 (2011): 189–214.

Gomez, Jewelle. "Representations of Black Lesbians." *Harvard Gay and Lesbian Review* 6, no. 3 (1999): 32.

Gorgos, Linda M., and Jeanne M. Marrazzo. "Sexually Transmitted Infections among Women Who Have Sex with Women." *Clinical Infectious Diseases* 53, no. suppl_3 (December 2011): S84–91. https://doi.org/10.1093/cid/cir697.

Gossett, Reina, Eric A. Stanley, and Johanna Burton, eds. *Trap Door: Trans Cultural Production and the Politics of Visibility*. Cambridge: MIT Press, 2017.

Gray, Kishonna L., and Anita Sarkeesian. *Intersectional Tech: Black Users in Digital Gaming*. Baton Rouge: Louisiana State University Press, 2020.

Griffin, Farah Jasmine. *Harlem Nocturne: Women Artists and Progressive Politics during World War II*. New York: Civitas, 2013.

Hall, Stuart, ed. *Representation: Cultural Representations and Signifying Practices*. London: Sage, 1997.

Hampton, Rachelle. "Years Ago, Black Feminists Worked Together to Unmask Twitter Trolls Posing as Women of Color. If Only More People Paid Attention." *Slate*, April 23, 2019. https://slate.com.

Harris, Nadine Burke. *The Deepest Well: Healing the Long-Term Effects of Childhood Adversity*. New York: Houghton Mifflin Harcourt, 2018.

Harris-Perry, Melissa V. *Sister Citizen: Shame, Stereotypes, and Black Women in America*. New Haven: Yale University Press, 2011.

Hartman, Saidiya V. *Lose Your Mother: A Journey along the Atlantic Slave Route*. New York: Farrar, Straus and Giroux, 2007.

Hayward, T. "Ecological Citizenship: Justice, Rights and the Virtue of Resourcefulness." *Environmental Politics* 15, no. 3 (2006): 435–46. https://doi.org/10.1080/09644010600627741.

Helm, Angela Bronner. "Ex-SC Cop Who Hurled Black Student over Desk Won't Face Criminal Charges." *Root*, September 3, 2016. www.theroot.com.

"Help Support Egypt!" Fundraiser organized by Dean Spade. GoFundMe, created May 8, 2013. www.gofundme.com.

Hersey, Tricia. "About." *Nap Ministry* (blog), January 5, 2018. https://thenapministry.wordpress.com.

Higginbotham, Evelyn Brooks. *Righteous Discontent: The Women's Movement in the Black Baptist Church, 1880–1920*. Rev. ed. Cambridge: Harvard University Press, 1994.

Hill, Marc Lamont. "Why Aren't We Fighting for CeCe McDonald?" *Ebony*, June 12, 2012. www.ebony.com.

Hine, Darlene Clark, and Kate Wittenstein. "Female Slave Resistance: The Economics of Sex." In *The Black Woman Cross-Culturally*, edited by Filomena Chioma Steady. Rochester, VT: Schenkman, 1981.

Hirschenbaum, Dana. "When CRACK Is the Only Choice: The Effect of a Negative Right of Privacy on Drug-Addicted Women." *Berkeley Women's Law Journal* 15 (2000): 327–37.

Hogarth, Rana A. *Medicalizing Blackness: Making Racial Difference in the Atlantic World, 1780–1840*. Chapel Hill: University of North Carolina Press, 2017.

Holland, Sharon Patricia. *The Erotic Life of Racism*. Durham: Duke University Press, 2012.

hooks, bell. *Black Looks: Race and Representation*. Boston: South End, 1999.

———. *Talking Back: Thinking Feminist, Thinking Black*. Boston: South End, 1989.

Hou, Kathleen. "Sephora Is Making a Big Move to Support Black Businesses." *Cut*, June 11, 2020. www.thecut.com.

Huddleston, Tom, Jr. "'Aunt Jemima' Heirs Sue Pepsi, Quaker Oats for $2 Billion in Royalties." *Fortune*, August 11, 2014. http://fortune.com.

Hull, Akasha, Patricia Bell-Scott, and Barbara Smith, eds. *All the Women Are White, All the Blacks Are Men, But Some of Us Are Brave: Black Women's Studies*. Old Westbury, NY: Feminist Press, 1993.

Human Rights Campaign. "Dismantling a Culture of Violence: Understanding Anti-Transgender Violence and Ending the Crisis." 2018. https://assets2.hrc.org.

Issa Rae. *The Misadventures of Awkward Black Girl*. TV series, 2011–. Accessed January 27, 2020.

Jackson, A. S., P. R. Stanforth, J. Gagnon, T. Rankinen, A. S. Leon, D. C. Rao, J. S. Skinner, C. Bouchard, and J. H. Wilmore. "The Effect of Sex, Age and Race on Estimating Percentage Body Fat from Body Mass Index: The Heritage Family Study." *International Journal of Obesity* 26, no. 6 (2002): 789–96. https://doi.org/10.1038/sj.ijo.0802006.

Jackson, Laur. "Memes and Misogynoir." *Awl*, August 28, 2014. www.theawl.com.

Jackson, Lauren Michele. "We Need to Talk about Digital Blackface in GIFs." *Teen Vogue*, August 2, 2017. www.teenvogue.com.

Jackson, Sarah J., Moya Bailey, Brooke Foucault Welles, and Genie Lauren. *#HashtagActivism: Networks of Race and Gender Justice*. Cambridge: MIT Press, 2020.

Jackson, Zakiyyah Iman. *Becoming Human: Matter and Meaning in an Antiblack World*. New York: New York University Press, 2020.

Jacobs, Julia. "Texas Jury Awards $68,000 to Black Girl Who Said Classmates Wrapped Rope around Her Neck." *New York Times*, November 1, 2018. www.nytimes.com.

Jarvie, Jenny. "Girl Thrown from Desk Didn't Obey Because the Punishment Was Unfair, Attorney Says." *Los Angeles Times*, October 29, 2015. www.latimes.com.

Jay Versace—On & On (Triller). YouTube, July 5, 2016. https://www.youtube.com/watch?v=VCyw7cp-tHI.

Jenkins, Candice Marie. "Queering Black Patriarchy: The Salvific Wish and Masculine Possibility in Alice Walker's *The Color Purple*." *MFS Modern Fiction Studies* 48, no. 4 (2002): 969–1000. https://doi.org/10.1353/mfs.2002.0075.

Johnson, Charmain. *Lovers and Friends: Season 1*. Wolfe Video, 2010.

Johnson, Rachel L., Debra Roter, Neil R. Powe, and Lisa A. Cooper. "Patient Race/Ethnicity and Quality of Patient–Physician Communication during Medical Visits." *American Journal of Public Health* 94, no. 12 (2004): 2084–90.

Jones, Edward P. *The Known World*. New York: Amistad, 2006.

Jordan, June. *Soldier*. Rev. ed. New York: Civitas, 2001.

Kaba, Mariame. "Transformative Justice." *Prison Culture Blog* 12 (2012).

Kaba, Mariame, and Shira Hassan. *Fumbling towards Repair: A Workbook for Community Accountability Facilitators*. Workbook edition. Project NIA, 2019.

Kapadia, Ronak K. *Insurgent Aesthetics: Security and the Queer Life of the Forever War*. Durham: Duke University Press, 2019.

Kasperkevic, Jana. "Private Violence: Up to 75% of Abused Women Who Are Murdered Are Killed after They Leave Their Partners." *Guardian*, October 20, 2014. www.theguardian.com.

Keeling, Kara. "'Ghetto Heaven': Sef It Off and the Valorization of Black Lesbian Butch-Femme Sociality." *Black Scholar* 33, no. 1 (2003): 33–46.

———. *The Witch's Flight: The Cinematic, the Black Femme, and the Image of Common Sense*. Durham: Duke University Press, 2007.

Kelley, Robin D. G. *Freedom Dreams: The Black Radical Imagination*. New ed. Boston: Beacon, 2003.

Kennedra. "Meet the Teen Who Bravely Shot the McKinney Pool Party Video." *CW33 Dallas/Ft. Worth*, June 8, 2015. https://cw33.com.

Kesslen, Ben. "Aunt Jemima to Change Name, Remove Image from Packaging." *NBC News*, June 17, 2020. www.nbcnews.com.

Klostermann, Philip. Profile. GitHub. Accessed August 7, 2019. https://github.com/philbot9.

Kohler-Hausmann, Julilly. "'The Crime of Survival': Fraud Prosecutions, Community Surveillance, and the Original 'Welfare Queen.'" *Journal of Social History* 41, no. 2 (2007): 329–54.

Kolata, Gina. "Why Do Obese Patients Get Worse Care? Many Doctors Don't See Past the Fat." *New York Times*, September 25, 2016. www.nytimes.com.

Kuumba, M. Bahati. *Gender and Social Movements*. Walnut Creek, CA: AltaMira, 2001.

Kwate, Naa Oyo A. "Fried Chicken and Fresh Apples: Racial Segregation as a Fundamental Cause of Fast Food Density in Black Neighborhoods." *Health & Place* 14, no. 1 (2008): 32–44.

Lane-Steele, Laura. "Studs and Protest-Hypermasculinity: The Tomboyism within Black Lesbian Female Masculinity." *Journal of Lesbian Studies* 15, no. 4 (2011): 480–92. https://doi.org/10.1080/10894160.2011.532033.

Lang, Cady. "How the 'Karen Meme' Confronts the Violent History of White Womanhood." *Time*, June 25, 2020. https://time.com.

Larson, Selena. "Welcome to a World with 280-Character Tweets." *CNNMoney*, November 7, 2017. https://money.cnn.com.

Laungani, Alexis, and Pierre Brassard. "Gender Confirmation Surgery: Cosmetic or Reconstructive Procedure?" *Plastic and Reconstructive Surgery Global Open* 5, no. 6 (2017). https://doi.org/10.1097/GOX.0000000000001401.

Lee, Chana Kai. *For Freedom's Sake: The Life of Fannie Lou Hamer*. Urbana: University of Illinois Press, 2000.

Levin, Sam. "California Woman Threatens to Call Police on Eight-Year-Old Black Girl for Selling Water." *Guardian*, June 25, 2018. www.theguardian.com.

Lewis, Brooke A. "Four Years Later, Sandra Bland's Death Casts Long Shadow over Prairie View." *Houston Chronicle*, July 9, 2019. www.houstonchronicle.com.

Liao, Shannon. "After the Porn Ban, Tumblr Users Have Ditched the Platform as Promised." *Verge*, March 14, 2019. www.theverge.com.

Lindsey, Treva B. "Negro Women May Be Dangerous: Black Women's Insurgent Activism in the Movement for Black Lives." *Souls* 19, no. 3 (July 2017): 315–27. https://doi.org/10.1080/10999949.2017.1389596.

Livingston, Jennie. *Paris Is Burning*. Documentary. 1990.

Lorde, Audre. "The Master's Tools Will Never Dismantle the Master's House." In *Sister Outsider: Essays and Speeches*, 10–14. Trumansburg, NY: Crossing Press, 1984.

———. *Zami: A New Spelling of My Name—A Biomythography*. Trumansburg, NY: Crossing Press, 1982.

Love, Bettina. *Hip Hop's Li'l Sistas Speak: Negotiating Hip Hop Identities and Politics in the New South*. New York: Peter Lang, 2012.

Lucas, Liza. "Illegal Butt Injections Carry Serious Health Risks." *CNN*, June 24, 2015. www.cnn.com.

Lyle, Timothy. "'Check with Yo' Man First; Check with Yo' Man': Tyler Perry Appropriates Drag as a Tool to Re-Circulate Patriarchal Ideology." *Callaloo* 34, no. 3 (2011): 943–58. https://doi.org/10.1353/cal.2011.0135.

MAJOR! Documentary. 2018. www.missmajorfilm.com.

Manne, Kate. *Down Girl: The Logic of Misogyny*. New York: Oxford University Press, 2017.

Mannix, Andy. "CeCe McDonald Murder Trial." *City Pages*, May 9, 2012. https://web.archive.org.

Marmot, Michael, and Richard Wilkinson. *Social Determinants of Health*. New York: Oxford University Press, 2005.

Martinez, Gina, and Tara Law. "Two Recent Murders of Black Trans Women in Texas Reveal a Nationwide Crisis, Advocates Say." *Time*, June 5, 2019. https://time.com.

McCracken, Allison, Alexander Cho, Indira Neill Hoch, and Louisa Stein. *A Tumblr Book: Platform and Cultures*. Ann Arbor: University of Michigan Press, 2020.

McDonald, CeCe. "Drama from the DOC and Snoop Lion, and March and April Quotes." *Support CeCe!* (blog), April 30, 2013. https://supportcece.wordpress.com.

———"Help Find Sage Smith!" *Support CeCe!* (blog), January 18, 2013. https://support-cece.wordpress.com.

———. "January 8, 2013." *Support CeCe!* (blog), January 15, 2013. https://supportcece. wordpress.com.

———. "Pursuit of Happiness." *Support CeCe!* (blog), November 5, 2011. https://supportcece.wordpress.com.

———. "Support Estrellita!" *Support CeCe!* (blog), January 9, 2013. https://supportcece. wordpress.com.

McGuire, Danielle L. *At the Dark End of the Street: Black Women, Rape, and Resistance—A New History of the Civil Rights Movement from Rosa Parks to the Rise of Black Power.* New York: Knopf Doubleday, 2010.

McIntyre, Hugh. "How Janet Jackson's Super Bowl 'Wardrobe Malfunction' Helped Start YouTube." *Forbes*, February 1, 2015. www.forbes.com.

McLeod, Elizabeth. *The Original Amos 'n' Andy: Freeman Gosden, Charles Correll and the 1928–1943 Radio Serial.* Jefferson, NC: McFarland, 2015.

Messinger, Adam M. *LGBTQ Intimate Partner Violence: Lessons for Policy, Practice, and Research.* Berkeley: University of California Press, 2017.

Mey. "Flawless Trans Women Carmen Carrera and Laverne Cox Respond Flawlessly to Katie Couric's Invasive Questions." *Autostraddle*, January 7, 2014. www.autostraddle. com.

Michaelson, Jay. "Media Ignores Rash of Assaults on Transgender Women." *Daily Beast*, June 6, 2012. www.thedailybeast.com.

Millward, Liz, Janice G. Dodd, and Irene Fubara-Manuel. *Killing Off the Lesbians: A Symbolic Annihilation on Film and Television.* Jefferson, NC: McFarland, 2017.

Mock, Janet. *Conversation with Janet Mock on #RedefiningRealness.* YouTube, February 14, 2014. https://www.youtube.com/watch?v=ooSJ_XdjRoI&feature=youtube_gdata_player.

———. "My Journey (So Far) with #GirlsLikeUs: Hoping for Sisterhood, Solidarity & Empowerment." May 28, 2012. www.janetmock.com.

———. *Redefining Realness: My Path to Womanhood, Identity, Love and So Much More.* New York: Simon and Schuster, 2014.

Morgan, Joan. *When Chickenheads Come Home to Roost: My Life as a Hip Hop Feminist.* New York: Simon and Schuster, 1999.

Morris, Monique W. *Pushout: The Criminalization of Black Girls in Schools.* New York: New Press, 2016.

Moye, David. "Black Texas Teenager Brutalized in 2015 Finally Gets Her Pool Party." *HuffPost*, June 20, 2018. www.huffpost.com.

"The Moynihan Report." *Social Service Review* 40, no. 1 (March 1966): 84–85.

Muzny, Christina A., Erika L. Austin, Hanne S. Harbison, and Edward W. Hook III. "Sexual Partnership Characteristics of African American Women Who Have Sex with Women: Impact on Sexually Transmitted Infection Risk." *Sexually Transmitted Diseases* 41, no. 10 (October 2014): 611–17. https://doi.org/10.1097/OLQ.0000000000000194.

Myers, Antoinette Luna. "On Your Time on Tumblr." Interview by Moya Bailey, October 23, 2019.

National Center for Education Statistics. "Degrees Conferred by Race and Sex." 2019. https://nces.ed.gov.

National Coalition Against Domestic Violence. "Domestic Violence and the LGBTQ Community." June 6, 2018. https://ncadv.org.

National Coalition of Anti-Violence Programs. *Lesbian, Gay, Bisexual, Transgender, Queer, and HIV-Affected Intimate Partner Violence in 2014.* New York: National Coalition of Anti-Violence Programs, 2015. http://avp.org.

National LGBTQ Task Force. "Injustice at Every Turn: A Report of the National Transgender Discrimination Survey, A Look at Black Respondents," September 5, 2012. www.thetaskforce.org.

———. "New Analysis Shows Startling Levels of Discrimination against Black Transgender People." September 16, 2011. www.thetaskforce.org.

Nelson, Alondra. *Body and Soul: The Black Panther Party and the Fight against Medical Discrimination.* Minneapolis: University of Minnesota Press, 2011.

———. "The Social Life of DNA." *Chronicle Review*, August 29, 2010. http://chronicle.com.

Nelson, Laura J. "As Demand for Illegal Silicone Injections Grows, So Do Deaths." *Los Angeles Times*, October 9, 2012. http://articles.latimes.com.

Nelson, Libby. "Donald Trump's History of Misogyny, Sexism, and Harassment: A Comprehensive Review." *Vox*, October 8, 2016. www.vox.com.

Nett, Danny. "For Trans Women, Silicone 'Pumping' Can Be a Blessing and a Curse." *NPR*, September 1, 2019. www.npr.org.

Newbury, Patience. "An Open Letter to Atlanta's Feminist Women's Health Center on Its Refusal to Treat Certain Women and Its Willingness to Treat Certain Men." *Cisnormativity* (blog), June 29, 2012. https://cisnormativity.wordpress.com.

Newkirk, Vann R., II. "What the 'Crack Baby' Panic Reveals about the Opioid Epidemic." *Atlantic*, July 16, 2017. www.theatlantic.com.

Nissen, Dano. "Lena Waithe on Jason Mitchell Allegations: 'I Wish I Would've Handled It Differently.'" *Variety*, May 30, 2019. https://variety.com.

Noble, Safiya Umoja. *Algorithms of Oppression: How Search Engines Reinforce Racism.* New York: New York University Press, 2018.

No One Is Disposable: Everyday Practices of Prison Abolition. YouTube, February 7, 2014. https://www.youtube.com/watch?v=Dexpp5oJoh4&feature=yout ube_gdata_player.

Office of Minority Health, US Department of Health and Human Services. "Obesity and African Americans." 2018. https://minorityhealth.hhs.gov.

Olayiwola, Porsha. *Porsha Olayiwola—"Rekia Boyd" (NPS 2015).* YouTube, August 30, 2015. https://www.youtube.com/watch?v=MNP7H6TxO7s.

Onuorah, Nneka. *The Same Difference.* Documentary. 2015.

Onyejiaka, Tiffany. "Why Is TV So Afraid to Show Black People Loving Black People?" *RaceBaitr* (blog), February 26, 2019. https://racebaitr.com.

Out2Enroll. "Plan Information for 2019." Accessed September 24, 2019. https://out2enroll.org.

Parham, G. P., and M. L. Hicks. "Racial Disparities Affecting the Reproductive Health of African-American Women." *Medical Clinics of North America* 89 (September 2005): 935–43.

Park, Madison, and Holly Yan. "Gorilla Killing: 3-Year-Old Boy's Mother Won't Be Charged." *CNN*, June 6, 2016. www.cnn.com.

Parker, Pat. *Movement in Black.* Expanded ed. Ithaca, NY: Firebrand Books, 1999.

Peoples, Whitney. "(Re)Mediating Black Womanhood: Tyler Perry, Black Feminist Cultural Criticism, and the Politics of Legitimation." In *Womanist and Black Feminist Responses to Tyler Perry's Productions*, edited by LeRhonda S. Manigault-Bryant, Tamura A. Lomax, and Carol B. Duncan, 147–62. New York: Palgrave Macmillan, 2014. https://doi.org/10.1057/9781137429568_10.

Perry, Imani. *Vexy Thing: On Gender and Liberation.* Durham: Duke University Press, 2018.

Perry, Tyler. *Daddy's Little Girls.* Drama, romance. 2007.

———. *Temptation: Confessions of a Marriage Counselor.* Drama, thriller. 2013.

———. *Why Did I Get Married?* Comedy, drama. 2007.

Piercy, Marge. *Woman on the Edge of Time.* New York: Fawcett, 1985.

Pilkington, Ed. "Black Americans Dying of Covid-19 at Three Times the Rate of White People." *Guardian*, May 20, 2020. www.theguardian.com.

Poland, Bailey. *Haters: Harassment, Abuse, and Violence Online.* Lincoln: University of Nebraska Press, 2016.

Police Officer Slams S.C. High School Student to the Ground. YouTube, October 27, 2015. https://www.youtube.com/watch?v=qBSrccdaqXo.

Racette, Susan B., Susan S. Deusinger, and Robert H. Deusinger. "Obesity: Overview of Prevalence, Etiology, and Treatment." *Physical Therapy* 83, no. 3 (March 2003): 276–88. https://doi.org/10.1093/ptj/83.3.276.

Ramsey, Franchesca. *Well, That Escalated Quickly: Memoirs and Mistakes of an Accidental Activist.* New York: Grand Central, 2018.

Raun, Tobias. "DIY Therapy: Exploring Affective Aspects of Trans Video Blogs on YouTube." In *Digital Cultures and the Politics of Emotion: Feelings, Affect and Technological Change*, edited by Athina Karatzogianni and Adi Kuntsman, 165–80. New York: Palgrave Macmillan, 2012.

Reid-Brinkley, Shanara R. "The Essence of Res(Ex)Pectability: Black Women's Negotiation of Black Femininity in Rap Music and Music Video." *Meridians* 8, no. 1 (2008): 236–60.

Richardson, Allissa V. *Bearing Witness While Black: African Americans, Smartphones, and the New Protest #Journalism.* New York: Oxford University Press, 2020.

Riggs, Marlon. *Tongues Untied.* Documentary. Signifyin' Works, 1989.

Riley, Jenelle. "Tyler Perry on Saying Goodbye to Madea, Calling Colin Powell and Reading Reviews." *Variety*, January 30, 2019. https://variety.com.

Roberts, Dorothy. *Fatal Invention: How Science, Politics, and Big Business Re-Create Race in the Twenty-First Century.* New York: New Press, 2012.

———. *Killing the Black Body: Race, Reproduction, and the Meaning of Liberty*. New York: Pantheon, 1997.

Robertson, Erin C. J. "Study: Eviction Rates for Black Women on Par with Incarcerations for Black Men." *Root*, June 19, 2014. www.theroot.com.

Robinson, Jeffrey. "Black Lives Matter Is Still Here—And Avoiding the Mistakes of Their Predecessors." *American Civil Liberties Union*, July 16, 2018. www.aclu.org.

Roose, Kevin. "Russian Trolls Came for Instagram, Too." *New York Times*, December 18, 2018. www.nytimes.com.

Rose, Tricia. *Longing to Tell: Black Women's Stories of Sexuality and Intimacy*. New York: Farrar, Straus and Giroux, 2003.

Roy, Jessica. "Must Reads: How Millennials Replaced Religion with Astrology and Crystals." *Los Angeles Times*, July 10, 2019. www.latimes.com.

Samuel, Sigal. "The Witches of Baltimore." *Atlantic*, November 5, 2018. www.theatlantic.com.

Sanders-Johnson, Grace. "A Good Drag?" Interview by Moya Bailey, January 12, 2019.

Santana, Dora Silva. "Mais Viva! Reassembling Transness, Blackness, and Feminism." *TSQ: Transgender Studies Quarterly* 6, no. 2 (May 2019): 210–22. https://doi.org/10.1215/23289252-7348496.

Sanusi, Victoria. "This Teen's Twitter Account Was Suspended after Her Response to Trump's Win Went Viral." *BuzzFeed*, November 21, 2016. www.buzzfeed.com.

Seelman, Kristie L., Matthew J. P. Colón-Diaz, Rebecca H. LeCroix, Marik Xavier-Brier, and Leonardo Kattari. "Transgender Noninclusive Healthcare and Delaying Care Because of Fear: Connections to General Health and Mental Health among Transgender Adults." *Transgender Health* 2, no. 1 (February 2017): 17–28. https://doi.org/10.1089/trgh.2016.0024.

Shange, Savannah. "Play Aunties and Dyke Bitches: Gender, Generation, and the Ethics of Black Queer Kinship." *Black Scholar* 49, no. 1 (January 2019): 40–54. https://doi.org/10.1080/00064246.2019.1548058.

———. *Progressive Dystopia: Abolition, Antiblackness, and Schooling in San Francisco*. Durham: Duke University Press, 2019.

Sharpe, Christina. *In the Wake: On Blackness and Being*. Durham: Duke University Press, 2016.

Sidibe, Gabourey. *This Is Just My Face: Try Not to Stare*. Boston: Houghton Mifflin Harcourt, 2017.

Simmons, Aishah Shahidah. *No! The Rape Documentary*. Documentary. 2004.

Skloot, Rebecca. *The Immortal Life of Henrietta Lacks*. New York: Crown, 2010.

Smith, Susan Lynn. *Sick and Tired of Being Sick and Tired: Black Women's Health Activism in America, 1890–1950*. Philadelphia: University of Pennsylvania Press, 1995.

Smythe, SA "Can I Get a Witness? Black Feminism, Trans Embodiment, and Thriving Past the Fault Lines of Care." *Palimpsest: A Journal on Women, Gender, and the Black International*, special issue, Black Feminism and the Practice of Care, 2020.

Sobande, Francesca. *The Digital Lives of Black Women in Britain*. New York: Palgrave Macmillan, 2020.

Solomon, Akiba. "CeCe McDonald: Attacked for Her Identity, Incarcerated for Surviving." *Ebony*, May 4, 2012. www.ebony.com.

Sommers, Zach. "Missing White Woman Syndrome: An Empirical Analysis of Race and Gender Disparities in Online News Coverage of Missing Persons." *Journal of Criminal Law and Criminology* 106, no. 2 (January 2016). http://scholarlycommons.law.northwestern.edu/jclc/vol106/iss2/4.

Sorrells, Billy. *Shit Black Girls Say*. YouTube, December 17, 2011. https://www.youtube.com/watch?v=fXDpfhehb6I.

Spillers, Hortense J. "Mama's Baby, Papa's Maybe: An American Grammar Book." *Diacritics*, 1987, 65–81.

Stanley, Eric A., and Nat Smith. *Captive Genders: Trans Embodiment and the Prison Industrial Complex*. Chico, CA: AK Press, 2015.

Statista. "Tumblr: Total Number of Posts 2019." Accessed June 25, 2020. www.statista.com.

Stillman, Sarah. "'The Missing White Girl Syndrome': Disappeared Women and Media Activism." *Gender and Development* 15, no. 3 (2007): 491–502.

Stowe, Harriet Beecher. "Sojourner Truth." *Atlantic Monthly* 473 (1863): 481.

Strings, Sabrina. *Fearing the Black Body: The Racial Origins of Fat Phobia*. New York: New York University Press, 2019.

Stroud, Hernandez D. "Our Opioid Crisis Reveals a Historical Racial Bias." *Time*, July 16, 2016. https://time.com.

Stuart, Tessa. "A Timeline of Donald Trump's Creepiness While He Owned Miss Universe." *Rolling Stone*, October 12, 2016. www.rollingstone.com.

Syd of OFWGKTA. YouTube, 2011. http://www.youtube.com/watch?v=ljE83rUouUI&feature=youtube_gdata_player.

Talusan, Meredith. "Unerased: Mic's Database of Trans Lives Lost to Homicide in the US." *Mic*, December 8, 2016. https://mic.com.

TEDMED Great Challenges: Transgender Health: An Evolution to Understanding. YouTube, December 12, 2013. https://www.youtube.com/watch?v=B8w-lt1Uhx0.

Telusma, Blue. *Skye's the Limit*. Ep. 8, "Feasting on Scraps." 2013. https://skye.bluecentric.com.

———. *Skye's The Limit*. Season 1 finale, "Bienvenidos a Miami!" 2013. https://skyesthelimit.vhx.tv.

Thompson, Sonia. "Despite Being the Most Educated, Black Women Earn Less Money at Work, in Entrepreneurship, and in Venture Capital. 3 Ways to Fix It." *Inc.*, August 22, 2019. www.inc.com.

Thompson, Wanna. "How White Women on Instagram Are Profiting Off Black Women." *Paper*, November 14, 2018. www.papermag.com.

Tinubu, Aramide A. "Disney's Racist Cartoons Won't Just Stay Hidden in the Vault." *NBC News*, April 25, 2019. www.nbcnews.com.

TiTi Do You Love Me. Zeus network. Accessed July 29, 2019. www.thezeusnetwork.com.

Trần, Ngọc Loan. "Calling IN: A Less Disposable Way of Holding Each Other Accountable." *Black Girl Dangerous* (blog), December 18, 2013. www.bgdblog.org.

TransformHarm.org. "Transformative Justice." Accessed December 1, 2019. https://transformharm.org.

Trudy. "Explanation of Misogynoir." *Gradient Lair* (blog), April 28, 2014. www.gradientlair.com.

Tuchman, Gaye. "The Symbolic Annihilation of Women by the Mass Media." In *Culture and Politics: A Reader*, edited by Lane Crothers and Charles Lockhart, 150–74. New York: Palgrave Macmillan, 2000.

Twenties. Comedy. Hillman Grad, 2020.

"*Tyler Perry's Atlanta Studio to Include a Compound for Displaced LGBTQ Youth and Trafficked Women.*" *CBS News*, October 8, 2019. www.cbsnews.com.

UC San Diego Center on Gender Equity and Health. "Measuring #MeToo: A National Study on Sexual Harassment and Assault." 2019.

Viglione, Jill, Lance Hannon, and Robert DeFina. "The Impact of Light Skin on Prison Time for Black Female Offenders." *Social Science Journal* 48, no. 1 (January 2011): 250–58. https://doi.org/10.1016/j.soscij.2010.08.003.

Volscho, Thomas W. "Sterilization Racism and Pan-Ethnic Disparities of the Past Decade: The Continued Encroachment on Reproductive Rights." *Wicazo Sa Review* 25, no. 1 (2010): 17–31.

Walker, Alice. *We Are the Ones We Have Been Waiting For: Inner Light in a Time of Darkness.* Reprint, New York: New Press, 2007.

Wallace-Sanders, Kimberly. *Mammy: A Century of Race, Gender, and Southern Memory.* Ann Arbor: University of Michigan Press, 2009.

Walsh, John. "11 Insults Trump Has Hurled at Women." *Business Insider*, October 17, 2018. www.businessinsider.com.

Walsh, Paul. "Graffiti Backing 'CeCe' Sprayed on County Jail; Prominent Transgender Author Arrested." *Star Tribune*, June 6, 2012. www.startribune.com.

Warith, Nadja. *Choiices: The Series Pilot Episode [LGBT Series].* YouTube, August 19, 2017. https://www.youtube.com/watch?v=OWtozDmfbLo&t=2s.

Washington, Harriet A. *Medical Apartheid: The Dark History of Medical Experimentation on Black Americans from Colonial Times to the Present.* New York: Doubleday, 2006.

Washington, Jasmine. "Lena Waithe Says She Talked to Jason Mitchell about Respecting Women." *Ebony*, May 30, 2019. www.ebony.com.

Weathers, Mary Ann. "An Argument for Black Women's Liberation as a Revolutionary Force." 1969. In *Words of Fire: An Anthology of African-American Feminist Thought*, edited by Beverly Guy-Sheftall. New York: New Press, 1995.

Weber, Paul J., and Clarice Silber. "Sandra Bland's Own Video of 2015 Texas Traffic Stop Surfaces." *AP News*, May 7, 2019. https://apnews.com.

Wells, Veronica. "Members of LGBT Community Refuse to Support Sandra Bland Doc Because of Her Homophobic Comments." *MadameNoire*, November 30, 2018. https://madamenoire.com.

"What CeCe's Reading." *Support CeCe McDonald!* Accessed January 25, 2020. https://supportcece.wordpress.com.

Wheeler, André. "He Pretended to Be a Black Woman Online and Became Famous—Then His Life Unraveled." *Guardian*, October 16, 2019. www.theguardian.com.

Wilkinson, Richard G., and Michael Marmot, eds. *Social Determinants of Health: The Solid Facts*. Copenhagen: World Health Organization, 2003.

Willis, Tasha Y. "'And Still We Rise . . .': Microaggressions and Intersectionality in the Study Abroad Experiences of Black Women." *Frontiers: The Interdisciplinary Journal of Study Abroad* 26 (2015): 209–30.

Wiltse, Jeff. "The Black–White Swimming Disparity in America: A Deadly Legacy of Swimming Pool Discrimination." *Journal of Sport and Social Issues* 38, no. 4 (August 2014): 366–89. https://doi.org/10.1177/0193723513520553.

Wise, Cat, and Kira Wakeam. "Millennials Are Leaving Organized Religion. Here's Where Some Are Finding Community." *PBS News Hour*, January 2, 2020. www.pbs.org.

Wootson, Cleve R., Jr. "A Black Yale Student Fell Asleep in Her Dorm's Common Room. A White Student Called Police." *Washington Post*, May 11, 2018. www.washingtonpost.com.

World Health Organization. "Preamble to the Constitution of the World Health Organization as Adopted by the International Health Conference." New York: World Health Organization, 1946. www.who.int.

World Health Organization and Commission on Social Determinants of Health. *Closing the Gap in a Generation: Health Equity through Action on the Social Determinants of Health: Commission on Social Determinants of Health Final Report*. World Health Organization, 2008.

Zaveri, Mihir. "Florida Deputy Charged with Child Abuse after Throwing 15-Year-Old to Ground." *New York Times*, November 5, 2019. www.nytimes.com.

Zhang, Jenny G. "After Aunt Jemima, Uncle Ben's, Cream of Wheat, Mrs. Butterworth's May Be Next to See Changes." *Eater*, June 18, 2020. www.eater.com.

INDEX

ABOUT THE AUTHOR

Moya Bailey is Associate Professor in the School of Communication at Northwestern University. Her work focuses on marginalized groups' use of digital media to promote social justice and she is interested in how race, gender, and sexuality are represented in media and medicine. She is the digital alchemist for the Octavia E. Butler Legacy Network and the Board President of Allied Media Projects, a Detroit-based movement media organization that supports an ever growing network of activists and organizers. She is a co-author of *#HashtagActivism: Networks of Race and Gender Justice* and is the author of *Misogynoir Transformed: Black Women's Digital Resistance*. She is an MLK Visiting Scholar at MIT for the 2020–2021 academic year.